Table of Contents

Table of Contents

Table of Contents

Table of Contents

Table of Contents

Table of Contents

Introduction:

Turning Clicks into Published Work

Welcome. If you're holding this book in your hands, chances are you're standing at one of these crossroads: maybe you've just opened Canva for the very first time and feel overwhelmed by a sea of colorful templates; maybe you've already played around with posts or a presentation or two, but you still don't have a clear method to save time and create with confidence; or perhaps you run a business, manage social media, or simply want a practical tool to design high-quality content without the steep learning curve of traditional software.

Whichever your starting point, this guide was built for you. What you're about to read is not another dry "click-here, then click-there" manual. It's a step-by-step journey that takes you from zero experience to published, real-world results. By the time you finish, you won't just know how to use Canva — you'll have a portfolio of deliverables you can actually use, share, or even sell.

This is the only 5-in-1 Canva Bible. Inside, you'll find five complete modules:

- **Canva for Beginners** — learn the fundamentals step by step and design your very first personal brand, complete with logo, colors, and social posts.
- **Canva for Social Media** — build a repeatable system to batch-produce a full month of content, from Instagram carousels to YouTube thumbnails, in a single session.
- **Canva for Business & Presentations** — create a professional Business Starter Kit: pitch decks, brochures, lead magnets, and branded materials ready to present or deliver.
- **Canva Advanced + AI** — unlock the power of Magic Studio and smart workflows to rebrand, repurpose, and bulk-generate assets in hours instead of weeks.
- **Canva for Video Editing** — transform ideas into scroll-stopping short videos with titles, captions, transitions, and hooks that hold attention.

Within each module, you'll complete a Final Project: 30 social posts, a business kit, a rebrand sprint with AI, or a 5-short video campaign. Each project is supported by QR codes that link to templates, checklists, prompt libraries, and storyboards — ready to duplicate and adapt.

What makes this book different?

- It's not about theory, but about publishing deliverables you can actually show to clients, followers, or colleagues.
- AI and video aren't side notes — they're core pillars. You'll learn to use Canva's Magic Studio and short-form video as your everyday tools.
- Instead of random tips, you'll learn systems that scale: batch workflows, content planners, brand kits, bulk creation, and SOPs you can repeat again and again.

By the final page, you'll have mastered a workflow that turns Canva into your design assistant. You'll be able to build a personal brand, keep social media consistently filled, pitch ideas to clients, rebrand with AI, and produce short videos — all with one single platform.

So, Before we dive into Module 1, let's get you ready. Think of this as stretching before a workout: a few simple steps to set your foundation, sharpen your focus, and give Canva a clear role in your life.

Quick Exercises to Kickstart Your Journey

These warm-up exercises may feel simple, but they plant the seeds for everything that comes next.

By the time you step into Module 1, you'll already have a clear sense of direction, a source of inspiration, and a project in mind that makes learning Canva both personal and purposeful.

1. Map Your Priorities

Take a piece of paper and list the areas where you most need design support: social media, presentations, marketing materials, or video. Circle the top two. This will keep you focused on the modules that matter most to you.

2. Build an Inspiration Folder

Open a folder on your computer (or inside Canva itself if you already know how to do it) and save five designs that you admire — they can be ads, posts, slides, or covers. Don't overanalyze. Just collect what inspires you. These examples will become your visual compass for your next projects.

3. Define Your First Design Goal

In your notebook, complete this sentence:

"The very first thing I want to create in Canva is..."

This is your anchor project — the design you'll keep in mind as you move through each exercise and tutorial.

4. Make Time for Exploration

Block out 30 minutes in your calendar this week to log into Canva and explore the dashboard. No pressure, no tasks — just a walk-through. The goal is to feel at home in the space before we start building.

Module 1 - Canva for Beginners

Opening the Door: Why This First Module Matters

Most people meet Canva at a moment of urgency: a presentation due tomorrow, a new Instagram post that should have launched yesterday, a flyer your community group needs by the weekend. You open the site, you see a flood of color and possibility, and you hope the software will somehow do the work for you. Sometimes it does—until the next design looks off, the text isn't aligned, or the export is blurry. That's where this module steps in.

Think of Module 1 as your calm introduction to a powerful workshop. We'll slow the pace, learn the layout of the room, and build a few early habits that save hours later. You'll discover that design is not about fancy tricks; it's about clarity: choosing the right format, selecting a readable font pairing, aligning elements so the eye can breathe, exporting in the correct quality so your work looks sharp everywhere. Those basics turn Canva from a "template machine" into your daily creative assistant.
This is not theory. **By the end of the module, you will have produced real work**: a simple logo, a color palette that feels like you, and three coordinated social posts you're proud to publish. You'll know why your decisions work—not just where to click. That confidence is the point. Once you understand the foundations, everything else in this book—social packs, business kits, AI rebrands, short videos—becomes faster, cleaner, and easier to repeat.
Before we dive in, set an intention. What do you most want from Canva right now: consistent social content, a clearer personal brand, or materials you can hand to a client or teacher? Keep that goal in a notebook. You can also use the notes from the previous wxercise. We'll return to it often as we build your skills layer by layer.

In this module, you will:

You're not reading for inspiration—you're reading to ship. Here's the journey we'll take, in plain language, so you can track progress as you go.

- Learn the space you'll work in every day: account, interface, dashboard, and how to find the right template fast.
- Shape your eye with typography and color: simple rules for pairing fonts, picking a palette, and using contrast with intention.
- Structure your page with grids, alignment, grouping, and sensible spacing so everything instantly looks more professional.
- Work with images and elements—uploading, cropping, layering, and using transparency without making a mess.
- Export correctly in PNG/JPG/PDF so your posts are crisp and your print files are clean.

It helps to picture the outcome. This is who you become by finishing Module 1. By the end, you'll be able to:

- Start any project from a template and make it yours—not a clone.
- Manage text, shapes, and images with confidence, keeping layouts balanced.
- Use grids and alignment so designs feel calm and intentional.
- Export in the right format and size without trial-and-error.
- Deliver a Mini Personal Brand: simple logo, palette, and 3 coordinated social posts.

Chapter 1

First Steps: Account, Interface, Dashboard & Template Search

Every Journey Starts With a Login. Every tool has a threshold moment—the second you open it for the first time. With Canva, that moment isn't about advanced features or polished exports. It's about the very basics: setting up an account that won't get lost, understanding an interface that looks simple but hides layers of power, and realizing that organization is not an afterthought but the foundation of creative speed.
Think of it like walking into a workshop. Before you can build furniture, you need a bench that's stable, tools that are sharp, and a shelf where everything belongs. Canva is the same. The dashboard is your workshop floor. The sidebar is your toolbox. Templates are your starter kits. If you rush past these, you risk building frustration instead of designs.

This chapter slows you down on purpose. We'll focus on four deceptively simple things: creating and securing your account, navigating Canva's interface without guesswork, taming the dashboard with folders before chaos arrives, and learning how to find templates that actually support your vision instead of trapping you in cookie-cutter design.

Why does this matter? Because the speed and polish you'll enjoy later—batching social posts, exporting campaigns, even rebranding an entire business—depend on these early habits. Beginners who skip setup often waste hours later searching for files, fighting the wrong fonts, or losing edits because they worked under the wrong login. Professionals never make those mistakes—because they invest ten careful minutes at the start.

By the end of this chapter, you'll no longer feel like someone "trying Canva for the first time." You'll feel like someone who owns a workspace, knows where the tools are, and understands how to start any project with clarity.

What You'll Do in 10 Minutes (and why it matters)

Before we build anything complex, you'll take a quiet tour through Canva's front door. The goal isn't speed; it's familiarity—because once the interface feels like home, you stop fighting the tool and start thinking like a designer. In this short warm-up you will:

- Create a single, reliable account so every project autosaves and shares cleanly across devices.
- Walk the interface, noticing how tools reveal themselves only when needed.
- Tidy the dashboard with two starter folders, avoiding chaos before it begins.
- Find and open a template that actually matches your intent, so you begin with structure instead of a blank page.

Your Canva Account: The Foundation You Don't Want to Rebuild Later

Every creative habit begins with a home.

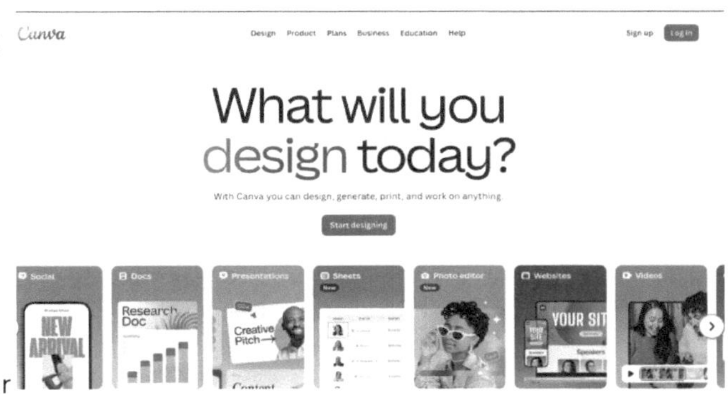

For your Canva work, that home is a single account you trust. Using multiple emails is like hiding your tools in different rooms—you will eventually lose something important.

Open canva.com and choose Sign up via email, Google, or Apple.

Pick the login you already use for professional or school work and stick to it. When Canva asks why you're here—personal, business, education—answer quickly.

This setting influences the templates you see first; it doesn't lock your account to one use.

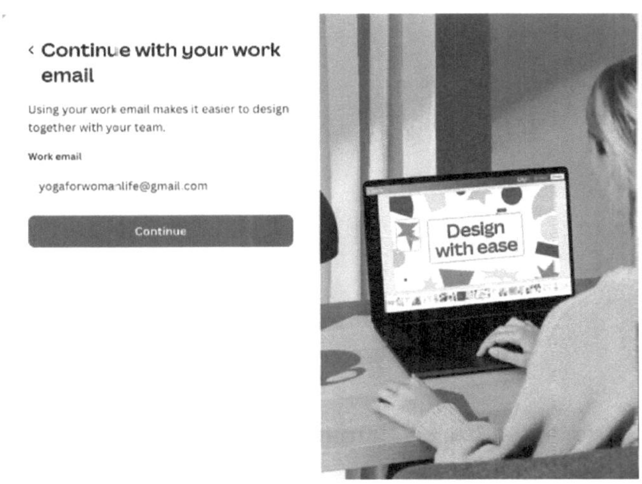

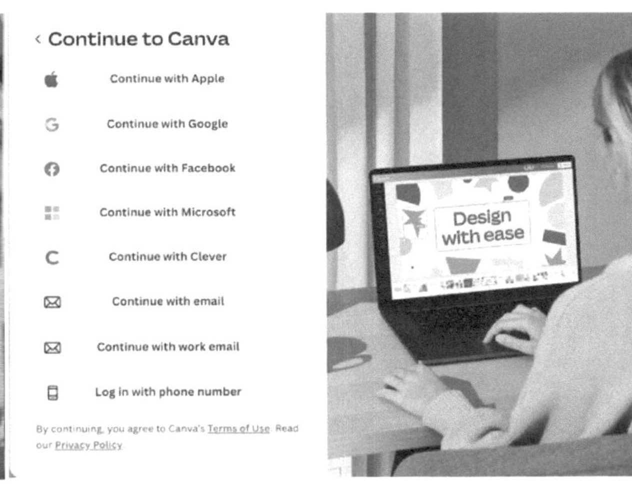

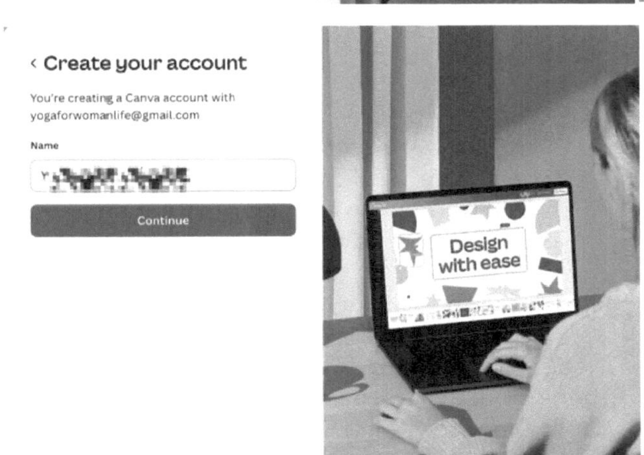

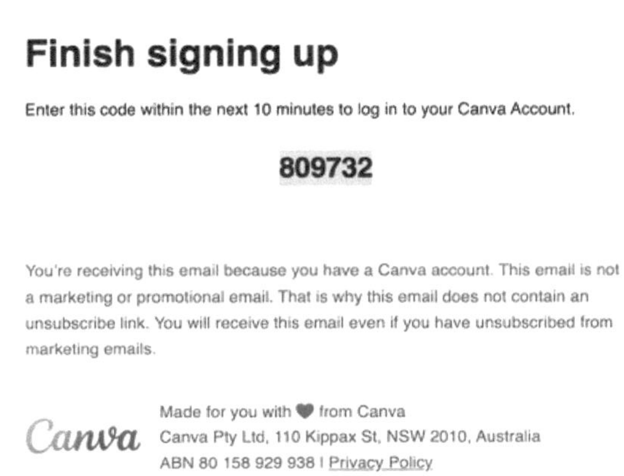

Your Canva Account: The Foundation You Don't Want to Rebuild Later

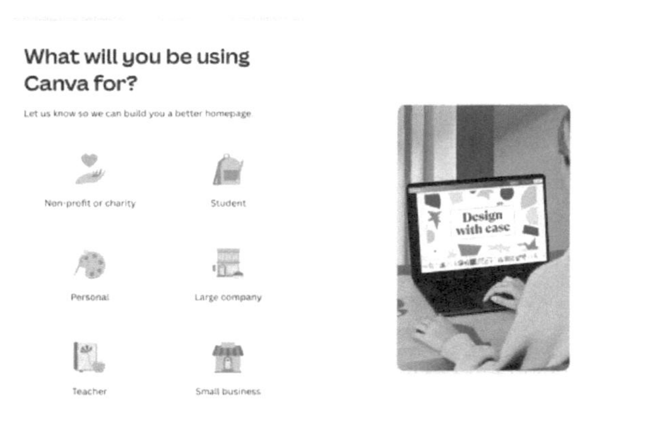

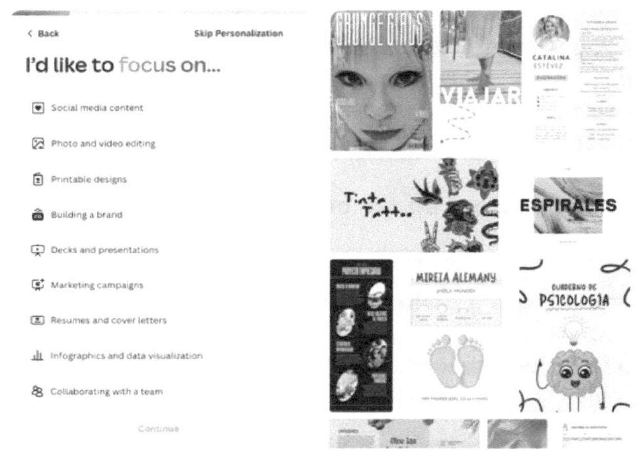

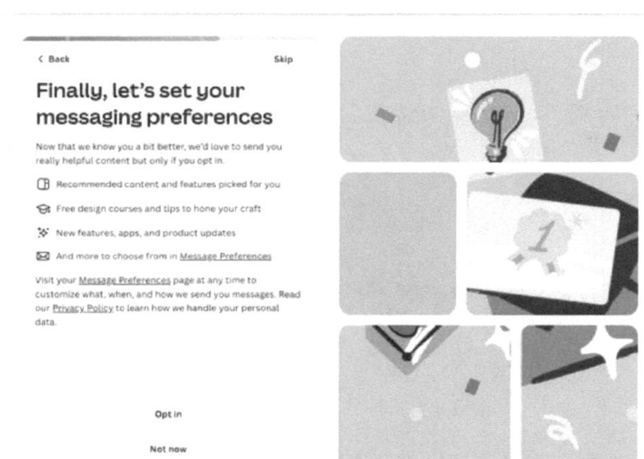

Complete your profile.

Add your name (or brand name) and, if you like, a simple avatar. It sounds cosmetic, but shared files look more credible when the author's name is clear. Later, when you export, that name helps you track drafts and versions without confusion.

Real Scenario — The "Lost Export" Problem

A student designed a presentation over two evenings: half on a laptop, half on a tablet. The slides looked great—until she couldn't find the final version on submission day. Two accounts, two sets of files. The fix was simple: one login, every device. Once she consolidated, the stress vanished. The work didn't change—only the system did.

Pro Tip — Start a Naming Habit Now

Before your library grows, pick a format for file names:

- YYYY-MM Project — Short Title — v01
- ClientName — Asset — Platform — v01
- Type it once; duplicate and update the version number. In a month, you'll thank yourself for the tidy history.

Mini Exercise — Make It Real

Create your account and confirm your email. Then create a blank design and name it: 2025-10 Canva Practice — First Steps — v01. You've just started your test archive.

Understanding the Interface: A Workspace That Stays Quiet Until You Need It

Traditional design software shows everything at once—icons, panels, hidden drawers. Canva takes a gentler approach: it reveals tools contextually, as you click. That means beginners can learn by doing, and experienced users aren't slowed by visual noise.

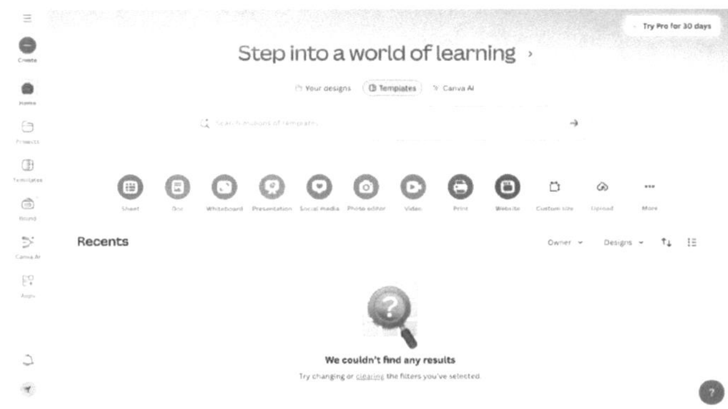

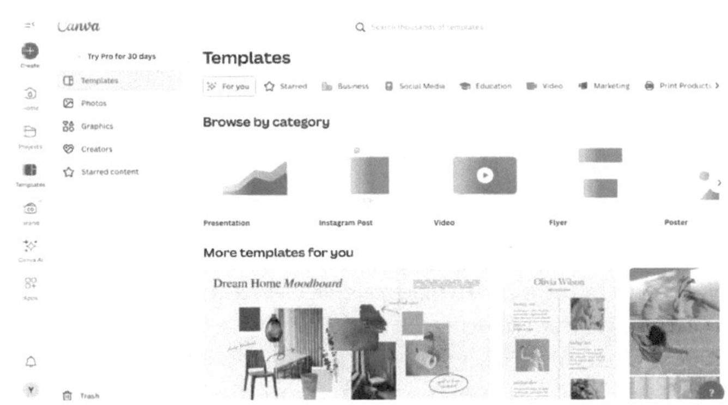

Here's the lay of the land, in plain language you will remember:

- **Left Sidebar:** your library. Templates, Projects, Brand, Folders, and Apps live here. Think of it as a well-labeled cupboard.
- **Top Search:** your radar. Type what you want—"Instagram carousel," "A4 flyer," "modern resume"—and jump straight to relevant formats.
- **Top Menu**: your global controls—undo/redo, file actions, resize (inside a design), version history.
- **Canvas (center):** where your design happens.
- **Contextual Toolbar**: appears when you select text, images, or shapes. It changes based on what you've clicked, keeping the interface calm.

What matters most is not memorizing names—it's forming a mental map. After a few sessions, your hand will move to the sidebar without thinking. That's when design speeds up: not because you rush, but because clutter disappears and decisions get clearer.

Attention — The "Click Wander" Trap. When you don't know where to look, you click everywhere. Pause for ten seconds instead. Ask: "What am I editing—text, an image, or the layout?" Then click the object first. The right toolbar will appear, every time.

Real Scenario — The Surprise Teacher. A non-designer opened a template and clicked on a headline by accident. The font toolbar appeared with size, weight, spacing. "Oh," she said, "it tells me what to do." Exactly. Canva teaches by showing only the tools you need in the moment.

Mini Exercise — A Three-Minute Tour

Log in. Open a design (any format).

1. Click a text box → notice the font controls.
2. Click an image → notice crop, flip, adjust.
3. Click outside everything → the toolbar vanishes.
4. Write this note: "When I select X, Canva shows Y." That sentence builds your mental model.

The Dashboard: Your Control Room (and Time Saver)

The dashboard is not a hallway to rush through—it's the room where you plan your day. Treat it well, and future-you will move at twice the speed. That's why you need to organize it well now for a quicker search later.

You'll see four zones that matter:

1. **Create a design —** the big purple button that picks your format and size.
2. **Recent projects** — autosaved designs you touched last.
3. **Folders** — your structure; absolutely worth five minutes now.
4. **Recommended templates** — suggestions that get smarter as Canva learns what you make.

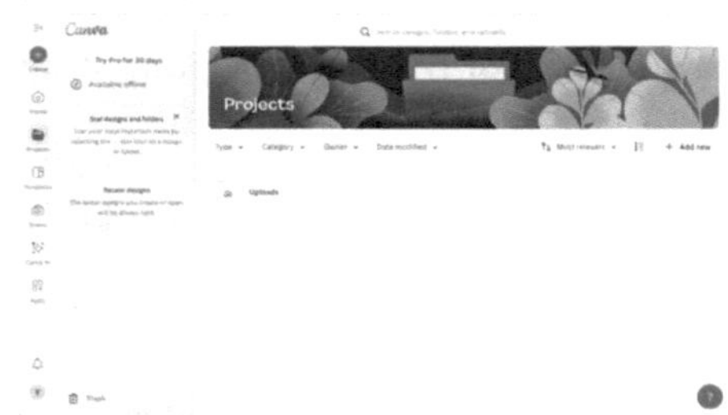

Dashboard and Projects

Start by creating two folders: Personal and Work/School. Almost every design you make belongs to one of these. Later, you can add subfolders (e.g., Personal → Social Posts, Work → Client A). Organization is not a personality trait; it's a workflow multiplier.

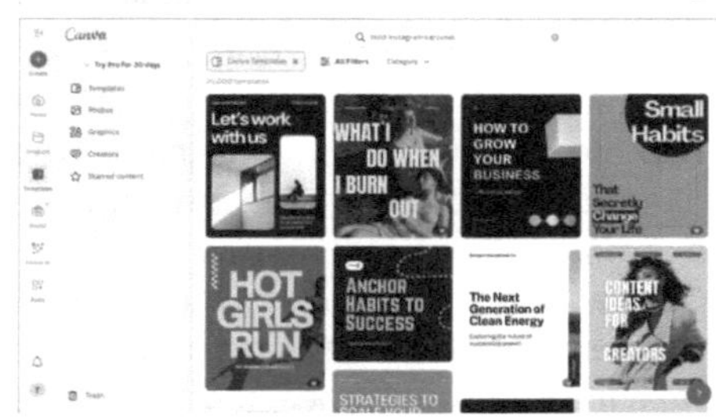

Common Pitfall — The "Recent Projects Graveyard"

New users let everything pile up in Recent Projects. After a few weeks, they scroll for minutes to find a file. That friction kills momentum. Move finished drafts into folders as soon as you stop working on them—even if you plan to return tomorrow. The habit is the point.

Real Scenario — Saving an Hour a Week

A freelancer had 120 designs floating in Recent. We built a quick structure: Clients, Marketing, Templates, Archive. Searching dropped from minutes to seconds. Over a year, that adds up to days of time reclaimed.

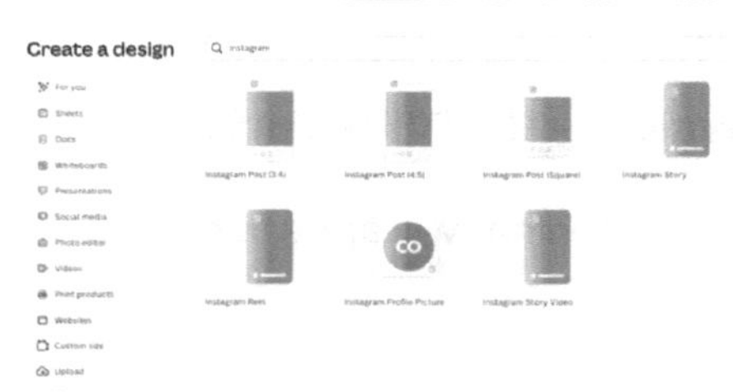

Pro Tip — Pin Your Active Files

If you work on three assets this week (say, a carousel, a slide deck, a flyer), add a "★ Active" folder. Pin it to the top. Move files out when they ship. You'll focus faster when your current work is always visible.

Mini Exercise — Two Folders, One Rule

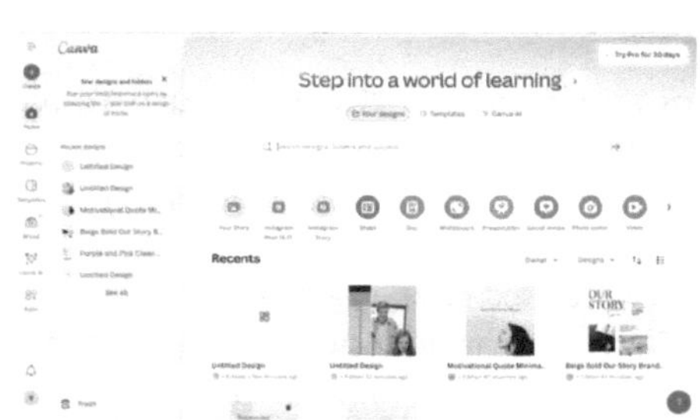

Create Personal and Work/School. Move your practice design into one. Write a tiny rule under each:

- Personal → Anything for me (social, hobby, study).
- Work/School → Anything shared with others (client, team, teacher).
- Small rules reduce decision fatigue later.

Finding and Using Templates: From Blank to Branded

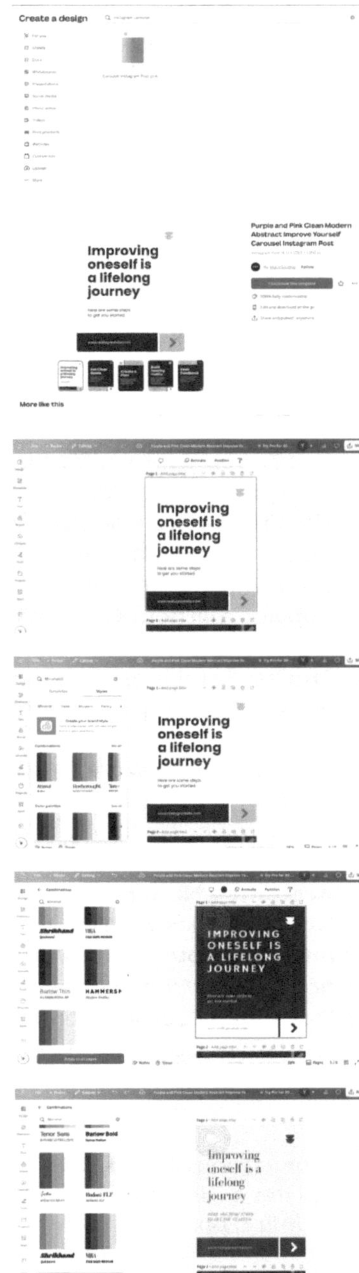

Templates are Canva's superpower. They remove blank-page anxiety and give you immediate structure—hierarchy, spacing, and rhythm you can study while you customize. But a template is scaffolding, not a finished building. Your job is to adapt it until it speaks in your voice.

Start with intent. Type what you actually need into the search bar: "minimal pitch deck," **"bold Instagram carousel,"** "A4 price list," "modern resume." Then apply filters—style (minimal/modern/elegant), color, and orientation. Narrowing options keeps your attention on quality rather than quantity.

Open three candidates and read them like a designer:

- **Hierarchy**: can you tell what's most important at a glance?
- **Spacing**: do the margins and gaps feel generous enough to breathe?
- **Readability**: are the font sizes and contrasts comfortable on a phone screen?

Pick your favorite and begin owning it. Change a palette color to match your taste, replace the hero image with something relevant, adjust the heading font weight if the default is too delicate or too heavy. Customize at least three elements (color, imagery, typography). This breaks the "I've seen this template before" feeling and moves the design into your world.

Attention — Don't Over-Edit All at Once
Change one variable at a time. First palette, then fonts, then images. If the design gets worse, undo the last change and try a different adjustment. Good design is often a sequence of small, reversible moves.

Real Scenario — The Quiet Upgrade
A bakery owner used a bright, playful template for a weekly specials post. It didn't match her cozy brand. We muted the palette, swapped the geometric font for a warm serif, and replaced stock sprinkles with her own croissant photo. Same layout, new voice. Customers noticed—and orders rose.

Pro Tip — Build a "Taste Board"
Create a single page with 5–6 swatches (your likely colors), 2 heading fonts, 2 body fonts, and 6–8 example images that feel on-brand. Keep it open while you customize templates. It's easier to adapt when your taste is visible.

Mini Exercise — Your First Owned Template

Search for "Instagram carousel."

1. Apply the Minimalist style filter and pick a set with clear margins.
2. Change the palette to two colors you love (plus black/white).
3. Replace the hero image on slide 1 with one of your photos.
4. Adjust the H1 size until it feels easy to read on a phone (aim for large and clean).
5. Export slide 1 as PNG and view it on your phone. Ask: "Would I pause to read this?" If not, increase contrast or simplify the text.

Recap — The First Milestone, Locked In

A quick recap solidifies new knowledge. The point is not to tick boxes; it's to feel how much smoother things already are.

- You have a single account that autosaves across devices.
- You can describe the interface in your own words and predict where tools will appear.
- Your dashboard now has the beginnings of a structure, so files don't disappear into "Recent."
- And you've taken a template from generic to personal by changing palette, fonts, and imagery.

Those are professional habits. Keep them, and every future chapter will feel easier.

Common Mistakes — Not Failures, Just Fixable Frictions

- Beginners don't ruin designs; they usually slow them down with avoidable friction. Here are the usual suspects and the antidotes that restore flow.
- Two Accounts, Two Worlds. If you've signed up with both email and Google, pick one and migrate. Share designs from the "old" account to the "new" one, then stop using the duplicate. Simplicity is speed.
- The Dashboard Pile-Up. When everything lives in Recent, scrolling becomes your daily exercise. Create Personal and Work/School now. Move anything older than two weeks into a subfolder called Archive. You can always search later.
- Copying Without Customizing. Templates are not your brand. Change at least three variables—color, typography, imagery—before you export. It's the difference between "nice template" and "your voice."
- Endless Scrolling, No Filters. The library is massive; your time isn't. Search with intent ("minimal investor deck," not just "presentation") and apply filters. Decision fatigue drops and quality rises.

"Do It Now" Homework — 20 Minutes That Change Your Next Week

End each major section with action, so learning sticks.

1. **Account + Naming.** Confirm your login method. Create a tiny text file pinned to your desktop: Canva — Naming Rules. Add your chosen pattern (e.g., YYYY-MM Project — Short Title — v01).
2. **Interface Tour.** Open a template and click text, image, and shape in turn. Write one sentence in your notebook: "When I select X, Canva shows Y."
3. **Dashboard Setup.** Create Personal and Work/School folders. Add a ★ to an Active folder and pin it to the top. Move your current file there.
4. **Owned Template**. Search, filter, like, save, start customizing. Change palette, headline font, and main image. Export slide 1 as PNG and review it on your phone. Tweak contrast if needed.

QR Bonus (end of module hub): First 60 Minutes Checklist + 10 Starter Templates + Dimensions & Export Table. Scan to duplicate the templates directly and print the checklist if you like working on paper.

Closing Thought

You've stepped from curiosity into practice. You now have a reliable account, a mental map of the interface, a dashboard that will scale with your work, and your first customized design.

The software didn't change—you did. In Chapter 2, we'll shape your eye so your designs read clearly at a glance. Good typography and honest contrast are quiet superpowers. You're ready for them.

Chapter 2

Typography & Color: Hierarchy, Font Pairing, Palettes & Contrast

Open any feed, slide deck, brochure, or landing page and notice what your brain does first: it doesn't read. It scans. It takes in big shapes, relative sizes, bolds versus regulars, darks on lights, and the temperature of color. In milliseconds, it decides: this looks trustworthy / this looks messy; this feels premium / this feels cheap; this is worth my time / this is noise. Typography and color are the two levers that drive those snap judgments. They are not decoration. They are the skeleton and blood of your message. **So, before they read your words, they read your design.**

Canva's promise is speed—and speed is a gift only if it comes with control. Click too quickly and you fall into the "font buffet" (six styles in the same design) or the "rainbow palette" (every hue shouting at once). That's how good ideas get dismissed as amateur. On the other hand, when you master hierarchy (what the eye sees first), pairing (which fonts sing together), palette (which colors feel like a brand), and contrast (whether people can actually read), your work stops looking like a template and starts reading like a brand.

This chapter slows you down—on purpose. We'll learn to stage a headline like a headline (commanding, spacious); to cast the right supporting font beside it (calm, legible); to assemble three or four colors that live well together across social, print, and slides; and to pressure-test every combination on the device that matters most: a phone. By the end, you won't be asking, "Which font looks nice?" You'll be asking, "Which hierarchy gets my idea read in three seconds?" You'll stop dabbling with colors and start carrying a palette that makes your work recognizable at a glance

Promise: the techniques here are simple, repeatable, and visible. Apply them once and you'll feel the difference: apply them for a month and others will feel the difference in you.

What You'll Do in 10 Minutes (and why it matters)

A small, focused sprint turns theory into muscle memory.

1. Set the stage (1 min).
2. Create a 1080×1350 (portrait) design in Canva—phone-first, so decisions are honest.
3. Build a three-step hierarchy (3 min).
4. Add three text boxes: Headline (largest, bold), Subhead (medium, regular), Body (small, regular). Place them with generous spacing.
5. Pick a proven pairing (3 min).
6. Set the Headline to a confident serif (e.g., Playfair Display or Merriweather). Set Subhead + Body to a clean sans (e.g., Inter, Open Sans, Montserrat). Already, you're 70% professional.
7. Load a 3–4 color palette (2 min).
8. From Canva's Color styles, choose: Primary (background), Secondary (headline), Accent (buttons/markers), Neutral (body text). Save to Brand Kit if available.
9. Make it readable (1 min).
10. Test contrast: white on navy; charcoal on pale beige. Preview on your phone. If you squint, it still reads? Good.

That one canvas now demonstrates hierarchy, pairing, palette, and contrast—the four decisions you'll refine for the rest of the chapter.

Section 1 — Hierarchy: The Map That Gets Your Message Read

Why it matters.

If everything speaks at the same volume, nothing is heard. Hierarchy is how you assign roles: the headline grabs, the subhead frames, the body explains, the CTA directs. Done right, your design reads itself in the viewer's mind before they consciously read it.

How to structure hierarchy in Canva (with intent).

- **Size**: Let the headline be decisively larger. Think 2.2–3× the body size for social, 1.6–2× for print.
- **Weight**: Bold for headlines, regular for body. Use italics sparingly (emphasis, not style).
- **Spacing**: Give each level breathing room. Tight spacing cheapens; air sells.
- **Position**: The eye lands high-left on Western layouts. Use that to your advantage.
- **Color**: One decisive color for the headline, then calm neutrals for body.

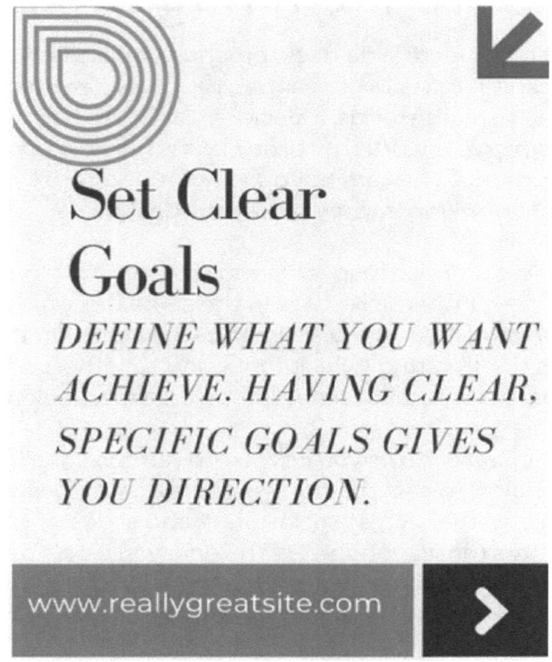

Real Scenario — "The Poster No One Read."

A community workshop poster placed date, title, and venue in the same size. People stared and kept walking. We rebuilt it: giant event name; medium-sized date/venue; small, crisp details. Same words, different ladder. Turnout doubled.

Pro Tip — The Three-Second Test.

Shrink your design to phone-thumbnail size in Canva's zoom. Can you grasp the headline (and only the headline) in three seconds? If not, increase size/weight and clear more space around it.

Mini Exercise — Ladder of Meaning.

Duplicate your 10-minute design into three copies.

A) Keep all sizes close (bad on purpose).
B) Make the headline 2.5× body, subhead 1.6× body.
C) Keep B's sizes but add more padding/space between levels.

Preview all on your phone. Which one feels most confident? That's the effect of hierarchy.

Section 2 — Font Pairing: Two Voices, One Message

Why it matters.

Fonts carry personality: serifs often read as editorial, premium, or classic; sans serifs read as modern, clean, or tech-forward; scripts whisper human warmth but can overwhelm legibility. The aim is to set two voices that harmonize—never competing solos.

Reliable pairings (start here, then evolve).

- **Editorial authority**: Merriweather (H1) + Inter (body).
- **Modern product:** Montserrat (H1) + Source Sans Pro (body).
- **Warm boutique**: Playfair Display (H1) + Lato (body).
- **Friendly educator**: Poppins (H1) + Noto Sans (body).

Rules that keep you safe.

- Cap yourself at 2 fonts (3 only if one is a tiny accent, like numerals or a script signature).
- Contrast, don't clash: pair categories (serif + sans). Avoid two loud display fonts together.
- Be consistent across assets: same pair on posts, decks, brochures. Repetition builds brand memory.

Real Scenario — The "Six Fonts, One Site" Freelance Portfolio.

Talented work, but the site felt chaotic. We cut to two: a dignified serif for headlines and a neutral sans for long reads. Inquiries rose the same month—not because the work improved, but because trust did.

Attention — Readability Across Weights.

Some sans look beautiful at 400 weight but fall apart at 700; some serifs are elegant in H1 but muddy in small sizes. Always test your exact sizes on phone.

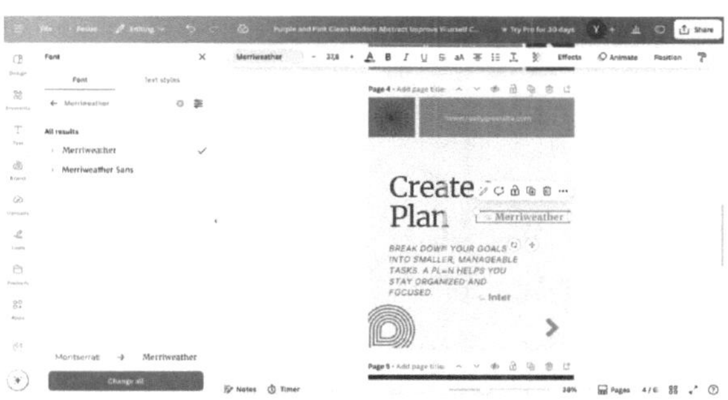

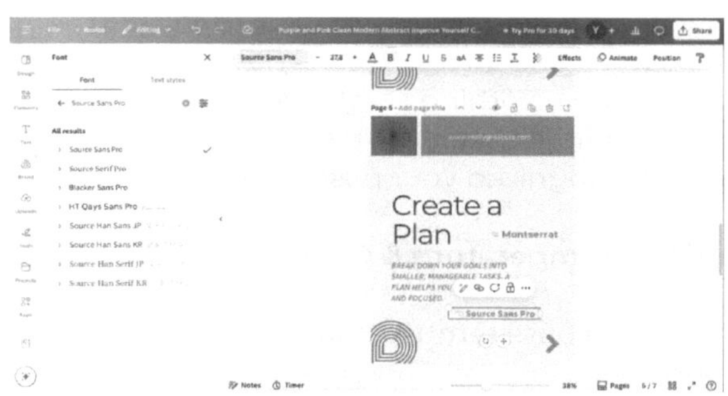

Pro Tip — Numerals Matter.

If your brand communicates numbers (pricing, metrics), compare numeral shapes. Pick the font with clean, unambiguous digits. It silently improves professionalism.

Mini Exercise — The Pairing Bake-Off.

Create one layout. Duplicate it four times, testing the four pairings above. Export a PDF with all five pages. Share with a friend or team and ask only: "Which version feels most us?" Choose by feel and legibility.

Section 3 — Palettes: Three or Four Colors That Behave Like a Brand

Why it matters.

Color sets mood instantly and creates memory over time. Chaotic color choices lead to forgettable brands; disciplined palettes lead to recognition. The best palettes are small, deliberate, and versatile.

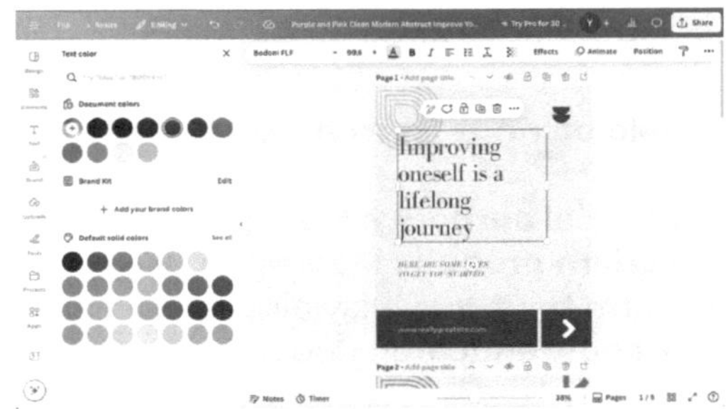

A simple, durable palette structure.

- Primary (60%) — background or dominant blocks (e.g., navy).
- Secondary (30%) — headline or key highlights (e.g., teal).
- Accent (10%) — buttons, bullets, small emphasis (e.g., coral).
- Neutrals — white/near-white and charcoal/near-black for text.

Where to find or build palettes in Canva.

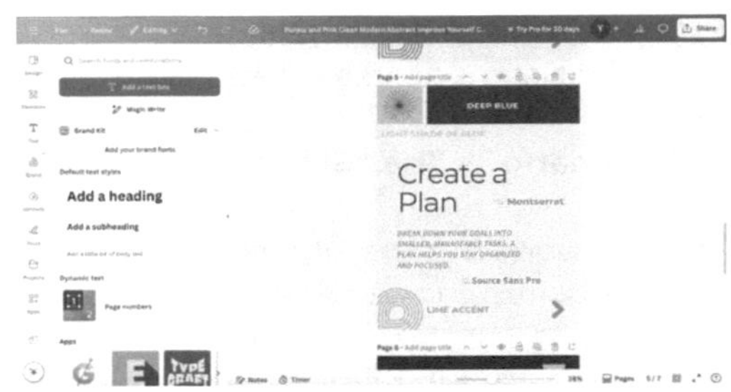

- Extract from Image: drop in a brand photo; save the suggested swatches.
- Color Wheel / Styles: search "calm," "bold," "vintage" to find curated sets.
- Brand Kit: lock your final four and stop experimenting every post.

Real Scenario — The Startup With Five Lives.

This creator's grid swung weekly: lavender, then orange, then mint, then red. Nothing stuck. We committed to deep blue + light slate + lime accent. Three weeks later, people started saying, "I recognized your post before I saw the handle."

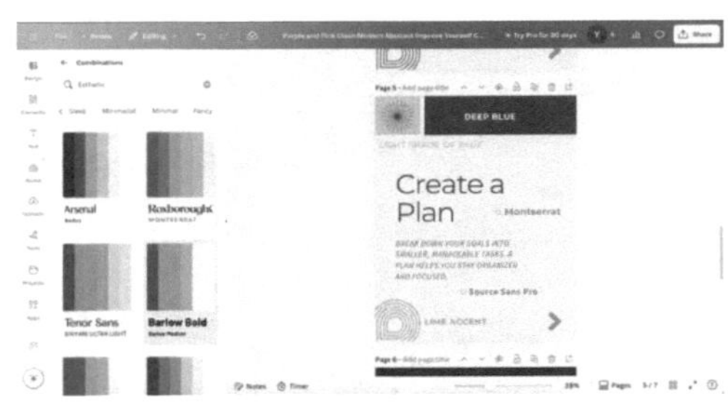

Pro Tip — Temperature & Contrast.

- Choose a base temperature (cool → trust, warm → energy) and keep contrast workable. Pale text on pale backgrounds will not survive mobile feeds.
- Alternative Fast Track — Monochrome + Accent.
- Pick one hue (e.g., blue) and live in its shades (navy, sky, slate). Add one pop accent (e.g., coral) for CTAs. Easy to manage, hard to mess up.

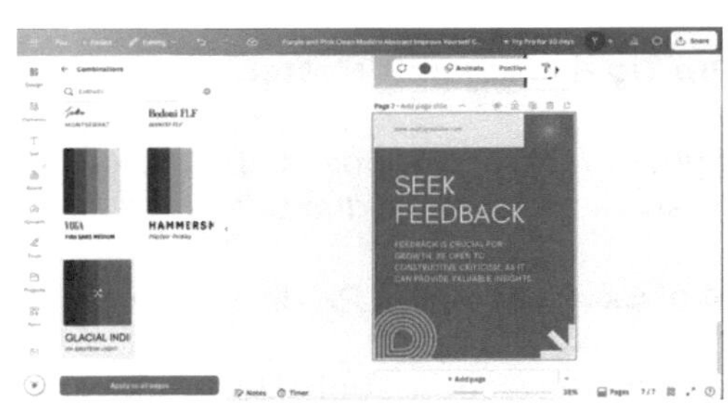

Mini Exercise — Palette in the Wild.

Search your camera roll for one photo that feels like your vibe (studio corner, product flatlay, city dusk). Use "Extract Palette" in Canva. Save those four colors to Brand Kit and apply them to a two-slide design. That's your first brand board.

Section 4 — Contrast: Legibility Is a Promise, Not a Preference

Why it matters.

If it isn't readable, it isn't communication. Low contrast is the silent killer of engagement: lovely aesthetic, zero comprehension. High contrast isn't about harshness; it's about clarity. **Practical ways to secure readability:**

- Dark on light or light on dark for body text. Avoid mid-tone on mid-tone.
- Overlays: place text over busy photos using a 30–60% translucent rectangle or gradient.
- Shadow/Outline with restraint: a 1–2 px text outline can rescue edge cases—but don't rely on it as a style.
- Phone preview: always, always check at hand-held size.

Real Scenario — The Pastel Problem.

A wellness brand loved pale sage on cream. Beautiful in the art board, invisible in Stories. We kept the vibe but flipped roles: charcoal text on sage blocks, sage accents around it. Same mood, new clarity.

Attention — Accessibility.

If your audience includes readers on dim screens or outdoors, push contrast up. It's inclusive and it converts better.

Pro Tip — CTA Contrast Multiplier.

CTAs need contrast in three ways: color (button vs background), weight (bold vs regular), and spacing (air around it). Treat the CTA like a mini headline; let it breathe.

Mini Exercise — The Contrast Ladder.

Create a 3×3 grid of small CTA buttons.

- Row 1: low-contrast combos.
- Row 2: medium.
- Row 3: high-contrast.
- Preview on phone in bright light. Which row survives? Make that your new baseline.

Section 5 — Putting It Together (With Reasoning, Not Only Rules)

Let's design a simple promo tile you could actually ship today—and explain why each choice works.

1. **Canvas**: 1080×1350 portrait (IG feed and LinkedIn-friendly). Phone-first reality.
2. **Hierarchy**: "Free Workshop: Build Your First Portfolio" as the H1. It's the job of the headline to earn the rest of the read. Make it large, bold, and short.
3. **Pairing**: Merriweather (H1) + Inter (body). Editorial authority + system clarity.
4. **Palette**: Navy background, off-white body text, teal subheads, coral CTA. Cool trust + one warm spark.
5. **Contrast**: White-on-navy for H1; charcoal-on-pale slate for body. No guessing.
6. **CTA**: "Save Your Seat →" in coral, bold, with comfortable padding.
7. **Spacing**: Bigger than you think. White space equals confidence.
8. **Consistency**: Save this as "Promo — Master Template." Duplicate for future workshops, swap only title/date.

Result: clear ladder of attention, two voices in harmony, a palette you can reuse, and legibility that survives a shaky bus ride.

Checklist — Typography & Color Locked

1. **Hierarchy** reads at a glance. **When you zoom out**—or hold your phone at arm's length—you can still identify the headline instantly, then the subhead, then the body. You no longer hope people read; you guide how they read.
2. **Two fonts,** one voice. Your chosen **pair** handles everything: headlines feel distinctive, body stays effortless, numerals look clean. Across posts, slides, and PDFs, the text feels like the same brand speaking in different rooms.
3. A **palette** you can live with. **Three or four colors r**ecur across assets without strain. Primary dominates, secondary supports, accent sparks action, neutrals carry text. Your grid begins to look like you, not like "whatever was cute today."
4. **Contrast** that respects readers and contexts. **Headlines and CTAs** are unmistakable; paragraphs don't fade; overlays come out when photos get busy. You've traded fragile aesthetics for durable clarity—especially on mobile.

When all four are true, your designs stop asking for attention and start earning it.

Common Mistakes — And How to Correct Them (for real-world freelancers & teams)

Mistake 1: The Font Parade.

- Six fonts, three scripts, every weight. It looks like indecision, which feels like inexperience.
- Fix: cap yourself at two (serif + sans). Save the pair to Brand Kit. Refuse "just one more" unless there's a functional reason.

Mistake 2: Mood Swings in Color.

- Every post a new palette. It might feel creative; it reads as unstable.
- Fix: adopt a 60-30-10 palette. If you're bored, vary layout, photography, or texture—not the base colors.

Mistake 3: Pretty but Illegible.

- Low-contrast aesthetics that die on phones.
- Fix: commit to readability. Use overlays, raise contrast, and test on mobile in sunlight. Beauty that can't be read doesn't sell.

Mistake 4: Flat Pages, Flat Sales.

- Equal sizes and weights, no visual path.
- Fix: make the headline decisively bigger, subhead supportive, body smaller with line-height tuned. Add air. Watch comprehension jump.

Why this matters.

None of these errors is fatal alone, but together they form an invisible wall of mistrust. Fix them, and clients see "professional" before they've processed a single sentence.

"Do It Now" Homework — 90 Minutes of Design That Sticks

1) Hierarchy Audit (20 min).
Open three past designs. Without changing words, rebuild the hierarchy: enlarge H1 dramatically, clarify subheads, add space. Export before/after. Note what changed in your gut reaction.

2) Pairing Decision (20 min).
Choose your long-term pair (serif + sans). Apply to: one IG post, one slide, one one-pager. Save to Brand Kit so future-you doesn't re-decide every time.

3) Palette Build (25 min).
Extract from a photo or pick a curated set. Lock Primary/Secondary/Accent/Neutrals. Create a one-page "Brand Board" with swatches, font pair, buttons, and a sample headline.

4) Contrast Stress Test (25 min).
Design a CTA block in three contrasts: low, mid, high. Export and test on your phone under bright light. Choose the one that survives the worst conditions. Make it your default.

Outcome: a practical typography + color system that speeds every future decision.

Closing Thought

Type and color look like cosmetics from a distance. Up close, they're governance. They create order without asking permission; they teach the eye where to go and how to feel. With a sturdy hierarchy, a faithful font pair, a palette you can live with, and contrast you can trust, you won't merely make "prettier" things—you'll make clearer ones. And clarity is the most generous thing you can give your audience. Next, we'll translate this clarity into structure on the canvas—grids, alignment, grouping, and placement—so that your pages not only speak well, they hold together under pressure.

Chapter 3

Layout & Levels: Grids, Alignment, Grouping, Positioning

A design can have beautiful colors, striking images, and clever text—and still feel wrong. The problem is often invisible: the layout. When elements float without connection, when text is misaligned, or when spacing is inconsistent, the viewer feels unease without knowing why. Good layout, on the other hand, is quiet and confident. It guides the eye naturally from headline to image to call-to-action.

In Canva, mastering layout is about learning how to place elements with intention. This chapter is not about decoration—it's about structure. Imagine building a house: typography and color are your paint and furniture, but the layout is the architecture. Without it, the whole thing collapses.

By the end of this chapter, you will know how to:

- Use grids to anchor your elements so they stay balanced.
- Apply alignment tools that make your text and images snap into place.
- Group elements so you can move, resize, or duplicate entire sections at once.
- Master layering and positioning, deciding what stays in front, what sits behind, and how depth creates focus.

This is where your work begins to look "professional." Most beginners struggle not because of creativity, but because of spacing and alignment. Once you fix that, your designs instantly look more polished—without changing a single font or color.

What You'll Do in 10 Minutes (and why it matters)

- Explore Canva's grid system and drop a few elements into place.
- Practice aligning text and shapes with the smart guides.
- Group two or more objects and move them together.
- Layer an image behind text and adjust transparency for balance.

These may sound simple, but they are the backbone of every design you will ever create.

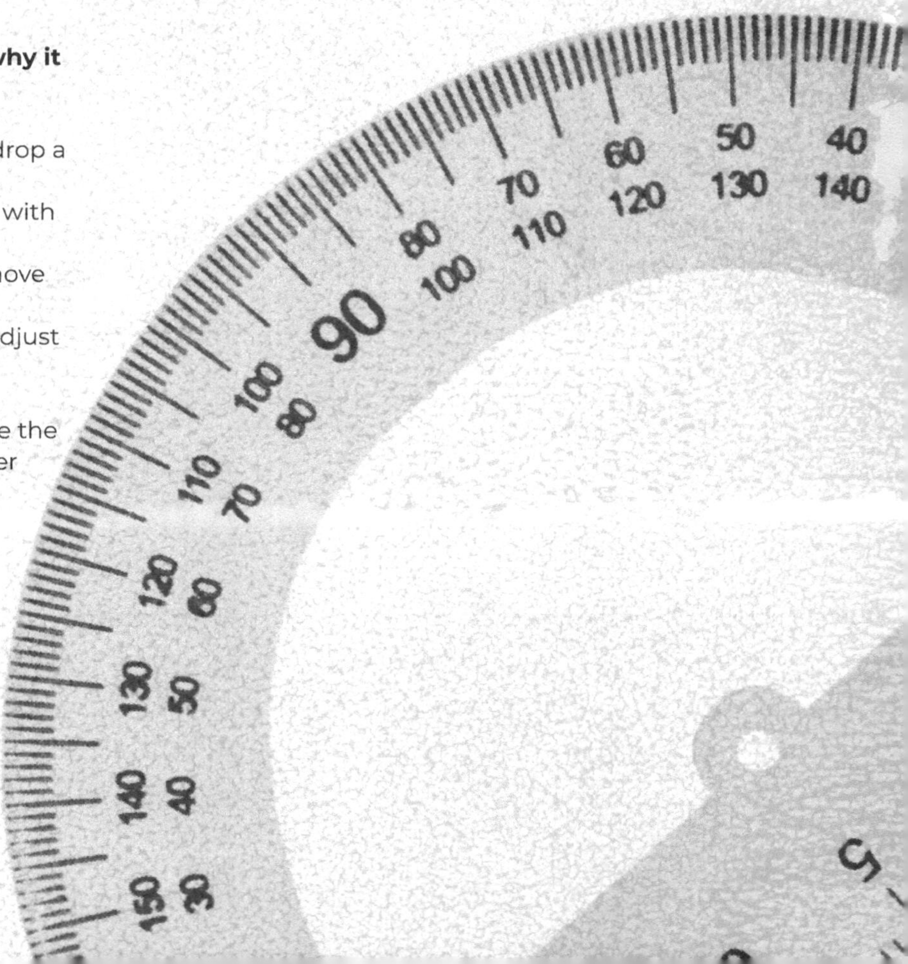

Grids: The Hidden Skeleton of Every Layout

Grids are invisible lines that organize content. Newspapers, websites, posters—all of them rely on grids. Canva offers a range of preset grid layouts (one column, two-column split, thirds, quarters) that help even beginners achieve professional spacing without measuring pixels.

To use grids:

1. From the sidebar, open Elements → Grids.
2. Drag a grid style onto your canvas.
3. Drop images or shapes into the grid slots—they'll automatically resize to fit.

The beauty of grids is consistency. Instead of guessing where to place a photo, you know it will always align. That frees your mind to focus on the message, not the math.

Real Scenario — Instagram Carousel That Feels Cohesive

A fitness coach wanted to post a 5-slide carousel of workout tips. Without grids, each slide looked slightly different—margins uneven, images cropped awkwardly. With a simple 2-column grid, every slide suddenly matched. The message felt cohesive, and engagement doubled.

Pro Tip — Break the Grid Intentionally

Rules matter until you're skilled enough to bend them. Use grids to anchor most elements, then allow one photo or headline to break the structure. That contrast draws attention.

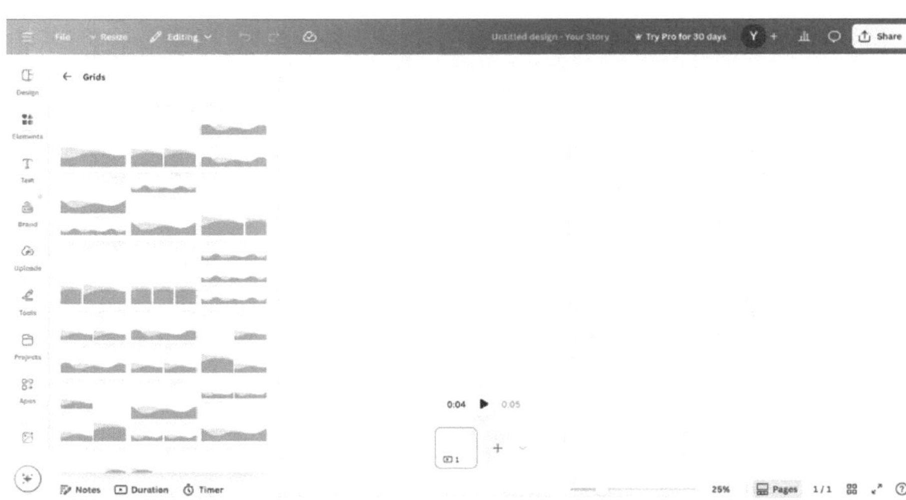

Mini Exercise

Open a blank Instagram Post (1080×1080). Insert a 2-column grid. Drop two photos inside. Then replace one photo with a colored background and text overlay. Export and look at it on your phone. Notice how balanced it feels.

Alignment: Snapping Into Place

Alignment is the invisible glue that holds design together. Canva's smart guides make it almost impossible to misalign—if you pay attention. When you drag an element, pink lines appear showing center points, edges, or equal spacing with other objects.

Why alignment matters:

- **Legibility**: aligned text is easier to read.
- **Professionalism**: aligned images show attention to detail.
- **Harmony**: aligned objects feel calmer and more intentional.

To practice alignment:

1. Add three text boxes.
2. Drag them until the pink lines show equal spacing.
3. Select them all, then use the "Align top" or "Align middle" options in the toolbar.

Common Pitfall — Eyeballing Alignment

Many beginners "eyeball" placements, thinking it looks fine. But one pixel off is visible on a phone screen. Trust Canva's guides—they exist for a reason.

Real Scenario — Pitch Deck Slide

A startup founder once showed investors a slide where bullet points were slightly staggered. The content was strong, but the visual chaos undermined credibility. After applying "Align left," the deck felt clean, sharp, and worthy of trust.

Mini Exercise

Create a flyer. Add a headline, subheadline, and call-to-action. Align all text boxes left. Then try aligning them center. Export both versions and compare: which looks calmer for your message?

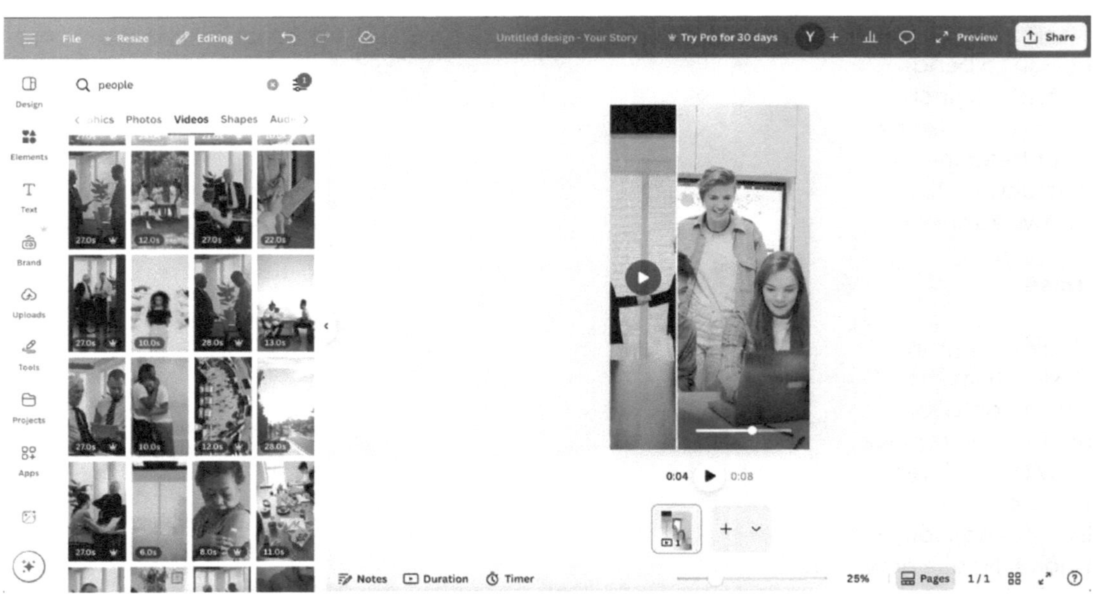

Grouping: Moving as One

Imagine trying to carry a stack of plates one by one. Grouping is like picking up the whole stack at once. In Canva, grouping lets you move or resize multiple elements together—headlines with subheads, icons with captions, photos with borders.

How to group:

1. Select multiple elements: Shift+click; Command+click (Apple) or drag across.
2. Click Group in the toolbar.
3. Now you can resize, duplicate, or move them as a unit.

Pro Tip — Use Grouping for Consistency

When you build a carousel, group the layout of one slide (image, text, button). Duplicate the grouped slide, then change the content. This keeps design consistent across slides.

Real Scenario — Event Flyer in Two Languages

A community organizer designed flyers in English and Spanish. By grouping the header, image, and CTA box, she could duplicate the entire layout and only replace the text. Both versions stayed identical in design—only the words changed.

Mini Exercise

Create a simple poster with a title, image, and button. Group them. Duplicate the group twice. Change the colors in each duplicate. Now you have three posters with identical structure but different moods.

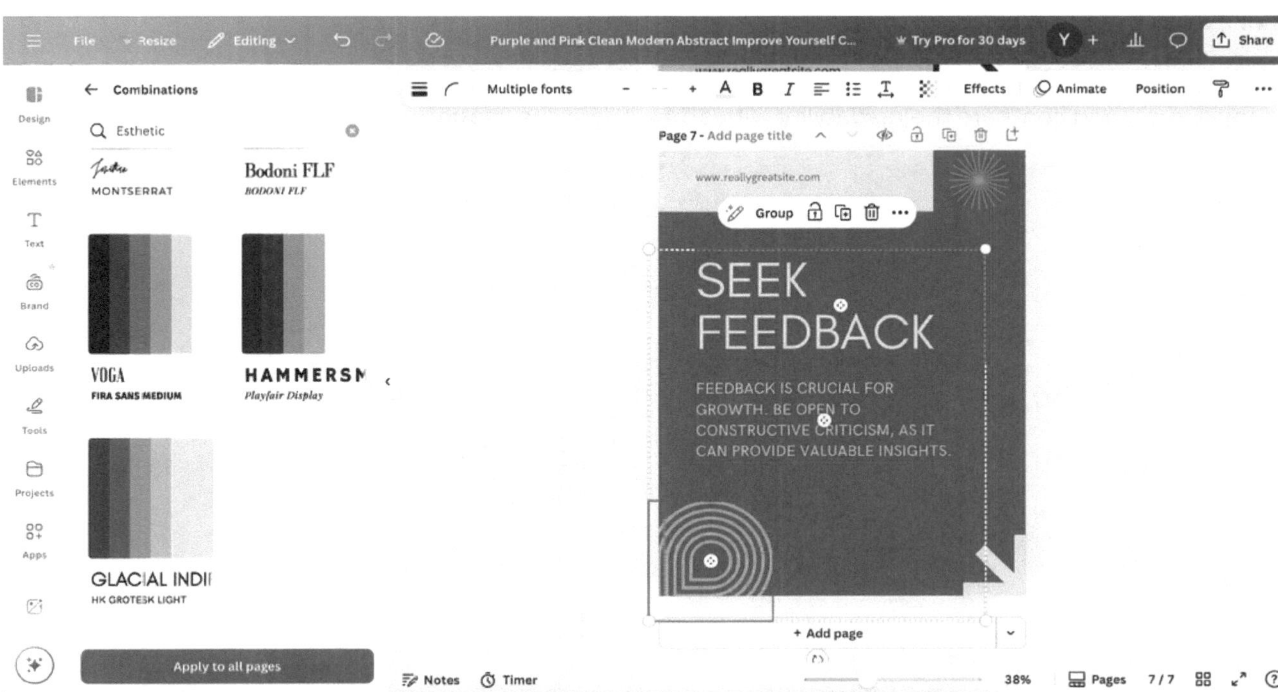

Positioning: Layers and Depth

Positioning determines what sits in front and what hides behind. Canva uses a simple layer stack, like sheets of paper. Every element you add goes on top by default. But you can send objects forward or backward to create depth.

Why it matters:

- Text should always sit above background images.
- Icons can overlap photos without hiding faces.
- Semi-transparent shapes can rest between background and text to improve readability.

How to use:

1. Right-click an element.
2. Choose "Arrange" backward or forward.
3. Adjust transparency if layering creates clutter.

Attention — Don't Overcrowd Layers

Too many overlapping shapes make a design heavy. Use layers with intention: one clear background, one focal image, one readable text area.

Real Scenario — YouTube Thumbnail That Pops

A gaming creator placed a character image behind bold text. The text was hard to read. We added a semi-transparent rectangle between them, adjusted transparency to 60%, and suddenly both text and character were visible. Click-through rates rose.

Mini Exercise

Create a social post. Add a background photo, a semi-transparent shape (rectangle at 60%), and bold text on top. Export and compare the readability with and without the shape.

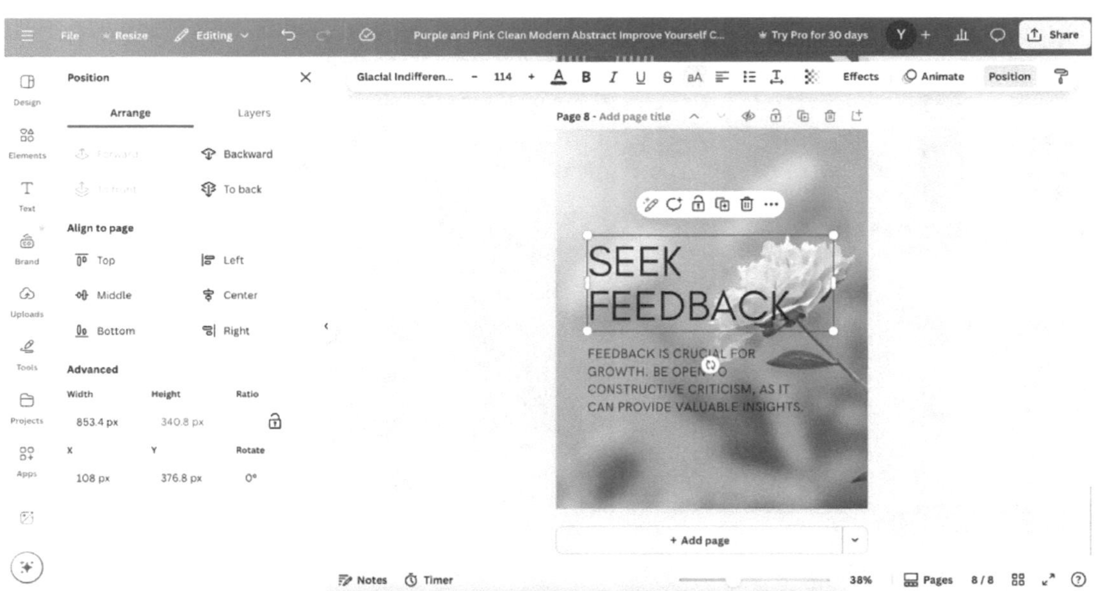

Checklist: Layout & Levels Locked In

Before moving on, confirm you can:

- Place images and text in grids for balance.
- Snap objects using alignment guides.
- Group elements to move or duplicate them together.
- Adjust layers to control depth and readability.

If these feel natural, your designs now have structure as well as style.

Common Mistakes — And Their Fixes

- Messy Spacing. Throwing objects randomly leads to chaotic layouts. Use grids as your training wheels until spacing feels natural.
- Ignoring Smart Guides. If you resist the pink lines, you're ignoring free help. Let Canva's guides do the math.
- Forgetting to Group. If you move text and image separately, they'll slip out of sync. Group and duplicate instead.
- Over-layering. Stacking too many shapes, images, and effects clutters the message. Keep depth intentional, not decorative.

Closing Thought

Mastering layout is like learning rhythm in music. Without it, even the best lyrics fall flat. With it, every design flows. By anchoring elements in grids, aligning them with guides, grouping logically, and layering with intention, you've crossed from "random" to "structured."

Next, we'll focus on Images & Elements—uploading, cropping, and using Canva's vast library to bring your designs to life.

Chapter 4

Images & Elements: Uploads, Cropping, Transparency, Libraries

Pictures carry the message—structure lets them speak. If layout is the architecture of your design, images are the windows that let light in. A single well-chosen photo can communicate mood, credibility, and context faster than a paragraph of text. **But images only work when they're handled well—imported at the right quality, framed with intention, layered with care, and stored in a system you can actually maintain.** This chapter is your guide to treating visuals like a professional: not as decorations, but as the core narrative components of your page.

We'll slow down and learn how images enter Canva (from your device, cloud drives, or Canva's built-in libraries), how to crop and frame them so the eye lands where you want, how to use transparency to balance text and background, and how to build a personal asset library that makes tomorrow faster than today. We'll also explore "elements"—icons, shapes, lines, frames—that quietly support your message.

Used well, these pieces reinforce hierarchy, rhythm, and clarity; used poorly, they add noise. By the end of this chapter, you'll move from "drag-and-drop" to directing the viewer's attention with purpose.

What You'll Do in 10 Minutes (and why it matters)

- A quick warm-up creates momentum and removes hesitation. In this short sprint you will:
- Upload one image from your device and one from Canva's stock library, so you can compare quality and style.
- Crop each image to a clear focal point and test a frame (circle or phone mockup) to see how it changes the story.
- Add a semi-transparent rectangle and place text on top, learning how transparency improves readability without killing the photo.
- Save both images to a Folder and Star them, so your asset library starts tidy and stays that way.

The point isn't to make something "perfect" yet—it's to feel how a few deliberate touches can turn a generic picture into a compelling, branded visual.

Uploads: Bringing Your World Into Canva

Why this matters.

Every brand—personal or business—has a visual fingerprint: your environment, your products, your face, your city.

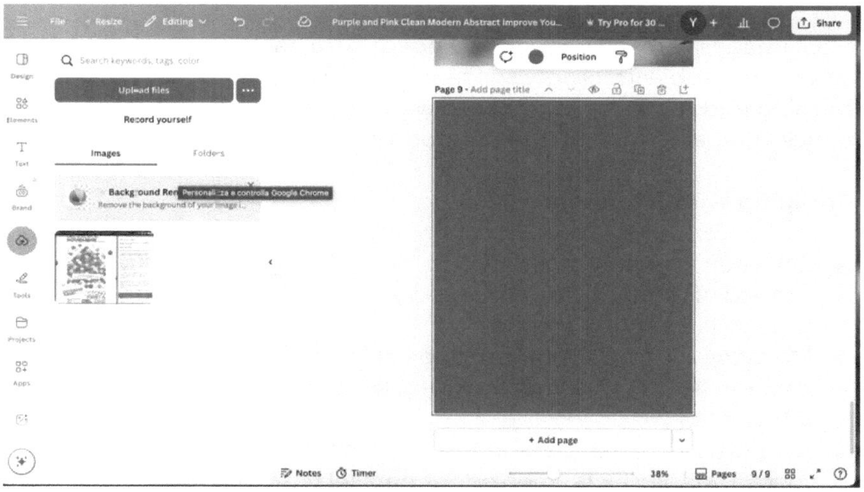

Uploading your own photos brings authenticity that stock cannot replicate. At the same time, Canva's built-in libraries are invaluable for filler images, conceptual shots, and quick experiments. You'll use both. The skill is choosing which source serves the message best.

How uploads work (with context).

- From any design, open the left sidebar and select Uploads.
- You can drag files in from your desktop or click Upload files to reach your computer, Google Drive, Dropbox, or Photos. Canva ingests common formats (JPG, PNG, SVG for vector icons, short MP4s/GIFs for motion), and it autosaves them to your account so you can reuse them later.

A few quality guardrails keep you out of trouble:

- **Resolution**: For social, aim for the design's native size (e.g., 1080×1080). For full-bleed A4 print, start with images at least 2500–3500 px on the long edge so they remain crisp.
- **Compression**: JPG is fine for photos; PNG is better for graphics with flat color or transparency. SVG stays razor-sharp at any size for icons and logos.
- **Color & tone**: If your brand is muted and warm, choose images with that mood. Consistency over time builds recognition—even with different subjects.

Real Scenario — The "Looks Fine on Desktop" Trap

A café owner loved a hero shot on her laptop. On mobile, it turned to mush—too dark, subject too small. We swapped it for a close, well-lit crop of a cappuccino pouring, with steam visible. Same theme, different framing; suddenly the headline popped and the photo looked premium on a phone.

Pro Tip — Upload in Sets

Don't upload one image at a time forever. Create small, themed sets: Team portraits, Behind-the-scenes, Product close-ups, Textures. Batch uploads help you design faster because the "next best" option is already waiting in the tray.

Mini Exercise — Dual Source Test

Upload a photo from your device and search Canva's library for a similar theme (e.g., "handmade ceramics studio"). Place both on a page. Which feels more you? Write down two reasons—lighting, authenticity, color tone. Keep that note as your sourcing rule.

Cropping & Framing: Directing the Eye to the Story

Why this matters.

Most images carry more than you need: extra background, competing subjects, empty space. Cropping creates focus; framing adds context. Together they decide what the viewer notices first and how the rest supports it.

Cropping with intention.

- Select an image and click Crop.
- Instead of randomly trimming edges, ask: "Where should the eye land in one second?"
- Move the crop box until your subject sits on a strong position (rule of thirds often works: key subject on an intersection).
- For portraits, leave space in front of the face (the "look room"); for products, keep edges parallel to the frame so the object feels stable.

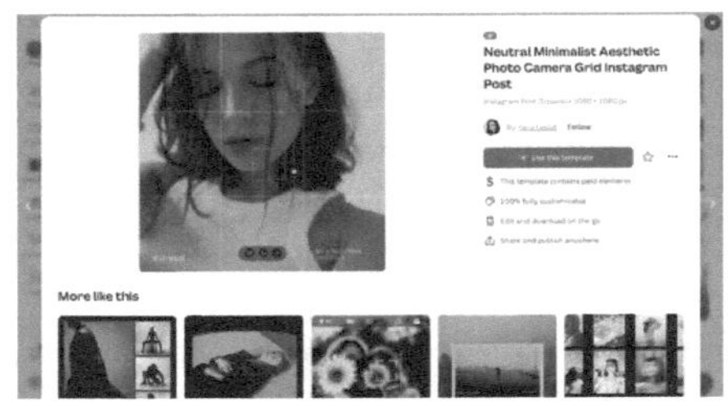

Framing to change meaning.

Frames in Canva (Elements → Frames) act like masks: drop an image into a circle to suggest "profile/identity," into a phone mockup to imply "app/tech," or into a torn paper frame for craft vibes. Frames provide instant context without adding text.

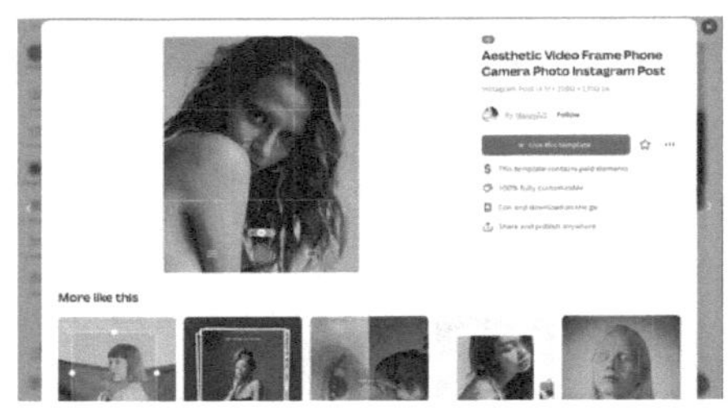

Alternative Fast Track — Use "Frames" for Carousel Consistency
When building a multi-slide carousel, pick one frame shape and use it across slides. The repeated silhouette becomes a rhythm the audience recognizes as "your series," even when photos change.

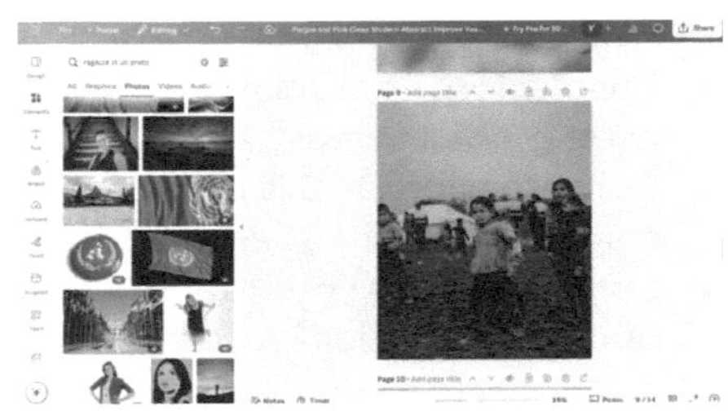

Real Scenario — From Noisy to Narrative

A travel creator used a wide cityscape on a 1080×1350 post. The skyline looked small; the caption fought for attention. We cropped tight to a single street corner with warm window light and placed the headline over a light area. Same image, but now the story was "this café at blue hour," not "a generic city."

Common Pitfall — Cropping to the Edges

If you crop a face or object too close to the edge, tension spikes and the design feels cramped. Leave breathing room—especially above headlines and around key details. Negative space is not wasted space; it's the frame that makes the subject readable.

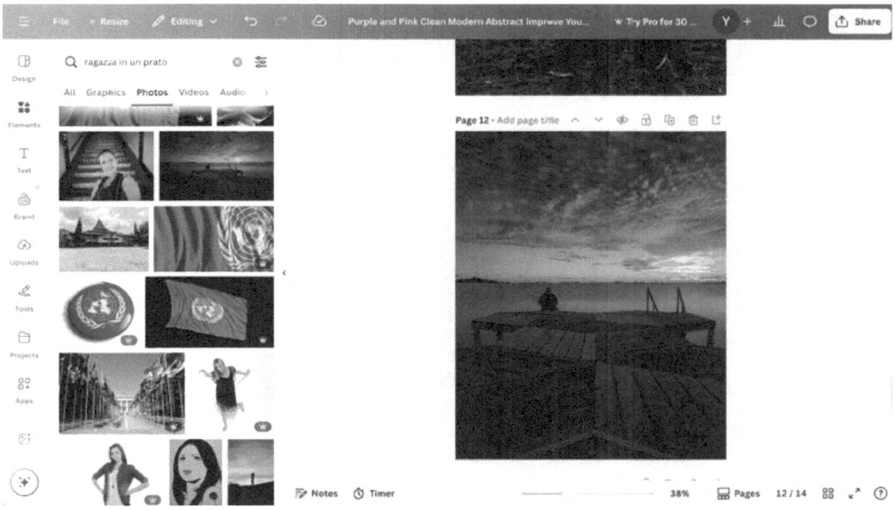

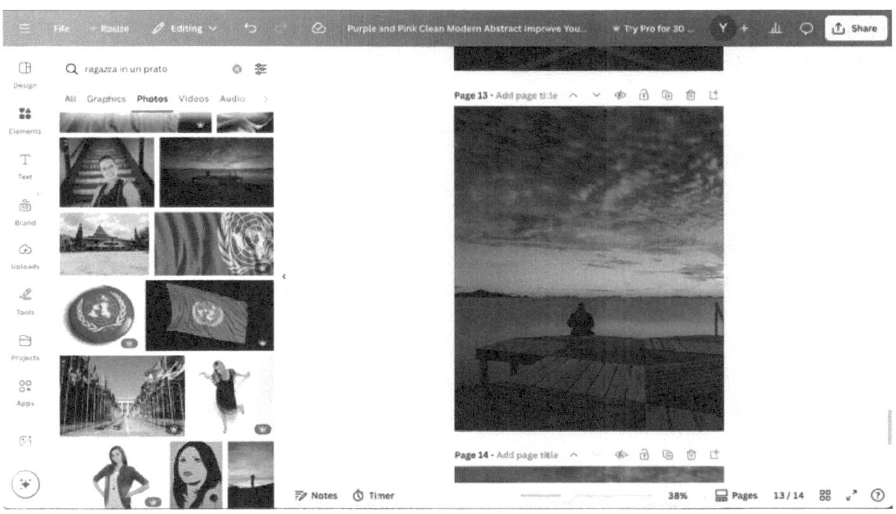

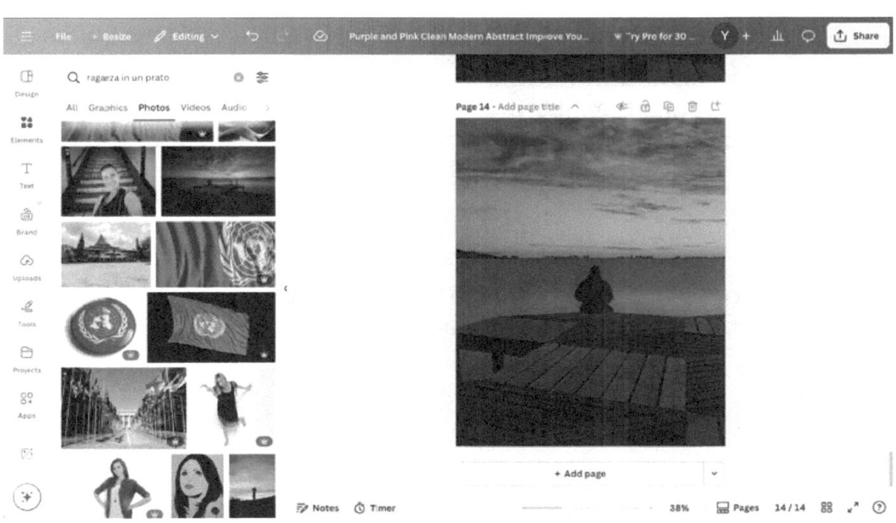

Mini Exercise — Three Crops, Three Stories

Pick one photo and create three crops:

1. Wide (environmental, subject small),
2. Medium (subject clear, some context),
3. Tight (detail shot).

Place all three on one page with the same headline.

Which tells the story best for social?

Which would you put in a brochure?

Write a one-sentence rule for when you'll choose each crop in the future.

Transparency: Balancing Photo Energy with Text Clarity

Why this matters.

Photos carry texture, contrast, and movement—great for emotion, tricky for text. Transparency lets you mediate between an energetic background and a legible message. Instead of lowering the image's brightness (which can make it dull), add a semi-transparent layer between image and text to preserve life and readability.

The practical recipe.

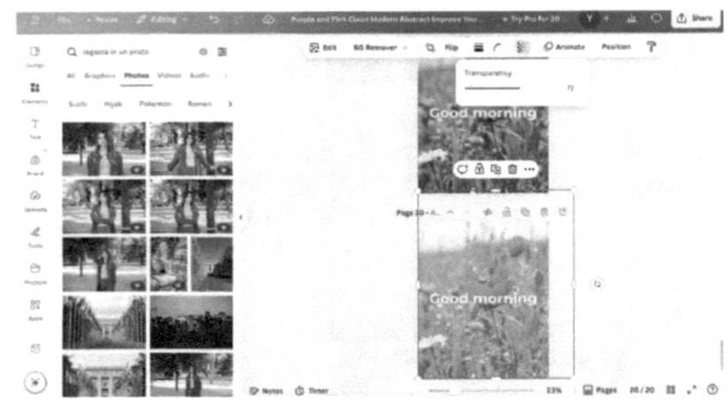

- Place a rectangle above the photo and below the headline.
- Open the transparency slider and test 30%–70% depending on background strength. Dark overlays work for light text; light overlays (or a subtle gradient) work for dark text. If your brand uses a key color, try that color at low opacity for a subtle, on-brand tint.

Beyond rectangles—shapes and gradients.

Hard rectangles are clean, but sometimes a soft gradient feels more natural, especially over complex backgrounds. A top-to-transparent gradient behind a headline can protect the first two lines while leaving the rest of the photo vibrant. Circles, ribbons, or angled shapes can also guide the eye—just use them sparingly so they support rather than compete.

Attention — Don't "Ghost" the Photo

Dropping a photo's opacity to 30% under text often kills its character. Keep the photo at 100% and adjust the layer above it. The image stays rich; the text gets its stage.

Real Scenario — YouTube Thumbnail Rescue

A tech creator had thumbnails with neon images and white text. On small screens, letters vibrated against bright details. We added a 60% dark gradient behind the title area, left the rest of the image untouched, and widened letter spacing slightly. CTR climbed—not because of clickbait, but because clarity won.

Pro Tip — Brand-Tinted Overlays

Pick your brand's darkest color and save a 40–60% overlay rectangle as a reusable component. You'll instantly harmonize mixed photo sources while reinforcing your brand palette.

Mini Exercise — The Readability Ladder

Take one busy photo and try three solutions:

1. Dark rectangle at 50% with white text,
2. Light rectangle at 50% with black text,
3. Vertical gradient (dark to transparent) at 60% under the headline.
4. Export small (1080 px) and preview on your phone. Which reads fastest? That's your default pattern.

Elements: Icons, Shapes, Lines, and the Quiet Design Grammar

Why this matters.

Elements are punctuation. They separate ideas, point attention, and create rhythm. In Canva, "Elements" includes icons, shapes, lines, stickers, and frames. These aren't decoration; they're tools for hierarchy and flow.

Icons that actually help.

Use icons when they replace repeated words or clarify categories: a phone icon before a number, a map pin for a location, a calendar for dates. Keep icon style consistent—outline with outline, solid with solid. Mismatched styles feel amateur even if the content is correct.

Shapes as structure.

Rectangles, circles, and lines build containers for text create columns, or form call-outs. A thin line under a heading adds emphasis without shouting. Rounded rectangles can hold short CTAs; full-width bars can divide sections gracefully.

Line weight & spacing.

Elements have weight just like fonts. A 1-px hairline under a bold headline often looks elegant; a 6-px bar might overpower. Match the weight of shapes to the typographic voice—light UI = light lines, bold poster = bold shapes.

Common Pitfall — Sticker Overload

Animated stickers and playful shapes can add charm in stories or casual posts. But too many moving parts drown the message. If everything moves, nothing moves the viewer.

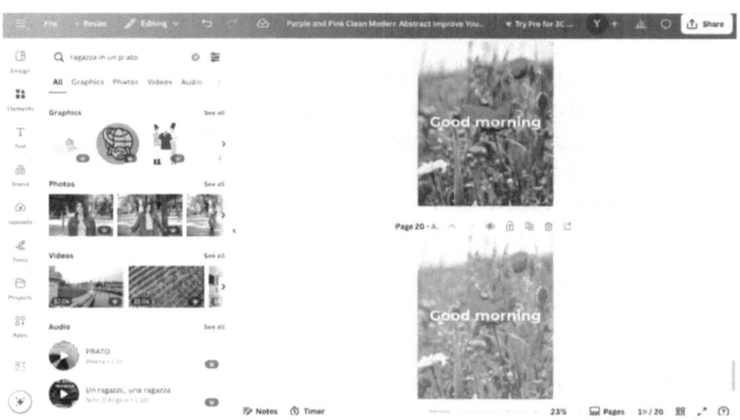

Real Scenario — A Clean Pricing Card

A founder used different icon sets for features—some rounded, some sharp. We replaced them with one consistent outline set, aligned the labels, and used a thin rule between tiers. The price card suddenly looked like the product was reliable.

Mini Exercise — Icon Consistency Audit

- Search "icons" in Elements and star a single consistent set (outline or filled).
- Build a tiny key (phone, email, map, clock). Save it to a folder named Brand → Icons. Use only those for one week.
- Notice how your designs start to feel unified.

Libraries & Asset Management: Designing Tomorrow's Speed Today

Why this matters.

A design habit without a library is a treadmill—you work hard, but don't move faster. Asset management turns creativity into a system: the images you trust, the icons that match, the overlays you reuse. When your future self logs in, the best choices are already within one click.

Folders and naming.

At minimum, create folders for Photos, Icons & Shapes, Textures/Overlays, and Brand (Logo, Palette, Fonts). Within Photos, consider subfolders by purpose (e.g., People, Product, Behind the Scenes). In Canva, you can Star assets and sort by "Starred" to quickly assemble a kit for a project.

Brand Kit (when available).

If you have Brand Kit access, load your logo, palette, and fonts. Even on free plans without full Brand Kit features, you can keep a Brand Board page—a single design with your colors, type choices, and key elements parked on it, ready to copy into any project.

Reusable components.

Save your favorite overlays, CTA buttons, dividers, and icon rows as master components on a "Components" page. When you start a new design, copy from that page instead of rebuilding. Micro-systems are how you scale.

Attention — Licensing & Mix-and-Match

If you combine Canva stock with your own photos, keep a quick note (in a text box off-canvas or a separate doc) about which assets are stock vs original. It helps maintain clarity for commercial use and handoffs to clients.

Real Scenario — The 2-Hour Weekly Batch

A creator used to spend entire evenings hunting for "the right photo." We built a library: 40 on-brand photos, a fixed icon set, and 3 overlay styles. She now batches a month of posts in two hours because the searching is over—most decisions are pre-made.

Pro Tip — Archive Aggressively

If an image never gets used, it clutters decisions. Once a month, spend ten minutes archiving or deleting unused assets. Space equals speed.

Mini Exercise — Your First System

Create a folder named Brand — Visual Library. Inside, add subfolders: Photos (People/Product/BTS), Icons & Shapes, Overlays, Components. Move at least 12 assets into the right places right now. Star your top 6. You just built tomorrow's momentum.

Putting It Together: A Small, Real Project (with reasoning)

Why this matters.

Knowledge sticks when it ships. You'll create one Instagram post that uses every idea above: honest sourcing, focused cropping, supportive elements, readable text, and clean asset management.

Step-by-step, with why.

1. **Start**: Open an IG Post 1080×1080. Choose a working title like "3 Morning Habits." Naming a purpose narrows style choices.
2. **Image sourcing:** Upload a genuine photo (your desk at sunrise) or pick one Calm, warm stock shot. You'll match your brand tone.
3. **Crop for story**: Tighten to the coffee mug + notebook, placing the mug on a thirds intersection so the eye lands there first.
4. **Overlay**: Add a dark brand-tinted rectangle at ~50% behind the headline area—readability without killing mood.
5. **Type**: Place a short headline (2 lines), then a smaller subhead. Keep line lengths short for mobile.
6. **Elements**: Add a thin line under the headline to anchor it; place a small icon (sun/clock) beside the subhead if it adds clarity.
7. **Balance & spacing**: Nudge elements until spacing is even. If the photo tugs the eye away, reduce its contrast slightly with Adjust.
8. **Library**: Save the overlay and line as components to your Components page. Star the photo if it suits your style.
9. **Export**: PNG for social. Preview on phone. If text vibrates, increase overlay opacity or tighten line spacing.

You've just transformed a generic picture into a clear, branded message—fast, and with choices you can repeat.

Checklist — Images & Elements, Locked In

A recap consolidates progress and keeps future chapters lighter to digest. If you can say "yes" to these, you're ready to move on.

- You can source images from Uploads and Stock, choosing based on tone and quality.
- You crop with purpose, using frames when they add context rather than clutter.
- You use transparency to balance energy and legibility instead of dulling photos.
- Your elements (icons, shapes, lines) match in style and weight and serve hierarchy.
- Your library has folders, starred assets, and a components page you can reuse.

Common Mistakes — Not Errors, Just Detours (and how to correct them)

- **Mismatched Image Tone**. One cool, bluish stock photo next to a warm, golden original screams inconsistency. Solve it by grading slightly toward your brand's temperature or choosing sets with similar lighting.
- **Over-cropping the Subject**. Faces and products need breathing room. If the layout feels tense, step back one notch and let negative space frame the hero.
- **Opacity Overkill.** If everything sits under a 70% black sheet, your feed will look lifeless. Use overlays precisely where text needs protection, and keep the rest vivid.
- **Icon Soup.** Mixing outline, filled, and hand-drawn icons on one page creates visual static. Pick one family and commit.
- **Folder Chaos.** "Uploads (3,284)" is a creativity tax. Ten minutes of sorting per week returns hours of focus later.

"Do It Now" Homework — 25 Focused Minutes

1. **Sourcing Rule (5 min).** Write your two sourcing rules (e.g., "Use my own photos for behind-the-scenes; stock only for conceptual backgrounds"). Pin them to your notebook or Brand Board page.
2. **3-Crop Study (8 min)**. Take one photo and make three crops: wide, medium, tight. Place the same headline over each. Decide which version you'll use for a carousel cover vs an inner slide.
3. **Overlay Kit (6 min).** Create three overlay components: dark brand color 50%, light brand color 40%, top-to-transparent gradient 60%. Save to Components and Star them.
4. **Library Sweep (6 min).** Build the Brand — Visual Library with subfolders and move 12 assets in. Star your top 6. You've started your system.

QR Bonus (module hub): Icon Starter Set (consistent style) + Overlay Components (3 styles) + Crop & Framing Guide (1-page). Duplicate from the QR and paste into your Brand Board.

Closing Thought

Great images don't rescue weak design—but they do supercharge strong structure. After this chapter, you can bring your world into Canva with confidence, frame it for attention, protect your message with subtle transparency, and store your assets in a system that gets faster every week. In the next chapter, we'll return to structure one last time—Export Without Errors—so that everything you've built leaves Canva looking as sharp as it does on your canvas.

Chapter 5

Export Without Errors: Formats, Quality, Dimensions, Transparency

Export is where designs stop being ideas and start being files that travel—into phones, inboxes, printers, feeds, storefronts. You can nail color, type, images, and layout, yet lose everything in a fuzzy JPG, a bloated PDF, or a logo boxed in white. **The last mile isn't glamorous, but it's decisive:** choose the right format, set sensible quality, match dimensions to destination, and use transparency when flexibility matters. Do this well and your work looks intentional everywhere; do it poorly and even brilliant concepts arrive tired.

In this chapter, we'll make **export choices visible and repeatable.** You'll learn when PNG outperforms JPG, when PDF Standard beats PNG slides, why "max quality" isn't always quality, what "bleed" is and when to enable it, and how one checkbox ("Transparent background") turns a good asset into a versatile one. By the end, you'll export with confidence—and your designs will finally look as sharp out there as they do inside Canva.

What You'll Do in 10 Minutes (and why it matters)

A quick experiment builds intuition you can trust. In this sprint you will:

- Export the same tile as PNG (with and without transparency), JPG at medium compression, PDF Standard, and—if print-bound—PDF Print with crop marks and bleed.
- Then open each file, zoom to 200%, and compare edges, type clarity, and file weight.
- In one pass, you'll see the trade-offs most beginners guess at, and you'll start forming your personal export defaults.

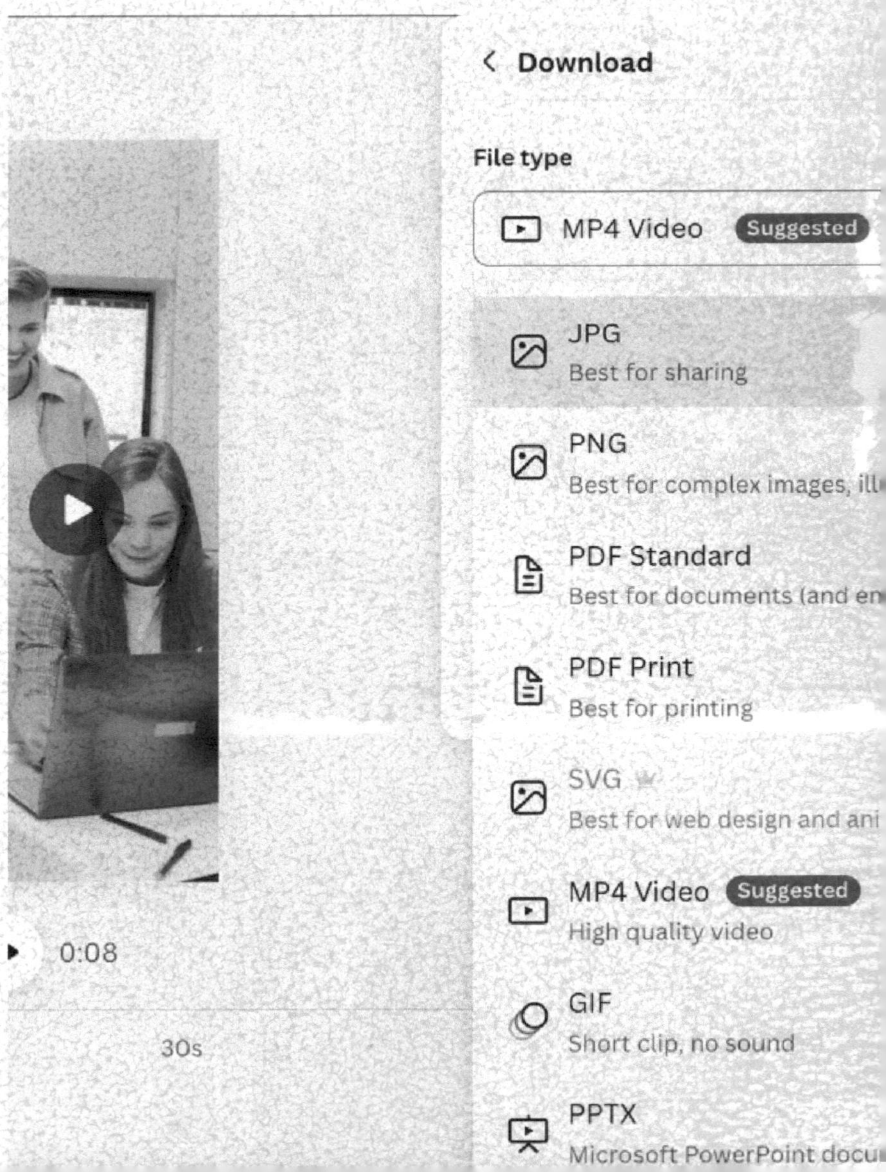

Formats: PNG, JPG, PDF — Use the Right Container

Why this matters.

Formats are containers with rules. PNG preserves crisp edges and can be transparent. JPG is compact and photographic but can't hold transparency. PDF locks layout and keeps text/vector sharp across pages and devices. When you pair message and medium correctly, you protect fidelity and reduce friction for everyone who opens your file.

PNG — crisp edges, optional transparency.

Logos, badges, stickers, UI elements, and graphics with flat color or type often look best as PNG. If the asset must float over photos or colored backgrounds, export PNG with Transparent background to remove the white box once and for all.

JPG — light weight for photos and gradients.

Photo-led posts, thumbnails, and blog images usually shine as JPG. The format compresses smoothly, keeping file sizes small and upload-friendly. Just remember: no transparency—a JPG logo will always carry a rectangle.

PDF — layout locked, vector intact.

Multi-page documents, presentations, brochures, and handouts belong in PDF. PDF Standard is perfect for screens and email; PDF Print adds crop marks and bleed for professional trimming at the printer.

Real Scenario — The Boxed Logo

A boutique exported its logo as JPG and placed it on a dark hero image. The white rectangle looked amateurish. Re-exporting as PNG with transparency solved it instantly—same design, professional result.

Pro Tip — Thumbnail vs Handout

If you're sending slides to be read on-screen, export PDF Standard (text stays vector-sharp, file stays light). If you're posting just the cover slide to social, export that single page as JPG for speed and platform-friendly compression.

Mini Exercise — Two Exports, One Truth

- Create a simple wordmark inside a rounded shape.
- Export as JPG and PNG (transparent).
- Place both over a photo background.

The difference you see is the rule you'll follow forever.

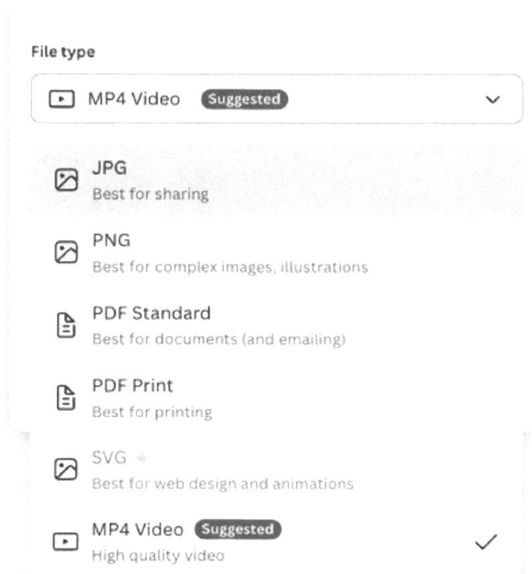

Quality: Sharp Enough, Small Enough

Why this matters.

"Max quality" isn't a strategy. Platforms compress uploads, clients dislike huge attachments, and printers need the right data—not the heaviest file. Quality is a dial you set per destination.

Social: photo-led posts.

For Instagram, LinkedIn, and Twitter/X, JPG around 80% often looks indistinguishable from lossless while cutting size dramatically. If your tile is mostly flat graphics or type, PNG may keep edges crisper—check both at 200% zoom.

Documents: screen reading.

Export decks and brochures as PDF Standard so body text stays vector-clean and images compress sensibly. Recipients can search, copy text, and print desktop-friendly handouts without ballooning file sizes.

Print: production-ready.

Use PDF Print, enable Bleed and Crop marks when a design runs to the edge. The printer will trim precisely to the final size; the bleed prevents unexpected white rims.

Real Scenario — The 10 MB Carousel

A creator exported a 10-slide carousel as max-quality PNGs; uploads stalled and IG recompressed anyway. Switching to JPG ~80% reduced each slide to ~1 MB with no visible loss on mobile.

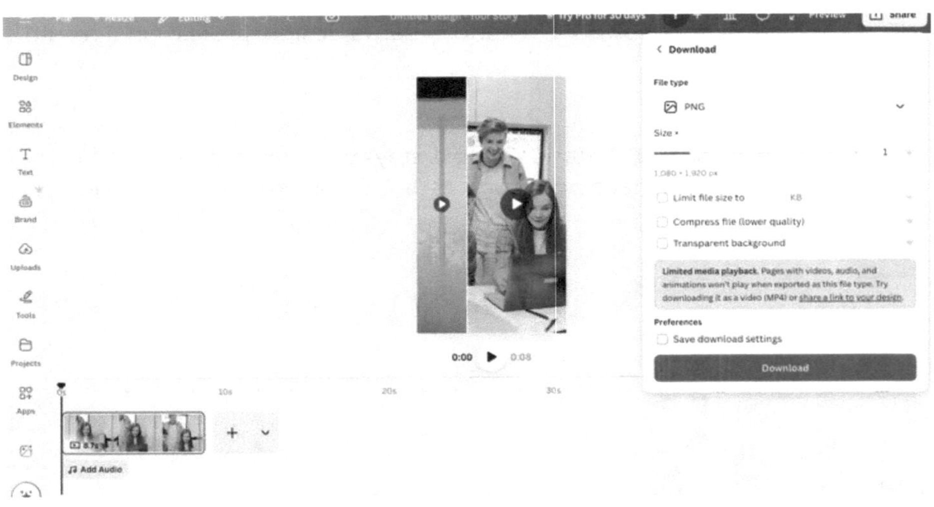

Pro Tip - The 200% QC Rule

Open your export and zoom to 200% on a headline and icon.

If edges look soft, bump quality up one notch. If they look identical across two settings, choose the smaller file.

Mini Exercise — A/B Compression

- Export the same tile as JPG 80% and PNG.
- Compare at 100%/200% on a phone and laptop.
- Record your default per asset type on your Brand Board ("Photo tiles → JPG 80%; Flat graphics → PNG.")

Dimensions: Design for the Destination

Why this matters.

Wrong dimensions force platforms to crop or scale your work, costing you clarity. Starting with the correct preset (1080×1080 Post, 1080×1920 Story, 1280×720 Thumbnail, A4/Letter) prevents cut-off headlines and awkward margins.

Start right; resize smart.

Choose the proper preset before you design. If you must adapt, use Resize to create the new canvas, then re-compose: adjust type sizes, nudge margins, reposition imagery. A good resize is a design act, not a stretch.

Safe zones and masks.

Stories need vertical flow with essential text away from top/bottom edges; thumbnails need central focus and big type; LinkedIn crops differently across placements. Designing for the real frame is the difference between "fine" and "professional."

Real Scenario — Cropped Call-to-Action

A square tile posted as a Story lost its bottom CTA to auto-cropping. Reframing in 1080×1920, lifting the CTA, and increasing top/bottom padding restored legibility and intent.

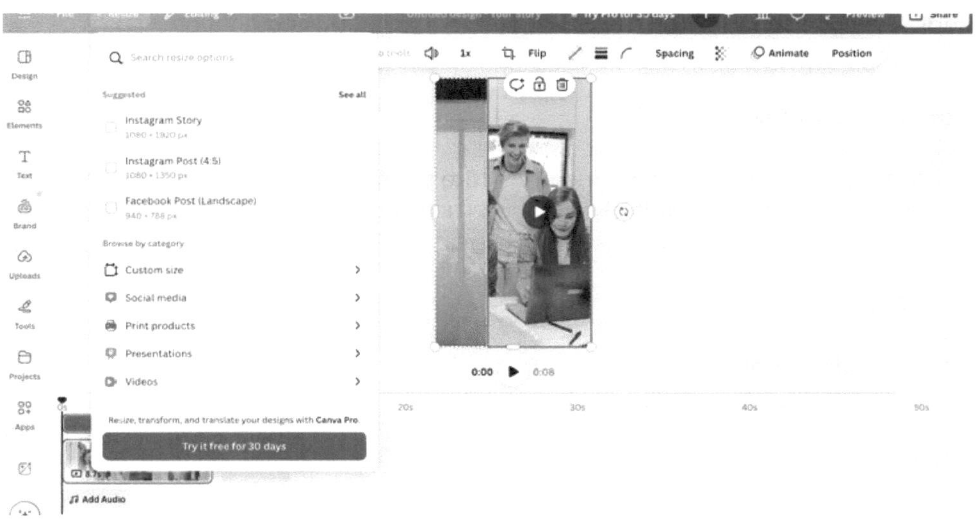

Pro Tip - Two Master Canvases

- Keep a Square Master (1080×1080) and a Story Master (1080×1920) template with guides and default type scales.
- Duplicating from masters saves time and preserves rhythm across formats.

Mini Exercise — Twin Composition Test

- Design one cover tile, then adapt it to Story.
- On your phone, compare where the eye lands first and how quickly the headline reads.
- Write a one-line rule you'll apply next time (e.g., "Story = larger lead line + higher CTA.")

Transparency: Make Assets That Work Everywhere

Why this matters.

When logos, badges, and sticker-style graphics need to sit on photos, colors, or video frames, transparency keeps them adaptable—and keeps you out of the white-box trap.

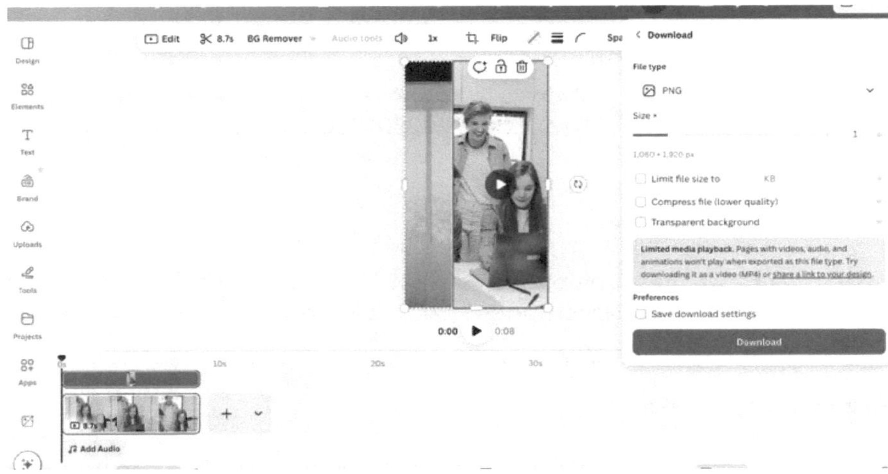

How to export with transparency.

Choose PNG, tick Transparent background, then export. You'll get only the marks—not the canvas. This is essential for overlays, mockups, and video lower-thirds.

Watch for halos.

If you designed on white, a faint fringe can appear over dark photos due to anti-aliasing. Test on white, black, and photo backgrounds. If halos show, tighten artwork edges or export placed on a neutral mid-gray background first.

Real Scenario — Apparel Mockup Fail → Fix

A merch designer placed a JPG logo on a t-shirt photo—instant white square. Re-exported as PNG (transparent), the mark blended naturally; a light Multiply effect on the mockup made it feel printed, not pasted.

Pro Tip — Three-Background Test

After exporting a transparent asset, drop it onto a white tile, a black tile, and a busy photo. If it reads on all three, ship it.

Mini Exercise — Badge to Everywhere

Create a small badge. Export PNG (transparent). Place it on three previous posts and one video frame. If it never carries a box and remains legible, your export is production-ready.

Checklist: Export, Locked In

You can now:

- Choose PNG / JPG / PDF deliberately,
- Dial quality to balance sharpness and size,
- Match dimensions to the destination (and re-compose when resizing),
- Export transparency for assets that must float over anything.

If you can explain why for each choice, you're no longer guessing—you're finishing like a pro.

Common Mistakes — And Gentle Fixes

- JPG Logos with White Boxes. Re-export as PNG (transparent) and update your Brand Board note so it never happens again.
- Overkill File Sizes. Social doesn't need lossless. Use JPG ~80% for photo-heavy tiles; reserve PNG for flat graphics and type.
- Wrong Canvas, Wrong Crop. Start with the right preset. If adapting, Resize → Re-compose (don't just stretch).
- No Bleed for Print. White rims are preventable. Export PDF Print with Bleed + Crop marks and confirm specs with your printer.

"Do It Now" Homework — 20 Focused Minutes

Defaults (6 min)
On your Brand Board, add a tiny table:
IG Post → JPG 80% | IG Story → PNG (type over photo) or JPG 80% (photo-only) | Print flyer → PDF Print (bleed).

Two-Zoom QC (4 min)

Export a finished tile. Inspect at 100%/200%. If edges blur, bump quality; if identical but heavy, step down.

Transparent Toolkit (5 min)

Export your logo, badge, and CTA button as PNG (transparent). Test on white, black, photo.

Dimension Sanity Check (5 min)

Duplicate a square tile to Story via Resize. Re-compose type and margins. Preview on your phone before shipping.

Closing Thought

Finishing well is a creative act. When you pair the right format with the right quality, choose honest dimensions, and use transparency with intent, your work arrives in the world exactly as you imagined it—crisp, confident, and trustworthy. Export is not an afterthought; it's the seal on your craft.

Module 2 - Canva for Social Media

From Random Posts to a Consistent Voice

Social media is where most brands live—or die. A website is static, a brochure is handed out once, but your **Instagram, LinkedIn, TikTok, or Facebook** feed is alive every single day. And yet, for most beginners, social media design is pure chaos: random colors, inconsistent fonts, posts that feel disconnected from each other. The result? Even good ideas look unprofessional, and followers scroll past without remembering who you are.

But here's the good news: consistency is not magic. It's a system. And Canva makes that system accessible to anyone—even if you've never studied design. With the right templates, palettes, and batching habits, you can produce a month of content in just a few focused hours. More importantly, your feed starts to look like a brand rather than a string of one-offs.

Think about what happens when your posts align: your colors repeat, your typography speaks with one tone, your logos sit in the same corner, your photos share a mood. Suddenly, people recognize your work at a glance. That recognition is trust. And trust is what social media, beneath all the noise, is really about.

This module will take you from sporadic posting to a **scalable content system.** You won't just design pretty posts; you'll learn how to batch 30 posts at a time, adapt them for multiple platforms, and keep everything on-brand without reinventing the wheel. Along the way, you'll create a Content Pack you can duplicate and adapt forever—your personal social media design engine.

What You'll Do in 10 Minutes (and why it matters)

To warm up, we'll start with a micro-sprint:

- Duplicate a social media post template.
- Swap in your logo and palette.
- Write three different headlines.
- Export the posts and preview them on your phone.

In just 10 minutes, you'll see how fast "one post" can become "a set." That shift—from single to system—is what unlocks scale.

What This Module Covers

By the end of Module 2, you will:

- Master Canva templates for social posts (static, carousel, story, reel cover).
- Batch-create 30 posts in a session, using duplication and small variations.
- Adapt posts across platforms, keeping brand voice consistent while respecting each format.
- Build a content calendar with your designs, so posting feels planned, not frantic.
- Export correctly for each platform, so posts look sharp everywhere.

Target Audience

This module is for beginners, solopreneurs, side hustlers, and students who want to look professional on social without hiring a designer. It's also for small businesses tired of inconsistent feeds and ready to build a visual system that scales.

Measurable Outcomes

By the end of Module 2, you will be able to:

- Design and export 30 coordinated social media posts in Canva.
- Apply your brand logo, palette, and fonts consistently across posts.
- Adapt a single design into at least three different formats (Post, Story, Carousel).
- Create a starter content calendar populated with your Canva designs.

Chapter 1

Formats & Consistency: IG, TikTok, YouTube, LinkedIn; Variants & Resizing

Imagine meeting someone who wears a different outfit every time you see them—so different you're not even sure it's the same person. That's how your audience feels when your posts look inconsistent across platforms. Instagram loves squares, TikTok thrives on tall verticals, YouTube runs on thumbnails, and LinkedIn expects polished professionalism. If you take one design and force it everywhere, you break recognition.

Consistency is not sameness—it's coherence. It means your colors, fonts, logo, and tone stay recognizable, while the format adapts to the frame. Canva's templates make this easy, but only if you understand each platform's native language.

In this chapter, we'll walk through the four **major social ecosystems—Instagram, TikTok, YouTube, and LinkedIn**—and break down their formats one by one. You'll learn how to design posts, stories, thumbnails, banners, and carousels that adapt without losing identity. By the end, you'll know how to translate one idea across multiple platforms so it feels like you everywhere, not a patchwork of random content.

What You'll Do in 10 Minutes (and why it matters)

- Take a single Canva design—say, a quote tile.
- Resize it four times: Squared Instagram Post (1080×1080), Instagram Post 4:5 (1080×1350); TikTok vertical (1080×1920), YouTube thumbnail (1280×720), and LinkedIn banner (1584×396).
- Export each, then preview them side by side. You'll see how the core identity survives, but the composition changes. This is the essence of format mastery: adapting, not forcing.

Instagram: The Post, the Story, the Carousel

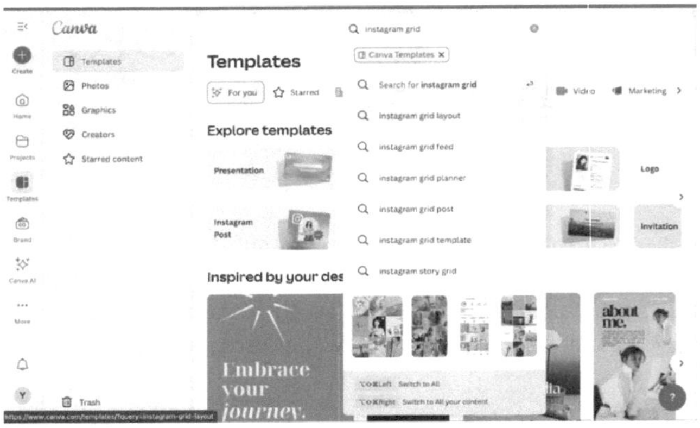

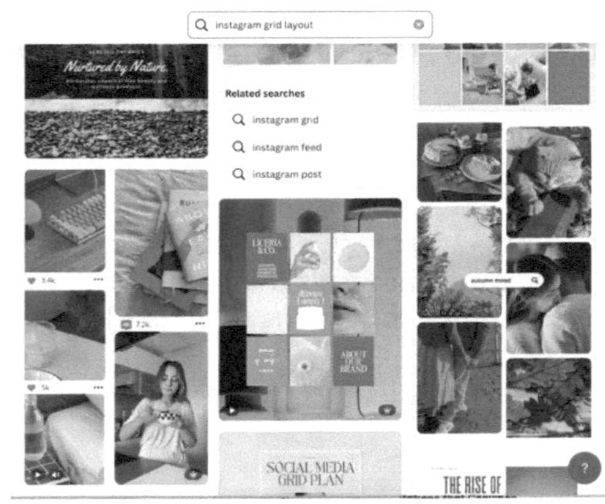

Why this matters.

Instagram is still the cornerstone for many creators and small businesses. The platform supports multiple formats, each with different rules: grid posts, carousels, stories, reels covers, highlights. Mastering all of them ensures your brand feels native, not recycled.

Core formats:

- **Grid post**: Instagram Post 4:5 (1080×1350) — new timeless, clean, consistent in profile view.
- **Carousel:** multiple 1080×1350 posts swiped in sequence, perfect for storytelling.
- **Stories/Reels:** 1080×1920 vertical, occupying the full screen.
- **Reel cover**: still 1080×1920 but must be designed with safe zones so the cover looks good in the square grid preview.
- **Highlights**: story icons, usually round, small (200×200 recommended).

Real Scenario — The Personal Trainer

A creator posted random sizes: sometimes 4:5, sometimes landscape. His feed looked chaotic. Once he locked everything to 1080×1350 and designed matching stories, his grid started to look like a polished portfolio.

Pro Tip — Safe Zone for Reels Covers

Always place text and logos in the center square of your reel cover. That way, when Instagram crops it for the grid, nothing gets cut.

Mini Exercise — Carousel Consistency

Create a 3-slide carousel with one headline repeated across all slides. Export and swipe on your phone. Does the flow feel smooth? Adjust margins until it reads like a story.

TikTok: Vertical First, Speed Always

Why this matters.

TikTok is full immersion: 1080×1920 vertical video. No side margins, no half-crops. Design here must respect safe zones—bottom for captions, right for buttons. Canva lets you make animated slides or short video posts that feel native.

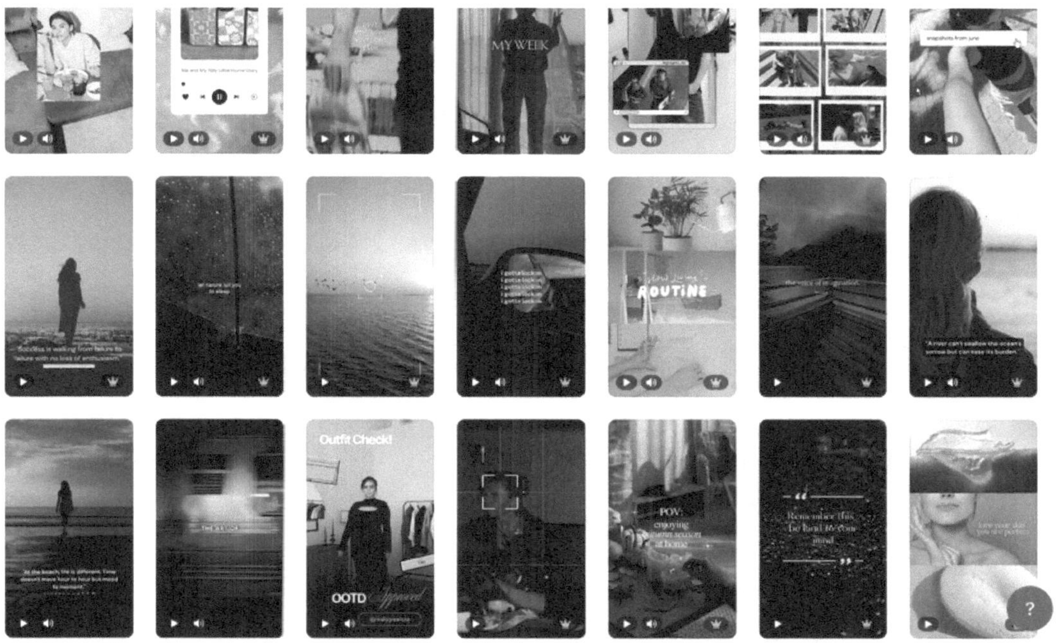

Core formats:

- **Vertical video**: 1080×1920 — main content.
- **Safe zones:** keep text and CTAs in upper-middle; avoid bottom third and right edge.
- **Profile picture & cover**: not designed in Canva but must harmonize.
- **Ad creatives (Spark Ads)**: same 1080×1920, but focus on strong hooks in first 3 seconds.

Real Scenario — The Language Tutor

You can repurpose Instagram slides by simply uploading them to TikTok. The text got covered by captions. After redesigning with safe zones in mind, retention rates doubled.

Attention — Platform Compression

TikTok compresses heavily. Export as MP4, 1080×1920 with medium compression; overloading quality often backfires.

Pro Tip — The “Upper Third Rule”

Always position text in the upper third. That area remains visible across most UI overlays.

Mini Exercise — Resize with Intention

Take a square quote tile. Resize to 1080×1920. Move headline to upper third, place logo top-left. Export and preview in TikTok mockup.

YouTube: Thumbnails, Banners, End Screens

Why this matters.

On YouTube, people click before they listen. Your thumbnail is your first handshake.

But the ecosystem also includes banners and end screens—spaces where brand consistency builds trust.

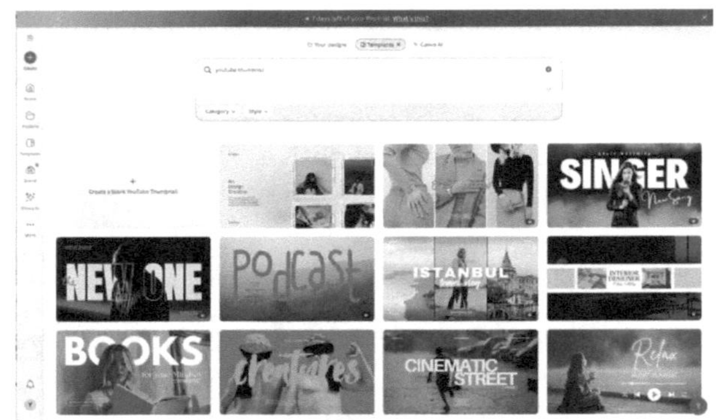

Core formats:

- **Thumbnail: 1280×720 (16:9)** — bold text, clear image, CTR driver.
- **Channel banner: 2560×1440 (safe area 1546×423)** — visible differently on TV, desktop, mobile.
- **End screen**: 1920×1080 overlay — design space for CTAs, playlists, or subscribe buttons.
- **Shorts**: 1080×1920 vertical video, but designed for scrollable feeds.

Real Scenario — Tech Reviewer

Their content was high-quality but thumbnails were dull screenshots. Once they designed custom thumbnails with bold type + brand accent, CTR rose 40%.

Pro Tip — The Blink Test

Shrink your thumbnail to 10% size. If it's still readable, it works. If not, simplify text.

Common Pitfall — Banner Safe Area

Many creators design banners too wide; text gets cut on mobile. Always check safe area guides.

Mini Exercise — Thumbnail Sprint

Design one 1280×720 thumbnail. Export and scale down to 100px. Does it still communicate?

LinkedIn: Professional Polish

Why this matters.

LinkedIn is where business credibility is judged. Poorly formatted posts or cut-off banners suggest carelessness. With the right formats, your profile becomes a portfolio.

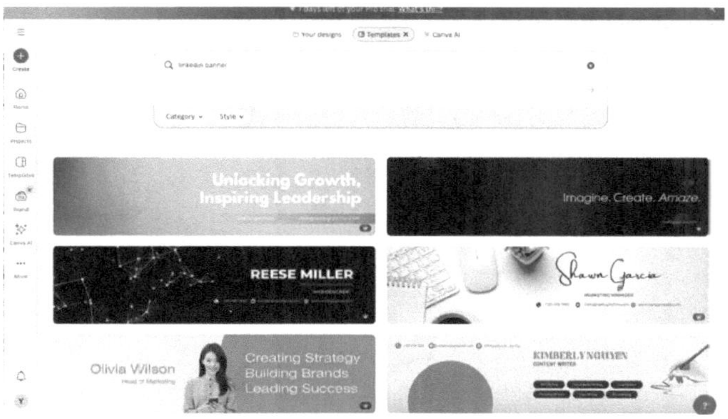

Core formats:

- **Feed post**: 1200×1200 (square) or 1200×628 (landscape).
- **Carousel posts**: uploaded as PDF multi-page (Canva export directly).
- **Company banner**: 1128×191 — narrow, needs clean type.
- **Personal banner:** 1584×396 — wide, must keep key info centered.

Real Scenario — Consultant Brand Upgrade

A consultant's banner had text pushed to the edge. On mobile, it cut off her website. Re-centered in Canva, the new banner read clearly across devices, improving credibility.

Attention — Text Hierarchy

LinkedIn users skim. Keep banners clean: logo, tagline, maybe one CTA. Posts should focus on clarity over decoration.

Pro Tip — PDF Carousels Win

Instead of static images, export educational content as PDF carousels. LinkedIn treats them like slide decks—perfect for storytelling.

Mini Exercise — Personal Banner Fix

Design a 1584×396 banner. Place text only in center safe zone. Export, preview on desktop and mobile. Adjust until consistent.

Checklist — Formats & Consistency

Checklist — Formats & Consistency

- Instagram posts, carousels, stories, reels covers designed natively.
- TikTok verticals with safe zones respected.
- YouTube thumbnails, banners, end screens sized correctly.
- LinkedIn posts, carousels, banners adapted to safe areas.
- Brand elements (logo, colors, fonts) coherent across all.

Common Mistakes — And How to Fix Them

- One-size-fits-all exports. Fix: resize with Canva's tool and re-compose.
- Ignoring safe zones. Fix: test with overlays before publishing.
- Overloading text. Fix: simplify, bold key words only.
- Banner cut-offs. Fix: always check mobile safe areas.

"Do It Now" Homework — 30 Minutes

1. Take one design (quote or CTA).
2. Resize it into Instagram (1080×1080, 1080×1920), TikTok (1080×1920), YouTube thumbnail (1280×720), LinkedIn banner (1584×396).
3. Export all.
4. Preview on each platform (mockup or actual upload).
5. Write down 3 rules for your brand ("Logo always top-right," "Text max 5 words in thumbnails," "Banners: text centered only")

.

QR Bonus (Module Hub):

- Dimension Cheat Sheet for all platforms.
- 20 Social Templates for posts + carousels.
- Thumbnail Starter Kit (5 styles) tested for CTR.

Closing Thought

Adapting formats isn't busywork—it's respect for the medium. When your posts fit every frame, your brand feels intentional and professional. Your followers won't think "nice resize"—they'll think "I know this brand, I trust them." And that recognition, across Instagram, TikTok, YouTube, and LinkedIn, is the first real step to social authority.

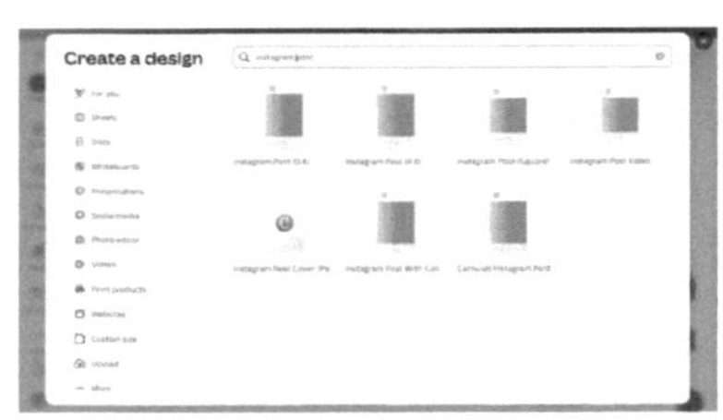

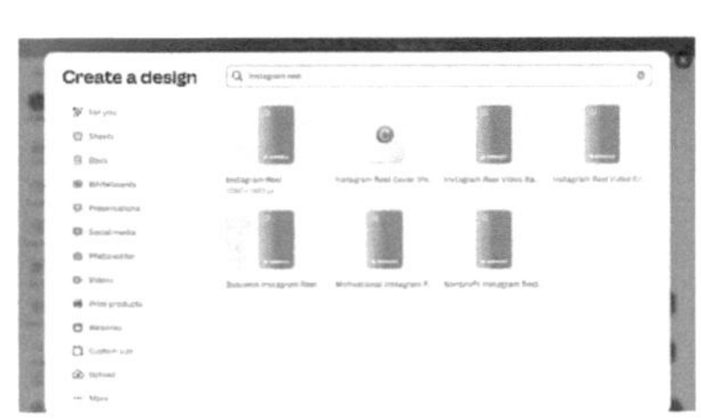

Chapter 2

Instagram & TikTok: Posts, Stories, Carousels, Reels Covers, Hooks & CTAs

If you want visibility today, **you can't ignore Instagram and TikTok**. These two platforms dominate the attention economy. They're where culture spreads, where trends begin, and where brands—personal or business—earn trust or vanish. But here's the catch: they reward speed, clarity, and emotion, not clutter.

A good design for Instagram or TikTok is not about decoration. It's about function: **grabbing attention in less than three seconds, delivering value fast, and leaving a clear next step** (a hook at the start, a CTA at the end). This isn't just design—it's choreography. Every slide, story, or reel cover is a move in a sequence that keeps viewers watching and acting.

Many beginners treat Instagram posts as random pretty cute designs, or TikTok covers as afterthoughts. But real creators know: consistency of brand + platform-native storytelling = growth. If you align your palette, fonts, and logo with strong hooks and calls to action, your content becomes recognizable, trustworthy, and sharable.

In this chapter, we'll walk through the main content types on IG and TikTok:

- Posts that fit the grid but also work in feed.
- Stories that invite interaction.
- Carousels that tell a story in swipes.
- Reel covers that protect recognition and readability.
- Hooks and CTAs that make people stop scrolling and take action.

By the end, you won't just be designing "pretty posts." You'll be creating narratives people engage with—a system of visuals and words tuned for platforms that never sleep.

What You'll Do in 10 Minutes (and why it matters)

Take one idea (e.g., "3 tips to stay focused").

- Make a square post (1080×1080) with headline + subtext.
- Duplicate as a Story (1080×1920) with vertical flow.
- Build a 3-slide Carousel version (same fonts/colors).
- Add a Reel Cover with logo centered and safe zones respected.
- Preview them side by side. You'll see the power of repurposing: one idea → four native assets.

Instagram Posts: Your Visual Anchor

Why this matters.

Posts are still the foundation of Instagram. They live in the grid, get shared in feed, and become your portfolio. They must be clear, consistent, and instantly recognizable.

Best practices:

- Size: 1080×1350 (4:5).
- Headline clarity: 3–5 words max, big and bold.
- Logo placement: consistent corner (usually bottom-right).
- Palette rotation: apply your chosen colors strategically, not randomly.

Real Scenario — The Fitness Coach

A creator used random Canva templates. Her feed looked mismatched. Once she locked a color palette (navy + neon green), her grid became coherent. Clients noticed: "I know it's your post before I read it."

Pro Tip — Grid View Audit

Duplicate 9 posts and arrange in Canva's grid. Does it feel like a family? If not, adjust palette and fonts.

Mini Exercise

Design 3 posts. Use same font, logo, color accents. Export and view on your phone grid. Do they hold together?

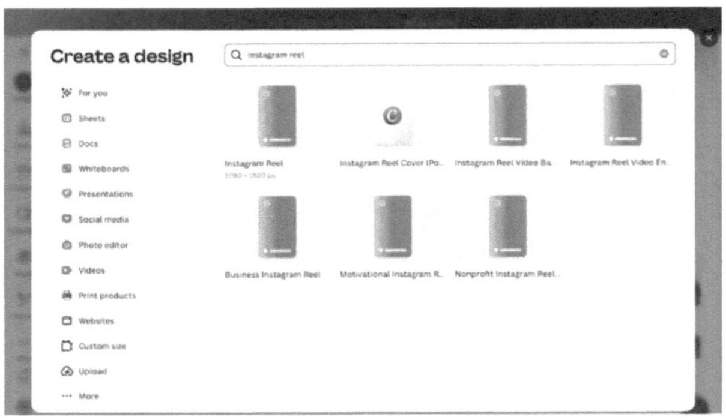

Instagram Stories: Interactive Flow

Why this matters.

Stories are full-screen, ephemeral, but powerful. They drive engagement, clicks, and personality. Design here must respect vertical flow and safe zones.

Best practices:

- Size: 1080×1920 (9:16).
- Hierarchy: one main message per story.
- Interactive elements: leave space for polls, stickers, questions.
- Visual rhythm: alternate static slides, short videos, and CTA slides.

Real Scenario — The Café Launch

A coffee shop announced a new latte via a 3-slide

- Story: Slide 1—photo of cup with headline. Slide 2—poll ("Would you try it?").
- Slide 3—CTA with swipe-up. Result: 300+ responses in one day.

Attention — Don't Overstuff

Stories are not posters. If everything screams, nothing is heard. Keep one clear idea per slide.

Mini Exercise

Turn one square post into a 3-slide Story sequence. Export and preview vertically.

Instagram Carousels: Swipe to Storytell

Why this matters.

Carousels are the secret weapon for engagement. People swipe more than they read captions. Each slide is a beat in your story.

Best practices:

- Size: 1080×1350 (4:5) for each slide.
- Slide 1: big hook.
- Slides 2–n: value bites (tips, steps, quotes).
- Final slide: CTA (follow, share, comment).

Real Scenario — Marketing Consultant

Turn blog posts into 8-slide carousels. Engagement tripled: same content, better delivery.

Pro Tip — Visual Rhythm

Alternate bold text slides with image slides. It keeps attention alive.

Mini Exercise

Build a 3-slide carousel: Hook → Tip → CTA. Export and swipe-test.

Reel Covers: Protecting Your Grid

Why this matters.

Reels are powerful, but their covers live on your profile grid. If covers aren't designed with safe zones, text gets cropped, leaving your grid messy.

Best practices:

- Size: 1080×1920, but design inside central 1080×1440 safe zone for grid view.
- Headline: short, bold, central.
- Logo: consistent corner.

Real Scenario — Lifestyle Creator

Imagine this: Anita is an influencer. She had random covers—her grid looked chaotic. Once she standardized covers with consistent fonts and palette, her profile felt professional.

Pro Tip — Use Templates

Create one Reel Cover template. Duplicate for each reel, only swap headline + image.

Mini Exercise

Design a Reel Cover with safe zone guides. Export and preview in grid mockup.

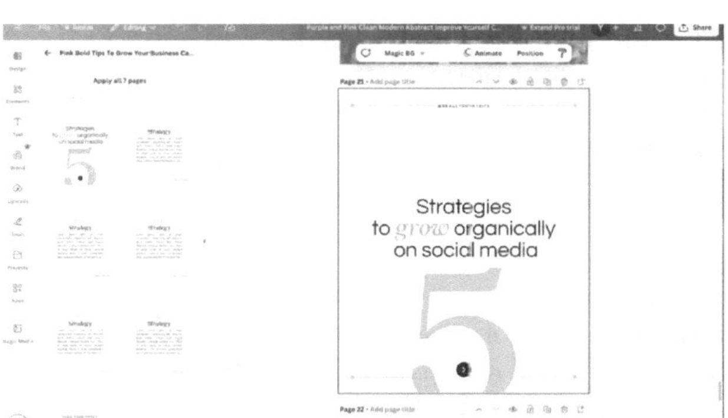

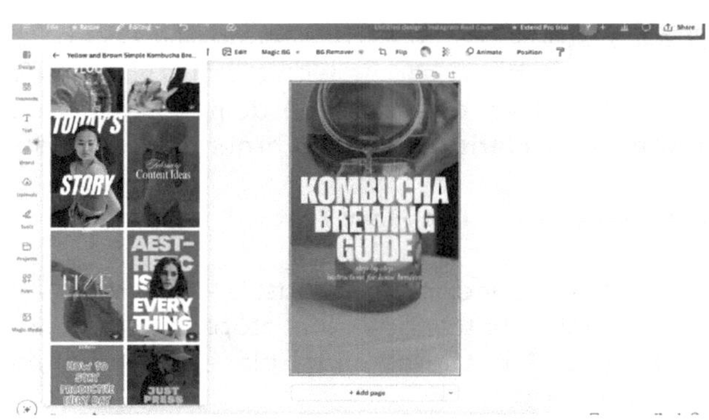

Hooks & CTAs: The Invisible Design Layer

Why this matters.

Great design fails if nobody stops to read. Hooks and CTAs are the invisible layer of design strategy: the words and placements that move people.

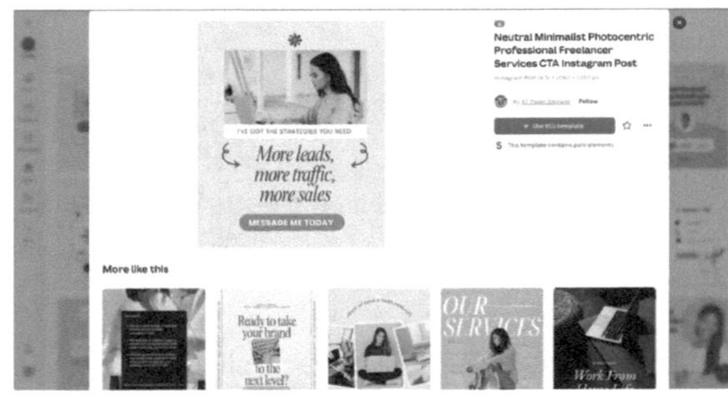

Hooks:
Hooks grab attention in seconds.
Think of them as your digital handshake:
bold, quick, and impossible to ignore. Effective hooks are:

- Short, bold, urgent. "Stop doing this..."
- Curiosity-driven. "Ever wondered why...?"
- Specific and numbered. "3 hacks you need today."

CTAs:

If hooks pull people in, CTAs tell them what to do next. Every piece of content needs a clear next step — simple, visible, and natural.

- Direct actions: "Follow for more," "Save this tip," "Click the link in bio," "Write this word and I'll send you freebies."
- Placed strategically: end of a carousel, final story frame, or caption of a reel.
- Visually emphasized: buttons, bold highlights, or standout typography.

Real Scenario — Small Biz Growth

A small bakery kept posting beautiful photos — cakes, pastries, specials — but nothing moved. People liked, scrolled, and left. Then they added one line to every carousel: "DM us to order." No redesign, no ads, no gimmicks.
Within a month, Instagram orders tripled. The visuals already worked; what was missing was direction. The CTA became the bridge between attention and action.
The design stayed the same — the strategy evolved.

Attention Rule — Don't Shout Twice
One of the biggest mistakes in design communication is trying to win attention with volume — stacking multiple hooks, arrows, and CTAs as if shouting louder would make people care more. It doesn't. It dilutes focus. Every asset should have a single moment of entry (the hook) and a single direction to exit (the CTA). The first stops the scroll. The second gives purpose to that stop. Anything in between should support those two anchors, not compete with them. If you have three messages shouting for attention, the viewer hears none. If you have one message, delivered with intent and clarity, it lands. **The formula is simple: one hook + one CTA = clarity.** And in communication, clarity always beats noise.

Mini Exercise — The Flow Test

Take one of your existing carousels — any topic works. Now, restructure it intentionally:

- On slide 1, write a hook that stops the scroll. Something bold, emotional, or curiosity-driven.
- On slide 3 (or the last slide), place a CTA that moves people — "Follow for more," "Save this," or "DM us for details."
- Then preview the flow as if you were the audience.

Does the message guide you smoothly from interest to action? Or does it feel scattered, heavy, or confusing? The goal isn't just to design slides — it's to design behavior. When every visual choice supports a clear psychological path, even the simplest post starts working like a mini sales funnel.

TikTok Posts: Fast, Native, Sticky

Why this matters.

TikTok thrives on immediacy. Text must live inside safe zones, content must grab attention in 3 seconds, and branding must be subtle but consistent.

Best practices:

- Size: 1080×1920 vertical video.
- Safe zones: avoid bottom third (captions) and right side (engagement buttons).
- Hook: first 3 seconds must stop scroll.
- Logo/branding: small, top corner.

Real Scenario — The Tutor on TikTok

This creator repurposed slides but didn't adjust safe zones—text got covered by captions. After moving text higher, her retention doubled.

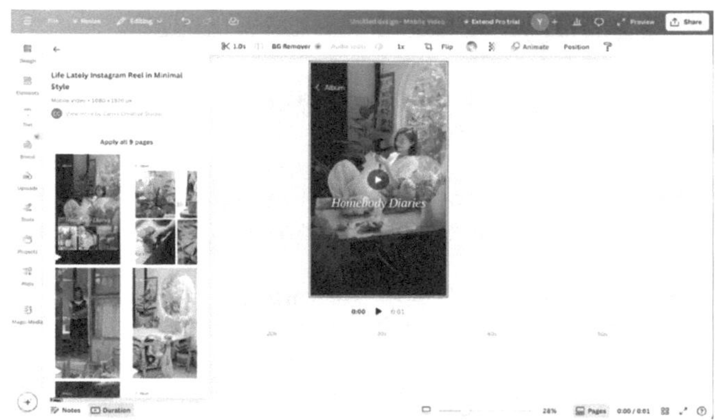

Common Pitfall — Using IG Reels as-is

IG posts often get cut on TikTok. Always adapt composition.

Mini Exercise

Resize one post to 1080×1920. Add bold hook top-center. Export as MP4 and preview.

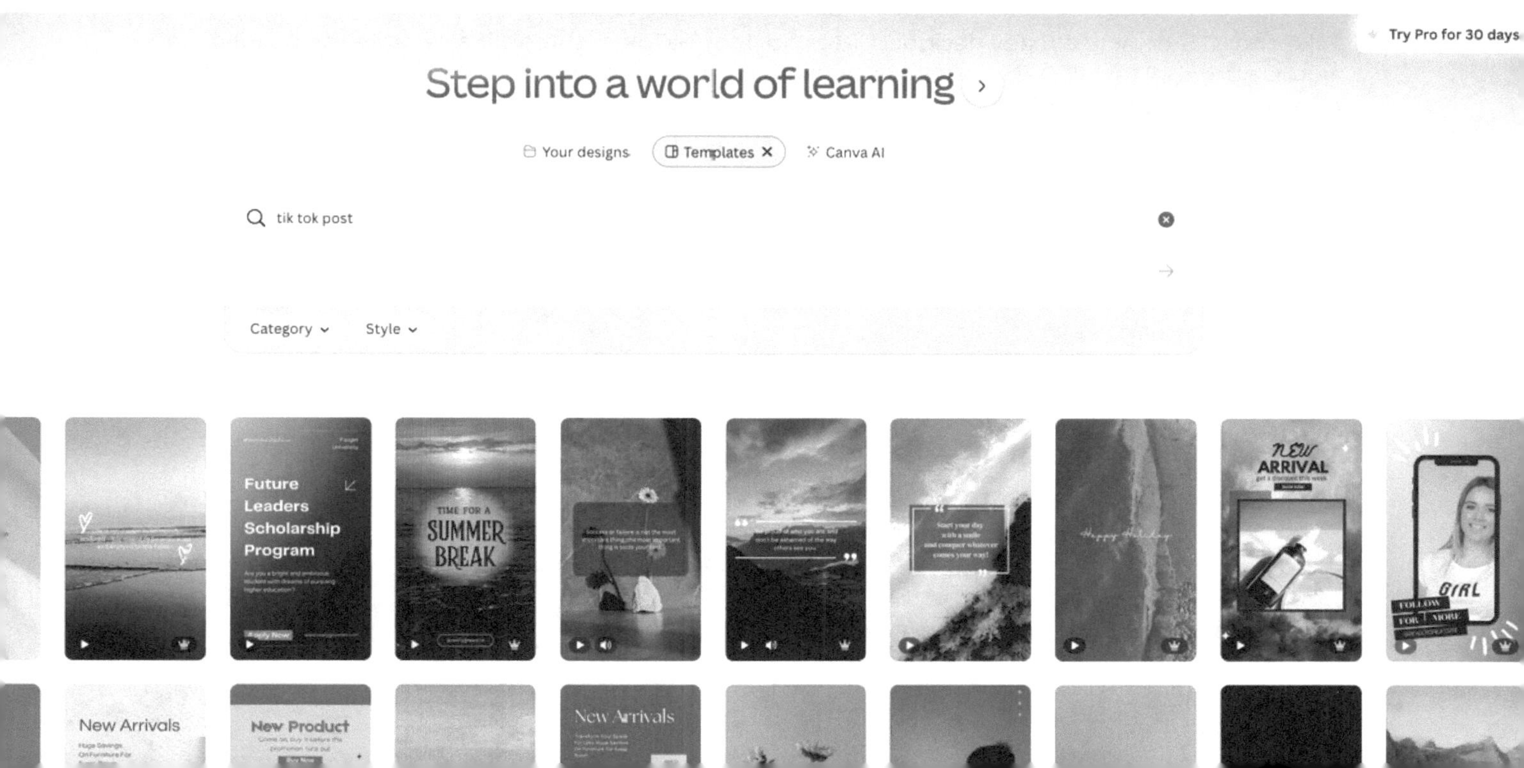

TikTok Stories-Style Sequences: Vertical Flow That Feels Native

Why it matters.

TikTok is built for uninterrupted vertical flow. Whether you have the Stories feature or you're stitching a short multi-clip video, the principle is the same: one idea, broken into clean beats that move quickly and leave no dead air. Your design job isn't to decorate; it's to keep the viewer's attention sliding forward—eyes high, text in safe zones, rhythm alive.

How to build it in Canva (and keep it native).

- Start with 1080×1920. Think in 3–5 beats: Hook → Proof/Visual → Payoff/Tip → CTA.
- Keep each beat to 2–4 seconds.
- Place text above the bottom caption bar and away from the right-side UI (likes/comments/share).
- Use large, high-contrast text and reinforce key words with a subtle highlight box at ~40–60% opacity.
- If you use stickers or polls (when available), leave negative space specifically for them—don't cram them on top of text.

Real Scenario — Micro-Tutorial That Didn't Drag.

A makeup creator turned a 30-second demo into four crisp beats: "Stop cakey under-eye" (hook), close-up of product dab (proof), two-swipe blend with timer overlay (payoff), "Save this for later" (CTA). Watch time jumped, saves spiked, and comments asked for shade recs—because the flow stayed single-task and fast.

Pro Tip — Build a 3-Beat Template.

Create a Canva file with three pages pre-laid: (1) big headline space, (2) mid-screen caption + room for B-roll, (3) oversized CTA with brand color bar. Duplicate for each idea; swap copy and clips. You'll ship twice as fast.

Mini Exercise.

Take one IG Story you already designed. Rebuild it for TikTok as three clips: re-write the headline to 5 words, nudge all text 200–250 px above the bottom edge, and remove any decorative elements near the right edge. Export and preview in TikTok's upload screen to verify nothing is covered.

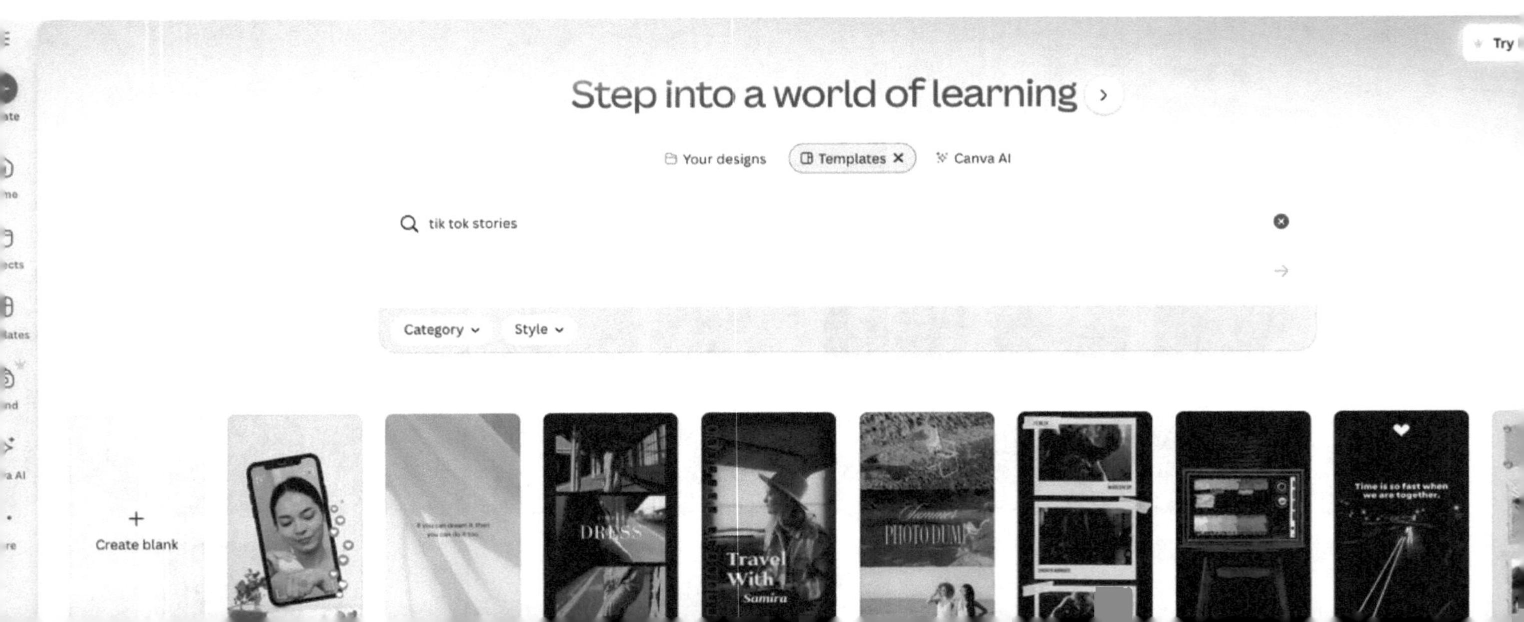

TikTok Carousels (Photo Mode): Swipeable Stories Without Video

Why it matters.

TikTok's Photo Mode (image carousel) lets you tell a story with stills. It's perfect for checklists, step-by-steps, recipes, or before/after sequences when you don't have video. The trap is treating it like a PDF: dense text, tiny type, no pacing. The win is to design it like a comic strip—big beats, one idea per card, and motion implied by the reader's swipe.

How to design it well.

- Create a multi-page 1080×1920 design in Canva: 6–10 cards is a sweet spot.
- Card 1 is a giant hook (promise + outcome)
- Cards 2–n deliver single-bite value (one step, one visual), and the final card is a CTA.
- Use the same type hierarchy across cards so the brain doesn't re-learn your layout each swipe. Keep margins generous, and never drop below 48–56 px for body text in 9:16—remember, thumbs are covering part of the screen.

Real Scenario — "3 Poses for Natural Portraits."

A photographer posted 7 cards: hook, three poses (each with a photo sketch), a "what to avoid" card, gear note, CTA to save. Saves crushed likes 3:1 (a good sign), and comments asked for a lighting sequel. The carousel worked because each card did one job.

Pro Tip — Export as PNGs, Keep Order Tight.

Export cards as individual PNGs labeled 01–10. When uploading to TikTok, keep sequence correct and repeat the hook language in the caption for search.

Mini Exercise.

Turn a 600-word blog tip into 6 cards: Hook → Tip 1 → Tip 2 → Tip 3 → Example → CTA. Design with the same headline size on every card; vary only imagery and subheads. Upload as Photo Mode and test swipe speed yourself.

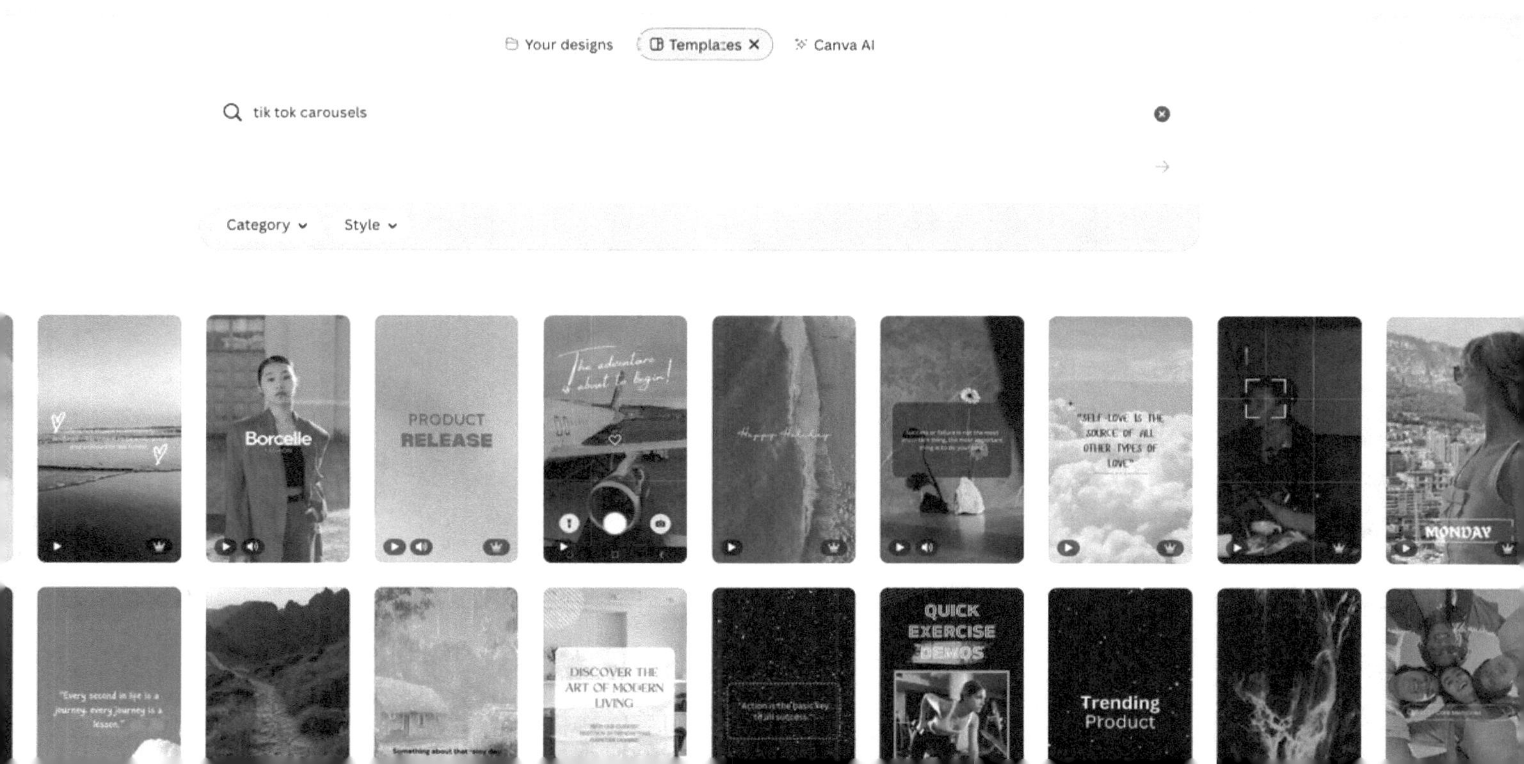

TikTok Covers/Thumbnails: Design the First Frame on Purpose

Why it matters.

On TikTok, your “cover” is usually a selected frame with optional text overlay—users meet your video in the grid and on your profile through that tile. If the cover is muddy (tiny type, busy background, words under UI), your best videos underperform. Plan the first frame as a cover, then build the video behind it.

How to do it in Canva (and respect UI).

- Design your opening frame at 1080×1920 with the title in the upper third and centered.
- Leave a clean right edge (TikTok’s engagement buttons) and avoid the bottom 250–300 px (caption bar). Keep the title to 3–6 words, high-contrast, and add a small brand mark in the top-left—consistency wins here more than cleverness.

Real Scenario — From Random Frame to Branded Tile.

A fitness coach switched from grabbing a mid-rep frame to a planned first frame: “Fix Your Plank” in big type, clean background, logo top-left. Click-throughs rose because the cover promised a specific outcome you could see at a glance.

Pro Tip — Make a “Cover Grid” Template.

Create one Canva page with faint overlays marking TikTok’s right-edge UI and bottom caption area. Use it to compose titles safely. Duplicate for every new video; change only the words and background.

Mini Exercise.

Design three cover variations for the same video: Result-first (“Fix Your Plank”), Problem-first (“Why Your Planks Hurt”), Curiosity (“This Plank Change Feels Wrong—Until It Works”). Export frames and ask a friend which they’d tap. Pick the winner and standardize the style.

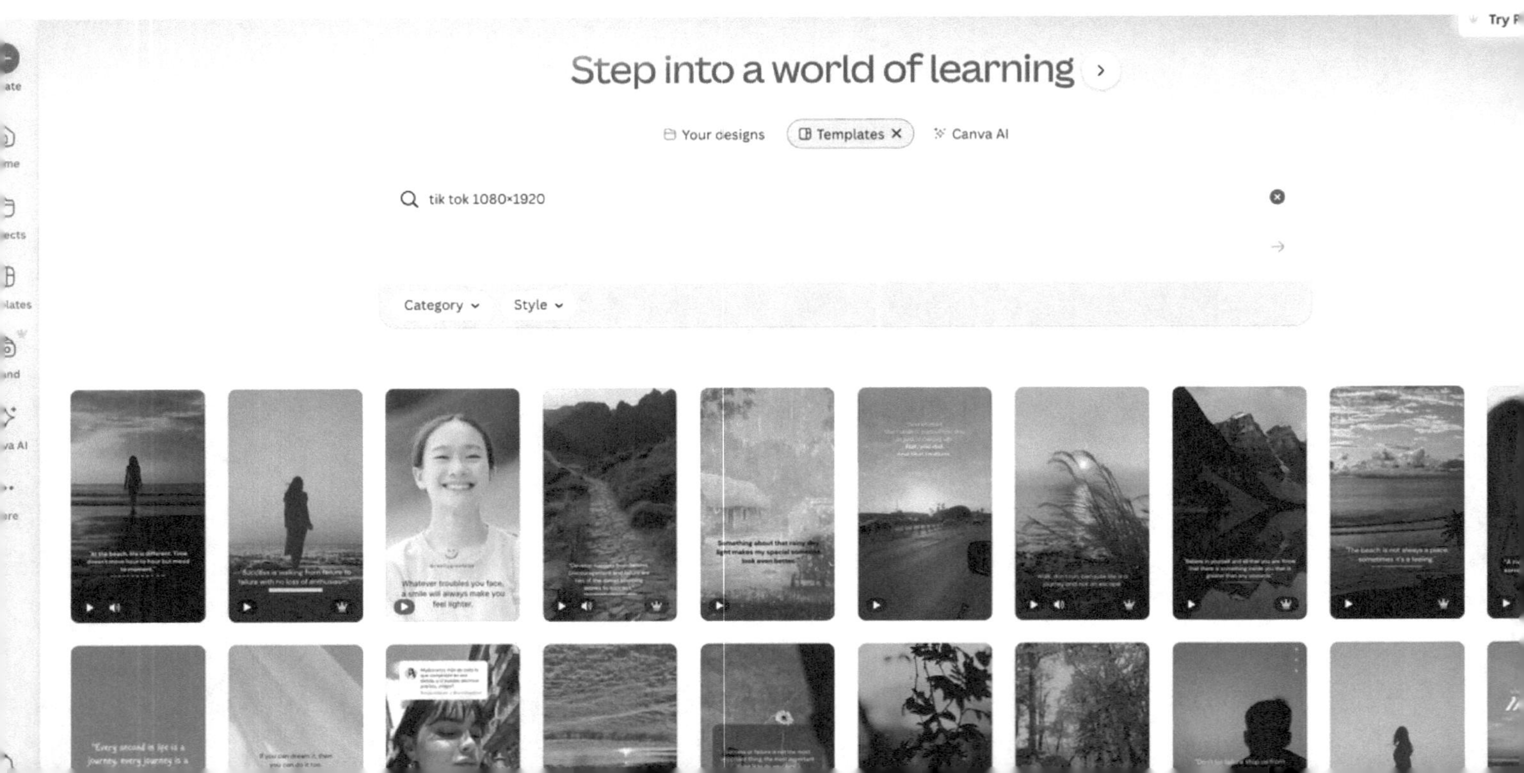

TikTok Hooks & CTAs: Words That Move Thumbs

Why it matters.

TikTok's algorithm rewards retention and replays. The hook buys you the first 3 seconds; the CTA converts interest into follows, comments, or saves. Design sets the stage, but language + timing win the watch.

Hooks that work (and why).

- Outcome + Time: "In 10 seconds, fix your color cast.' → Clear promise with a clock.
- Stop Doing X: "Stop exporting at 720p." → Pattern interrupt + authority.
- Mistake Reveal: "3 Canva mistakes beginners still make." → Curiosity with built-in value.
- Show, Don't Tell: Start with the after visual, then reveal the before—instant proof.

Place your hook on-screen in the first frame (big type) and say it out loud if you speak on camera—dual-channel hooks stick better. Keep it five to seven words, and make sure the text sits above the caption bar.

CTAs that feel native (not needy).

Use one CTA per video and time it in the final 1–2 seconds: "Save this for your next edit," "Comment 'preset' for the settings," "Follow for the full workflow." Echo the CTA in the caption with a skimmable first line (TikTok surfaces keywords for search).

Real Scenario — Saves Over Likes.

A cooking creator shifted her CTAs from "like and follow" to "save this for Sunday prep." Saves exploded, and so did replays—because the CTA matched user intent.

Pro Tip — Comment Bait That Helps.

Invite a specific response: "Type 'export' if your files look mushy and I'll drop the checklist." You'll drive comments and learn what to make next.

Mini Exercise.

Write five hooks for the same idea, each in 7 words or less. Drop them into your cover frame template and preview on your phone. Pick the one you understand without reading twice—that's your keeper. Then write one CTA that matches the value (save, comment, or follow—not all three).

Checklist — Instagram/TikTok Mastery

- Posts: bold, branded, correct size.
- Stories: one idea per slide, vertical safe zones.
- Carousels: narrative flow, clear hook + CTA.
- TikToks: full-screen, hooks in first 3 seconds, safe zones respected.
- Reels Covers: central safe zone, grid-friendly.
- Hooks & CTAs: sharp, minimal, consistent.

Common Mistakes — And Fixes

- Posts as decoration, not strategy. Fix: always start with hook/CTA in mind.
- Stories overloaded with text. Fix: one idea per slide.
- Carousels too long without rhythm. Fix: alternate text and visuals.
- TikTok ignoring safe zones. Fix: always preview.
- Reel covers messy. Fix: centralize text/logo.

"Do It Now" Homework — 45 Minutes

1. Posts (10 min): Design 3 branded posts with same font/palette.
2. Stories (10 min): Turn one post into 3-slide Story sequence.
3. Carousel (10 min): Build 3 slides with Hook → Value → CTA.
4. TikTok (10 min): Resize one design to 1080×1920, adjust safe zones.
5. Reel Cover (5 min): Create a cover with central safe zone.

QR Bonus (Module Hub):

- Swipe file of 100 Hooks & CTAs tested for social.
- 20 Starter Templates for IG + TikTok.
- Content Pack Calendar (30-day planner).

Closing Thought

Instagram and TikTok aren't just platforms—they're attention machines. If your designs fit natively, respect formats, and lead with strong hooks and CTAs, you don't just look professional—you earn attention, trust, and action. From now on, every post, story, carousel, or reel cover is part of a coherent system: one idea, many formats, one brand.

Chapter 3

YouTube: Thumbnails that Convert, Banners that Frame, End Screens that Keep People Watching

On YouTube, your content isn't discovered because it's good—it's discovered because it's clicked. And the click depends almost entirely on the thumbnail. In a crowded sidebar filled with videos, the human brain doesn't read titles first—it scans images. That's why creators say: "The video starts with the thumbnail."

But thumbnails alone don't build trust. When viewers land on your channel, the banner is your storefront. It signals professionalism, niche focus, and whether they should subscribe. And once someone finishes your video, the end screen decides whether they leave or stay in your world. That extra 20 seconds of design can be the difference between one isolated view and a binge session of three or four videos.

Many small creators underestimate this. They spend hours editing content but upload with a random screenshot as a thumbnail, a banner cropped badly on mobile, and no end screen. The result? Low CTR, weak retention, poor growth—even if the content itself is fantastic.

This chapter is about treating YouTube visuals as seriously as the content itself. You'll learn how to:

- Create thumbnails that stop the scroll and raise CTR.
- Design banners that work on desktop, mobile, and TV without cutting text.
- Build end screens that funnel viewers deeper into your channel.
- Adapt content into Shorts with proper safe zones and hooks.

By the end, you won't just have better-looking assets—you'll have a system for YouTube design that earns clicks, builds recognition, and keeps people watching.

What You'll Do in 10 Minutes (and why it matters)

Take a single video idea (e.g., "5 Canva Hacks"):

- Design a thumbnail (1280×720) with a bold headline and one focal image.
- Create a channel banner (2560×1440) with your tagline in the safe area.
- Build a 1920×1080 end screen with placeholders for "Next Video" and "Subscribe."
- Resize one of your IG Stories into a YouTube Short (1080×1920).

Export all four. Place them in one folder called "YouTube Kit." You now have the essential brand system for YouTube—not just a random video upload.

Thumbnails: The Art of the First Impression

Why this matters.

CTR (click-through rate) is one of YouTube's strongest signals. If 10,000 people see your video but only 200 click, the algorithm decides it's not engaging. If 2,000 click, it pushes your video to more people. Thumbnails are the gateway.

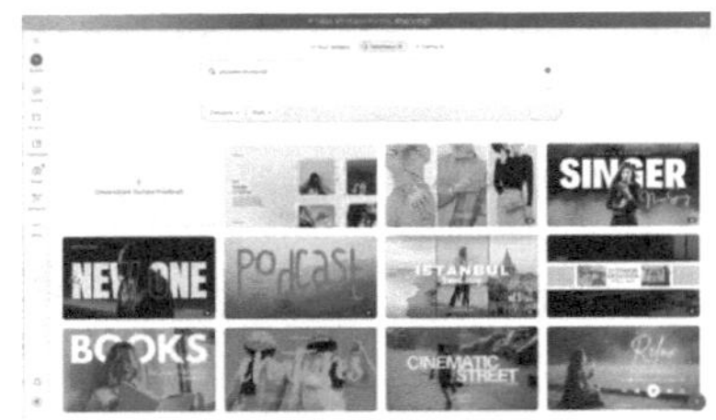

Design Principles:

- Size: 1280×720, always 16:9 ratio.
- Headline: 3–5 words max, large, high-contrast.
- Image: one clear subject (close-up face, product, or bold object).
- Colors: bright or contrasting; use your brand accent consistently.
- Consistency: build a recognisable style so viewers spot your videos instantly.

Real Scenario — Tech Reviewer

A reviewer used bland screenshots for thumbnails. His CTR was under 2%. After redesigning thumbnails with yellow highlights, bold type, and close-up reactions, CTR rose to 6%—triple the clicks, same content.

Pro Tip — The Blink Test

Shrink your thumbnail to 10% size. Can you still read it? If not, simplify text or increase contrast.

Attention — Don't Compete With Titles

Your video title appears right below the thumbnail. Don't repeat it. Use the thumbnail to tease, not to explain.

Common Pitfall — "Poster Syndrome"

Beginners try to cram too much into one thumbnail—multiple images, long sentences, logos everywhere. Result: clutter. The best thumbnails look almost too simple.

Mini Exercise

Design three thumbnail variations for the same video. Change color schemes and headline phrasing. Export and preview at small size. Which one grabs your eye?

Channel Banners: Your Storefront on Every Device

Why this matters.

When viewers click to your channel, they're deciding: "Should I subscribe?" The banner is your brand's handshake. On desktop it's wide, on mobile it's cropped, on TV it's enormous. If you don't respect the safe zone, text gets chopped.

Design Principles:

- Size: 2560×1440.
- Safe Zone: 1546×423 (center strip). Keep all important text here.
- Content: Logo, tagline, upload schedule, maybe social links.
- Tone: Reflect your niche—fun and vibrant for lifestyle, minimal for business, bold for entertainment.

Real Scenario — Fitness Channel

A trainer put "New videos every Monday" at the far right. On mobile, it vanished. After centering it in the safe zone, subs increased—viewers trusted the consistency.

Pro Tip — Schedule Signal

Adding "New videos weekly" or "Tutorials every Tuesday" builds anticipation and loyalty.

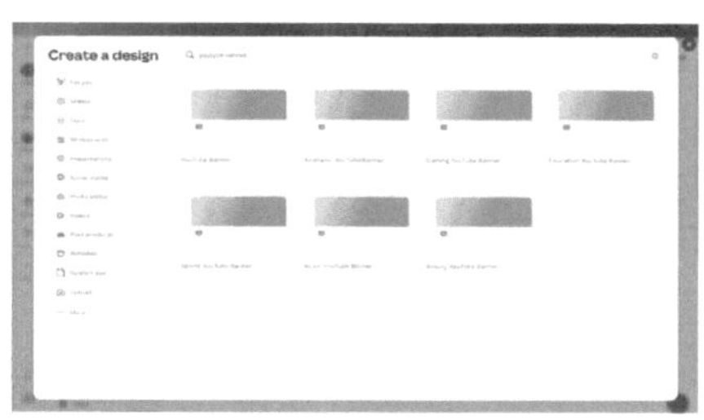

Attention — Mobile First

70% of YouTube traffic is mobile. Always preview your banner in Canva mockups and on your phone.

Common Pitfall — Empty Banners

Some creators leave banners plain or with blurry stock images. It wastes a huge branding opportunity.

Mini Exercise

Design a 2560×1440 banner. Place your logo + tagline in center safe zone. Export and preview on desktop + mobile. Adjust until consistent.

End Screens: Holding Viewers for the Next Step

Why this matters.

Most viewers leave at the end of a video. End screens give them a reason to stay—suggesting another video, playlist, or subscribe button. Retention is key: if viewers watch more of your channel, YouTube rewards you.

Design Principles:

- Size: 1920×1080.
- Placement: Dedicate one side to "Next Video," keep subscribe button in same spot across all videos.
- Background: gradient, brand color, or blurred video still.
- Text: simple CTA ("Watch Next," "Subscribe for More").

Real Scenario — Gaming Creator

A social media manager ended videos with black screen. Viewers dropped instantly. After adding bright end screens with fun CTAs, watch time rose 15%.

Pro Tip — Branded Template

Make one end screen layout in Canva. Reuse it for all videos. Consistency = recognition.

Attention — Too Many Options

Offering four links overwhelms viewers. Keep it to one "Next Video" and one "Subscribe."

Mini Exercise

Design a 1920×1080 end screen. Add a "Watch Next" area and "Subscribe" icon. Export and overlay on a test clip.

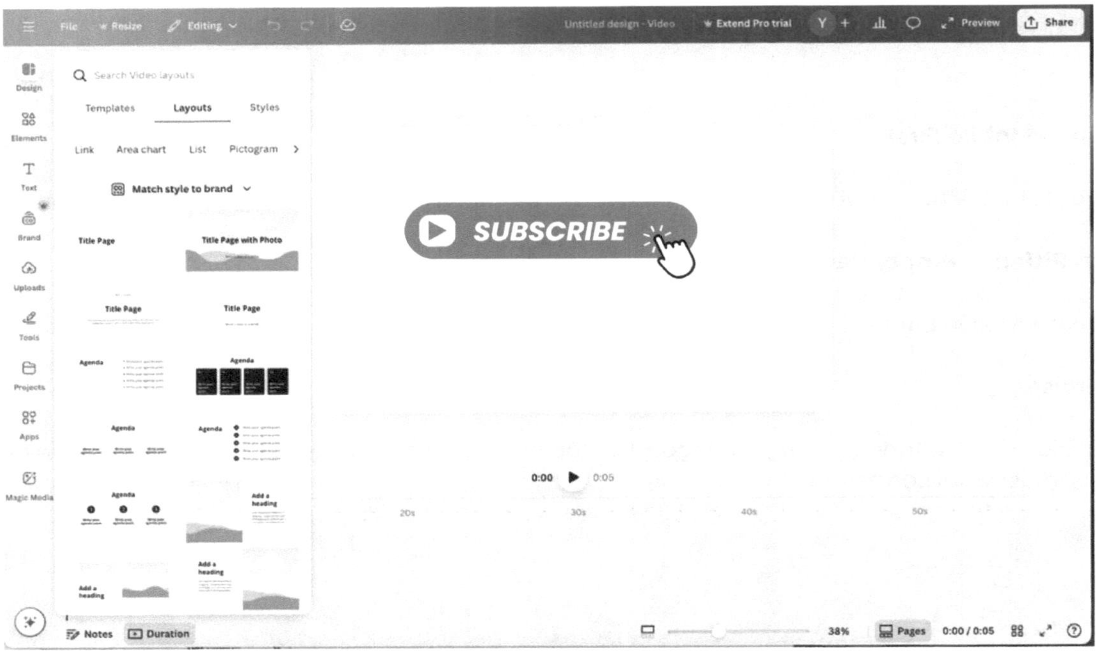

Shorts: YouTube's Answer to TikTok

Why this matters.

YouTube Shorts (1080×1920) drive massive exposure. They appear in a separate feed and reach audiences who may never see your long videos. Shorts thrive on hooks in the first 3 seconds.

Design Principles:

- Size: 1080×1920 vertical.
- Safe zones: avoid bottom caption + top cropping.
- Hooks: place big text top-center.
- CTA: add "Subscribe for full video" at end.

Real Scenario — Educator

A creator clipped 30-second moments from lectures, added bold titles, and posted as Shorts. Subscriber growth tripled.

Pro Tip — Reuse Stories

IG Story templates adapt perfectly into Shorts. Just adjust for YouTube's pacing.

Mini Exercise

Take one IG Story. Resize into 1080×1920 Short. Add bold headline at top. Export and preview.

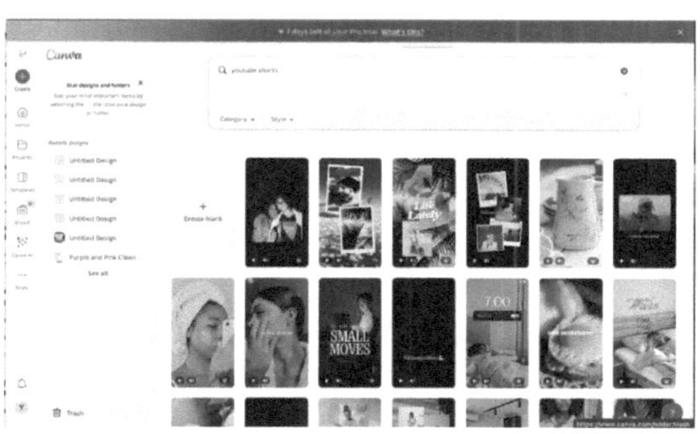

Checklist — YouTube Design Kit

- Thumbnails: bold, short text, clear focal point, brand accent.
- Banner: safe zone respected, tagline centered.
- End screens: consistent template, max two CTAs.
- Shorts: hooks in first 3 seconds, safe zone text.

Common Mistakes — And How to Fix Them

- Thumbnail text too long. Fix: keep ≤5 words.
- Banner text cut on mobile. Fix: stay inside safe zone.
- End screens overcrowded. Fix: stick to two CTAs.
- Shorts without hooks. Fix: add bold opening headline.

"Do It Now" Homework — 60 Minutes

1. Thumbnail Sprint (20 min): Create 3 thumbnail variations for one video. Test at small size.
2. Banner Build (15 min): Design banner with tagline and upload schedule. Test on phone.
3. End Screen Layout (15 min): Create branded template. Save for reuse.
4. Shorts Adaptation (10 min): Repurpose one Story as a Short.

QR Bonus (Module Hub):

- 5 Thumbnail Templates (CTR-tested).
- Banner Safe Zone Guide.
- Reusable End Screen Template.
- Shorts Storyboard Template.

Closing Thought

A strong thumbnail earns the click. A clean banner builds trust. An end screen extends retention. Shorts expand reach. Together, they form a design system that amplifies your content.

Chapter 4

Planner & Batch: Duplications, Calendars, and Reusable Libraries

Scroll through the feeds of the creators or businesses you admire most. You'll notice something: their content feels planned. Posts appear in rhythm, stories connect to promotions, carousels drop on the same day each week, and there's no sense of panic. It feels like they're always prepared.

Now contrast that with the average beginner's feed: bursts of activity followed by silence, a random motivational quote next to a blurry product shot, stories that feel improvised. The difference isn't creativity—it's systems. Professionals don't sit down each day asking "What should I post?" They already know, because they've batched, scheduled, and built libraries that do half the work for them.

This chapter is about building your hidden engine. Canva gives you the tools—duplication, content planner, and folders—but the mindset is what matters: stop reinventing, start scaling. With duplication, you multiply designs quickly. With a planner, you turn designs into a timeline. With libraries, you create a system that accelerates every future session.

By the end, you'll have a repeatable workflow:

- One idea becomes five posts in minutes.
- A month of content sits ready, mapped and labeled.
- Your future self doesn't hunt for logos, colors, or CTAs—they're already in place.

This is how creators free up time, small businesses look professional, and social media managers stay sane. Consistency isn't luck. It's a machine. And you're about to build it.

What You'll Do in 10 Minutes (and why it matters)

- Pick one post design.
- Duplicate it 5 times.
- On each version, change just one thing—headline, image, background color, CTA box, layout spacing. Export the set.

You've just created a micro-pack of content. What seemed like "one post" has become "a week of posts." That small shift in thinking—system, not scramble—is the foundation of every social brand that grows.

Duplication: More Posts, Less Effort

Why this matters.

Beginners often confuse "original" with "effective." In reality, audiences don't need a brand-new layout every day. They need clarity and repetition. Duplication saves time, keeps style consistent, and allows you to focus on message instead of decoration.

How to do it.

- Start with a master design. Build one strong post that feels aligned with your brand.
- Duplicate inside Canva. Click "Duplicate page" or "Make a copy."
- Vary one element per version. Example: headline text, background color, image, or CTA phrasing.
- Batch export. Export all in one folder, naming clearly (Post01, Post02...).

Real Scenario — The Online Coach

An online coach used to design every single post from scratch. It took hours. Once she started duplicating and varying one element, she produced 15 posts in the same time it used to take her to make 3. Her audience didn't see "repetition"—they saw a consistent brand voice.

Pro Tip — Theme Packs

Instead of single posts, think in packs: "5 Tips," "3 Myths," "4 Quotes." Duplicating the design gives you a family of content that feels coherent.

Attention — Cosmetic vs Strategic Variation

Don't change so much that the posts feel random. Small, consistent shifts build rhythm. Keep fonts, logos, and layout steady.

Mini Exercise — The 5-Variation Sprint

Take one design. Duplicate it five times. Version A: new headline. Version B: new image. Version C: rotate brand color. Version D: change CTA box. Version E: adjust spacing. Export all and compare side by side. Do they look like siblings?

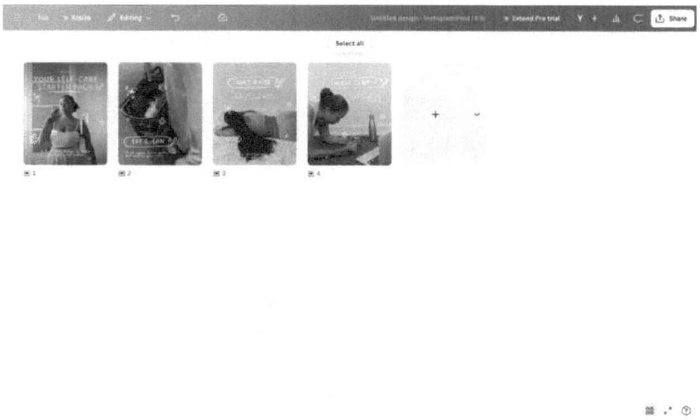

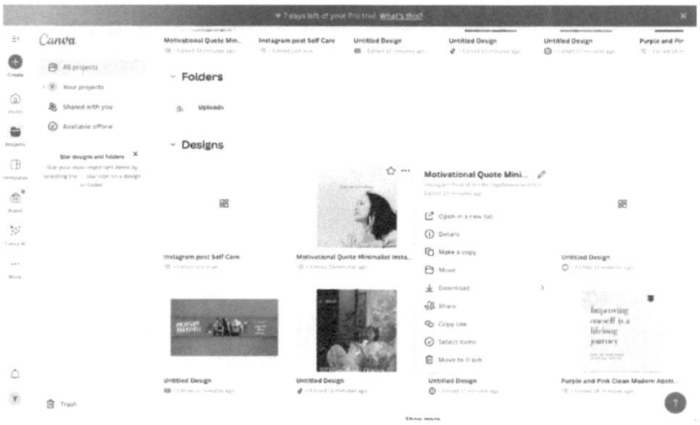

Calendars: Turning Designs Into Strategy

Why this matters.

Great content dies if it's not posted at the right time. A content calendar shifts you from "reactive" to "proactive." Instead of waking up to design something for today, you map your month in advance. This creates rhythm, variety, and space for creativity where it matters.

How to use Canva's Content Planner.

Inside Canva, after finishing a design, click "Share → Schedule." Pick your platform, write your caption, and set the date. Repeat for your batch of posts. In the Planner view, you'll see a monthly grid filled with your scheduled designs.

How to do it manually.

If you prefer external tools, export your posts, drop them in a folder labeled by month (e.g., "Nov 2025 Social Pack"), and create a Google Sheet with columns: Date, Platform, Theme, Post File. This gives you control across multiple platforms.

Real Scenario — Local Bakery

The bakery used to post whenever they remembered. Engagement was low. After mapping a calendar—Mondays for product highlights, Wednesdays for tips, Fridays for promotions—their audience started expecting content. Customers even messaged on Fridays waiting for the new promo post.

Pro Tip — Theme Days for Momentum

Assigning categories to days prevents burnout: "Motivation Monday," "Tip Tuesday," "Feature Friday." Audiences love rhythm, and you design faster when categories are fixed.

Common Pitfall — Overstuffed Calendars

Ambition kills consistency. Don't plan 50 posts if you can realistically create 20. Consistency beats volume.

Mini Exercise — Build a Month View

Take 12 designs. Assign them to a monthly grid (either in Canva Planner or Google Sheets). Label by theme. Export the calendar and pin it above your desk.

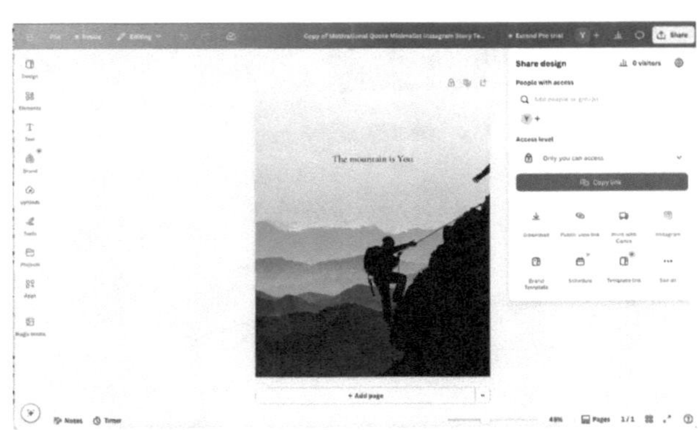

Libraries: Your Personal Design Warehouse

Why this matters.

Imagine cooking a meal where every time you had to find a new knife, pan, or ingredient from scratch. That's how beginners treat Canva: every session, they search for logos, fonts, colors, icons. A library turns chaos into flow.

How to do it.

- **Brand Kit**: If you have Canva Pro, load your fonts, colors, and logos once. Every new design starts branded.
- **Folders**: Create folders for Photos, Icons, Overlays, Carousels, Reels. Label them clearly.
- **Components page**: Build one Canva page with reusable assets—CTA buttons, dividers, overlays. Copy them into new projects.

Real Scenario — Content Creator

A content creator wasted 20 minutes each session hunting for the "right" arrow icon. After making a components page with her go-to icons and overlays, design time dropped by 50%.

Pro Tip — Star What You Actually Use

In Canva, you can "Star" assets. Do this for icons, photos, and templates you love. Your starred items become a quick library inside search.

Attention — Clean the Clutter

A messy library slows you down. Once a month, archive unused elements. The less you see, the faster you choose.

Mini Exercise — Build Your Library Now

Create a folder called "Brand Library." Add your logo, brand colors, and 10 reusable icons. Create one "Components Page" with at least 3 overlays and 2 CTA buttons. Star them all.

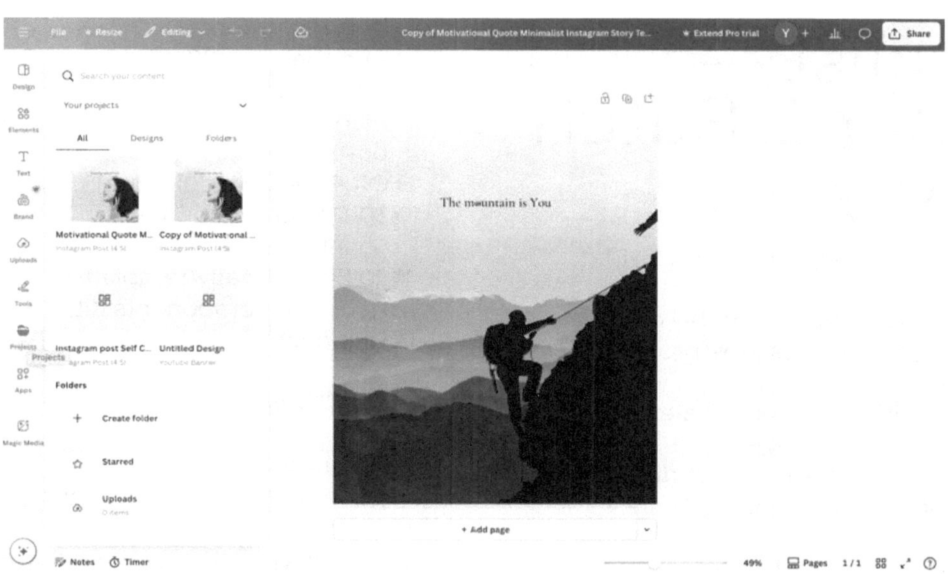

Connecting the Three: Duplication + Calendar + Library

Why this matters.

Each element is powerful on its own, but the system comes alive when they work together:

- Duplication produces volume.
- The calendar organizes that volume.
- The library speeds up creation each time.

Together, they form a loop: design once, multiply, schedule, repeat faster.

Real Scenario — Marketing Agency Workflow

A small agency created 40 posts for a client in two days by combining these three: duplicated templates, scheduled them in Canva Planner, and pulled assets from a pre-built brand library. What looked like magic was simply systems.

Mini Exercise — The Loop Test

Pick one design. Duplicate 5 versions. Assign them to dates. Export to your Brand Library folder. You've just run the cycle once. Repeat monthly, and posting becomes routine instead of stress.

Checklist — Planner & Batch Mastery

1. One design can be multiplied into 5–10 variants.
2. Posts are mapped into a monthly calendar.
3. Themes assigned to days (tips, promos, quotes, stories).
4. Library built with logos, fonts, palette, reusable icons and overlays.
5. Components page ready for fast duplication.
6. Workflow loop established: Duplicate → Schedule → Store.

Common Mistakes — And How to Fix Them

- Designing from scratch every time. → Fix: Duplicate and vary.
- Random posting. → Fix: Use planner or spreadsheet.
- Cluttered library. → Fix: Clean monthly, star essentials.
- Overambitious calendars. → Fix: Plan realistically, then scale.
- Inconsistent logos/colors. → Fix: Always use Brand Kit or Brand Library.

"Do It Now" Homework — 60 Minutes

1. 5-Variation Pack (15 min).
2. Choose one design. Duplicate 5 versions with slight changes. Export as "Variation Pack."
3. Monthly Calendar (20 min).
4. Take 12 designs. Assign them to specific dates (via Canva Planner or Google Sheets). Add categories (Tip, Testimonial, Promo).
5. Brand Library Setup (15 min).
6. Create folder with logo, fonts, swatches, 10 icons. Add a Components page with CTA buttons + overlays.
7. Run the Loop (10 min).
8. Take one variation, schedule it in Canva Planner, store it in your folder. Repeat for 3 posts.
9. QR Bonus (Module Hub):
10. 30-Day Content Calendar Template (Google Sheet + Canva).
11. 20 Batch-Ready Templates.
12. Reusable Components Kit.
13. Brand Library Folder Starter Pack.

Closing Thought

Calendars save your consistency. Libraries save your energy. Build this once, and your creative work stops being a daily struggle and starts being a machine that runs smoothly.

Chapter 5

Basic Metrics & Publishing: CTR, Naming, and Versioning

In this chapter, we go from pretty pictures to measurable results. There's a hard truth in the world of digital content: nobody cares how much time you spent designing a post. The only thing that matters is whether the post worked. **But how do you define "worked"? Was it about likes? Comments? Shares?** For a designer, those numbers may feel validating. Yet for a brand or a business, the real indicator is whether the design moved someone to act. Did they click? Did they open? Did they watch? Did they move one step deeper into your ecosystem?

This is where metrics come in—not as cold numbers, but as the mirror that reflects how your audience reacts to your work. Metrics transform design from an artistic exercise into a growth engine. They don't kill creativity; they guide it. They help you distinguish between what looks good to you and what actually works for your audience.

The most important of these is CTR—Click-Through Rate. CTR is the lifeline of design on digital platforms. A carousel that gets people swiping, a thumbnail that makes someone click play, a story that drives a tap forward—CTR is the thread connecting your visual to the next action. You could think of it as the heartbeat of your design: if it's strong, the design is alive; if it's weak, the design is flat.

But numbers without order are noise. That's why naming conventions and versioning strategies matter just as much. If you don't name your files properly, you'll never know which design produced which result. If you don't version systematically, you'll never learn what change improved performance. Without these practices, your "data" is useless—just a cloud of posts you can't trace.

And then comes publishing. Publishing is not just pressing "post." It's about rhythm. It's about telling a story in time, building anticipation, creating predictability for your audience and reliability for algorithms. A publishing schedule is a silent signal: "We're serious, we're here, and you can trust us to show up."
In this chapter, you'll discover how metrics, naming, versioning, and publishing work together to turn chaos into clarity.

We'll explore how to track CTR and use it as design feedback, how to build a naming system that makes analytics usable, how to version like a scientist, and how to publish with rhythm instead of randomness.

By the end, you won't just design posts—you'll design outcomes.

CTR: The Metric That Speaks the Loudest

Why this matters.

Imagine two posts: one garners 1,000 likes but only 3 link clicks. The other has 200 likes but 50 clicks. Which one did its job? The second. CTR cuts through the vanity of "vanity metrics." It's not about applause—it's about action.

The anatomy of CTR.

On Instagram, CTR might show up as "Profile Visits" or "Website Clicks." On YouTube, it's thumbnail CTR—impressions vs actual views. On LinkedIn, it's clicks on a carousel PDF. CTR is always the ratio between exposure and action: how many saw it, and how many cared enough to act.

Real Scenario — The Webinar Flyer

A coach designed a beautiful post crammed with details: date, time, benefits, testimonials. CTR was 0.7%. When she stripped it down to a bold headline, one key benefit, and a clean CTA button, CTR shot up to 3.5%. The offer didn't change—only the design did.

Pro Tip — Treat CTR as Creative Feedback

Low CTR isn't an insult. It's feedback. Maybe the headline was too small, maybe the CTA button blended in, maybe the image was irrelevant. Each low CTR is a clue.

Common Pitfall — Blaming the Algorithm

It's easy to say, "The platform doesn't like me." But often, the audience didn't see value quickly enough. CTR forces you to confront that gap.

Mini Exercise — A/B Testing for Designers

Take one post. Create two versions: Version A with headline focus, Version B with image focus. Publish both. After a week, compare CTR. Write down two lessons from the results—what worked, what didn't. This turns every post into a learning lab.

Naming: Order in the Midst of Chaos

Why this matters.

Without naming conventions, you're lost in the wilderness. Files called "final-final-v3.jpg" don't tell you anything. Six months later, you won't remember what that file was, let alone how it performed. Naming conventions create traceability. They allow you to connect designs to metrics and learn over time.

How to name with purpose.

Adopt a formula: Date + Platform + Campaign + Version.

- Example: 2025-10_IG_FocusTips_V1.jpg
- Carousel example: 2025-10_LI_CarouselProduct_V2_Slide03.pdf

Real Scenario — The Agency in Chaos

A small agency couldn't tell which designs had worked for a client. CTR reports came in, but they didn't know which visuals they referred to. After enforcing naming rules, they matched performance to specific designs and doubled down on what worked.

Attention — Naming as Future-Proofing

Don't name for today. Name for six months from now, when you've forgotten. Name for the colleague who will join your team. Name for the campaign you'll revisit next year.

Mini Exercise — Build a Named Set

Create 3 posts. Save them with naming convention: 2025-10_IG_Mindset_V1, 2025-10_IG_Mindset_V2, 2025-10_IG_Mindset_V3. Drop them in a folder. Notice how clarity emerges instantly.

Versioning: The Designer's Science Lab

Why this matters.

Great design isn't guessing—it's iteration. Versioning means creating small, deliberate variations to test what works. It's design turned into science.

The rules of versioning.

- Change one variable at a time: color, image, headline.
- Label clearly: V1, V2, V3.
- Publish or schedule side by side.
- Record results.

Real Scenario — The SaaS Startup

A startup tested two thumbnails: one with founder's smiling face, one with abstract illustration. CTR on face: 8%. CTR on illustration: 3%. From then on, they always used faces.

Pro Tip — Document Every Test

Use a simple spreadsheet: Date, Platform, Campaign, Version, CTR, Notes. Over time, patterns emerge—like "faces beat objects" or "yellow outperforms blue."

Common Pitfall — Changing Too Much

If you change font, color, image, and text all at once, you won't know which caused the result. Discipline in versioning is everything.

Mini Exercise — Three Versions, Three Lessons

Create three versions of the same post: V1 with color change, V2 with font change, V3 with image change. Export, name properly, and track.

Publishing: Rhythm Builds Trust

Why this matters.

Random posting feels chaotic to audiences and invisible to algorithms. Consistency, not volume, is what builds trust. A publishing rhythm makes you predictable—in a good way.

The publishing mindset.

Think of publishing as music. The posts are notes, but the schedule is the rhythm. Without rhythm, it's noise. With rhythm, it's a song your audience learns to expect.

How to execute.

- Use Canva's Content Planner to assign dates.
- Or export posts into folders and schedule with tools like Buffer, Later, or Meta Business Suite.
- Better to post 3× a week consistently than 7× in one week and silence the next.

Real Scenario — The Lifestyle Blogger

A creator posted sporadically: three posts in one week, then nothing for a month. Engagement lagged. After scheduling weekly posts in Canva, her audience began to anticipate her content. "Love your Monday tips!" followers said. Predictability became part of her brand.

Pro Tip — Build Cadence, Not Perfection

Don't obsess over "best times." Algorithms reward consistent presence. Your brand's heartbeat matters more than timing tricks.

Mini Exercise — Map a Week

Take 5 designs. Schedule them across one week in Canva Planner. Preview the calendar. Notice the relief that comes with clarity.

Checklist: From Chaos to System

- CTR is tracked regularly, not ignored.
- Naming conventions applied to all files.
- Versioning done with discipline (one variable per change).
- Publishing rhythm established (weekly cadence).
- Planner or spreadsheet used to schedule.

Common Mistakes — And How to Fix Them

- Focusing on likes instead of CTR. Solution: train yourself to look at actions, not applause.
- Files with random names. Solution: enforce naming conventions.
- Testing too many variables. Solution: one change at a time.
- Posting when inspired only. Solution: set rhythm, not mood.

"Do It Now" Homework — 60 Minutes

1. CTR Test (20 min).
2. Design two versions of the same post. Publish both. After one week, compare CTR and write down 3 lessons.
3. Naming Audit (10 min).
4. Take 10 of your existing files. Rename them using the convention: Date + Platform + Campaign + Version.
5. Versioning Sprint (15 min).
6. Create three versions of one design: change only one element each. Save with V1, V2, V3.
7. Publishing Rhythm (15 min).
8. Map out a week of content. Assign each post to a day in Canva Planner or a Google Sheet.

QR Bonus (Module Hub):

- CTR Tracking Sheet (Google Doc).
- Naming & Versioning Guide.
- Weekly Publishing Calendar Template.

Closing Thought

Design is only half the job. The other half is learning from results, organizing your work, and showing up with rhythm. Metrics are your compass, naming is your map, versioning is your experiment, and publishing is your drumbeat. Master these, and your social media stops being guesswork—it becomes growth.

Module 3 – Canva for Business and Make Money

From Posts to Serious Business

If the first modules of this book gave you the ability to create and schedule content, this module changes the playing field. Here, design is no longer about chasing likes—it's about winning trust, persuading clients, and opening new revenue streams. For freelancers, small businesses, and professionals, Canva isn't just a creative playground. It becomes the backbone of your business identity.

Think about it: a customer doesn't judge you only on the quality of your service. They judge you on your brochure, your presentation, your proposal PDF, your website header. They may not say it out loud, but their brain is making decisions in seconds: "Does this brand feel reliable? Does it look polished? Do I trust them with my money?" That judgment isn't emotional—it's visual. And consistency across your business materials is what tips the scale in your favor.

In this module, you'll stop thinking like a casual creator and start thinking like a business. You'll learn how to set up a Brand Kit that locks in your identity. You'll build presentations that follow a persuasive rhythm instead of a messy slide dump. You'll create a Marketing Pack—brochures, product sheets, headers—that give you professional polish at every customer touchpoint. You'll even design a simple but powerful one-page website with CTA and SEO basics, showing that you can operate online without paying thousands to developers.

And then, we'll go a step further. Because Canva isn't just about using design for your own business—it's also a platform to make money. We'll show you how to package digital products like templates or mini-ebooks, sell them on platforms like Etsy or Gumroad, and price them smartly. Not with hype, but with practical, concrete steps.

By the end of Module 3, you'll walk away with a complete Business Starter Kit—brand kit, pitch deck, brochure, and lead magnet—ready to use with clients or prospects. More importantly, you'll understand how to monetize your Canva skills without chasing trends.

What You'll Do in This Module (and why it matters)

- Set up your Brand Kit & governance: palettes, fonts, logos, asset libraries, and rules that protect your brand identity.
- Design persuasive presentations: learn how to structure, pace, and deliver slides that sell, not bore.
- Build a Marketing Pack: brochures, product sheets, email headers—tools that make you look like a business, not a hobby.
- Launch a one-page site: domain, CTA placement, SEO basics—your digital storefront in hours, not months.
- Explore Make Money strategies: create and sell digital products (templates, ebooks), price them, and deliver them professionally.
- Implement workflows: approvals, file naming, versioning—so your system scales, even with a team.

By the end of this module, you won't just know how to "design with Canva." You'll have the tools, the confidence, and the system to run a professional brand and even generate new revenue streams.

Chapter 1

Brand Kit & Governance: The Foundation of Business Design

When people think of "branding," they often imagine creativity: a striking logo, a catchy tagline, maybe an unusual color. But the secret behind the strongest brands in the world is not creativity—it's consistency.

Think about Coca-Cola. Their logo hasn't changed significantly in over a century. Starbucks uses green everywhere: cups, aprons, signage. Apple? You recognize their sleek typography and clean layouts in a fraction of a second. These brands aren't improvising; they're repeating themselves, over and over, with surgical precision.

Now compare that to the average small business. Their Instagram posts are blue one week, orange the next. The brochure uses Times New Roman, while the website headline uses Comic Sans. Their logo appears stretched on a proposal, cropped on an invoice, and pixelated in a presentation. What does this communicate? Not "creativity." It communicates inconsistency, and inconsistency kills trust.

The paradox is that small businesses often think governance is for "big companies with manuals." But Canva has changed the game. You no longer need a hundred-page PDF called "Visual Identity Guidelines." You need a simple but effective Brand Kit inside Canva, with your palette, fonts, logos, and rules locked in place. You need a culture—whether it's just you, a small team, or a group of freelancers—that respects consistency as the foundation of trust.

This chapter is where you build that foundation. We'll go step by step: how to choose and save a brand palette, how to lock in fonts, how to manage logos, how to create libraries that accelerate work, and how to set light but powerful governance rules. By the end, you won't just be "designing with Canva." You'll be running a brand, not a hobby.

Section 1 — Palette: Choosing Colors That Tell Your Story

Why this matters.

Colors aren't decoration; they're language. In fact, color is processed in the brain faster than words. Before someone reads your flyer, their subconscious has already judged whether your red feels bold or cheap, whether your blue feels trustworthy or cold. If your Instagram feed flips between random shades, you communicate chaos. A defined palette communicates identity.

Building it in Canva.

Inside the Brand Kit panel, set your primary palette. Start with:

- **2 primaries**: the colors that appear in your logo and dominate your brand.
- **2–3 secondaries**: supporting shades for backgrounds or highlights.
- **Neutrals:** one dark (black/charcoal) and one light (white/cream).

Real Scenario — The Boutique Bakery

A local bakery had a pink logo but posted flyers in red and brown. Customers asked, "Did you rebrand?" They hadn't—it was just random Canva choices. Once they set their palette to soft pink, cream, and espresso brown, everything aligned. Suddenly, their Instagram looked like a premium patisserie, not a flea market.

Pro Tip — Emotional Anchors

Each color carries associations. Blue = trust, green = growth, orange = energy. Choose colors that align with your values, not just what you like.

Attention — The "Favorite Color" Trap
Founders often pick their favorite color. But your personal love for purple may not say "luxury real estate." Choose for audience, not ego.

Mini Exercise — Palette in Action
Pick two primaries, two secondaries, one neutral. Apply them to a flyer, a post, and a brochure. Ask: "Do these look like siblings?" If not, adjust saturation or tone.

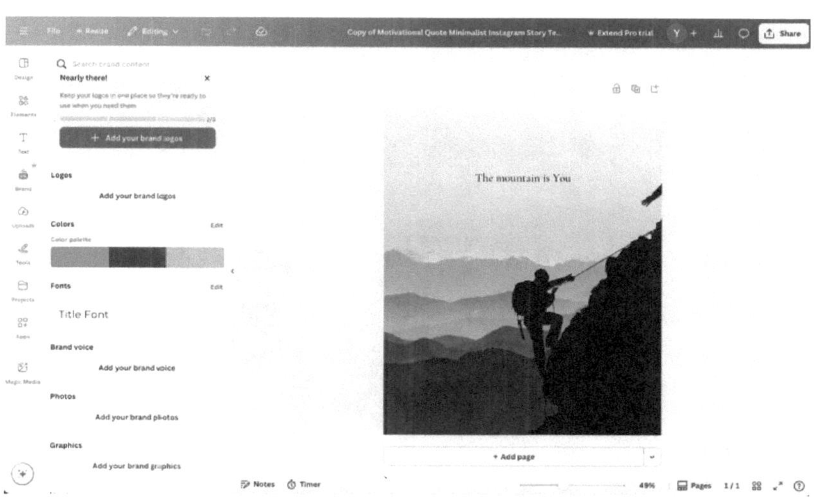

Section 2 — Fonts: Giving Your Brand a Voice

Why this matters.

Typography is your brand's voice in text form. Bold sans-serif fonts shout modernity and confidence. Elegant serifs whisper tradition and expertise. Script fonts suggest intimacy or playfulness. If your posts speak one way but your brochure speaks another, your voice cracks.

How to set it up.

In Canva's Brand Kit, define:

- **Header font:** bold and distinctive, for attention.
- **Body font:** clean, legible, for longer text.
- **Accent font (optional)**: for quotes or highlights.

Real Scenario — Freelance Designer

A freelancer used different fonts every time. One proposal was in Arial, another in Lora, a flyer in Lobster. Clients never felt continuity. After locking Montserrat for headers and Open Sans for body, everything clicked—her "brand voice" finally sounded consistent.

Pro Tip — Font Families Save Sanity

Choose fonts with multiple weights (light, regular, bold). That way, you get flexibility without changing families.

Attention — Don't Overdecorate

Using five fonts feels amateurish. Two, max three, is enough. Your goal is identity, not variety.

Mini Exercise — Lock Your Voice

Pick one header font, one body font, and one optional accent. Apply to a brochure, a presentation slide, and an Instagram post. Do they sound like the same voice?

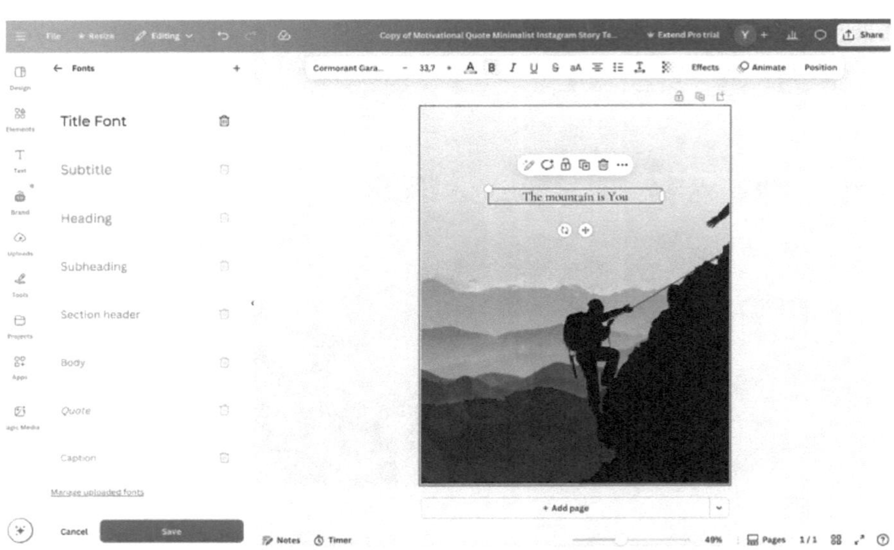

Section 3 — Logos: Your Signature, Standardized

Why this matters.

Your logo is your handshake. If it appears pixelated, stretched, or inconsistent, you send a sloppy first impression.

How to manage logos in Canva.

Upload multiple clean versions:

- Full logo (with wordmark).
- Icon version (just symbol).
- Black/white version for light/dark backgrounds.
- Transparent PNGs for overlays.

Real Scenario — The Consultancy Firm

A consulting team sent proposals with stretched logos. Their competitor's logo looked sharp on every page. Guess who looked credible? Once they uploaded a clean logo set to Canva, the difference was night and day.

Pro Tip — Label Clearly

In Canva, rename files "Primary Logo," "Dark Background," "Icon Only." Don't leave them as "logo-final-v3.png."

Attention — Always Keep Vector Originals

Even if you upload PNGs to Canva, store the vector (SVG, AI, EPS) elsewhere. For scaling, nothing beats vector.

Mini Exercise — Logo Audit

Upload 3 versions of your logo. Place each on a white, black, and photo background. Which works? Adjust your library until each has a use case.

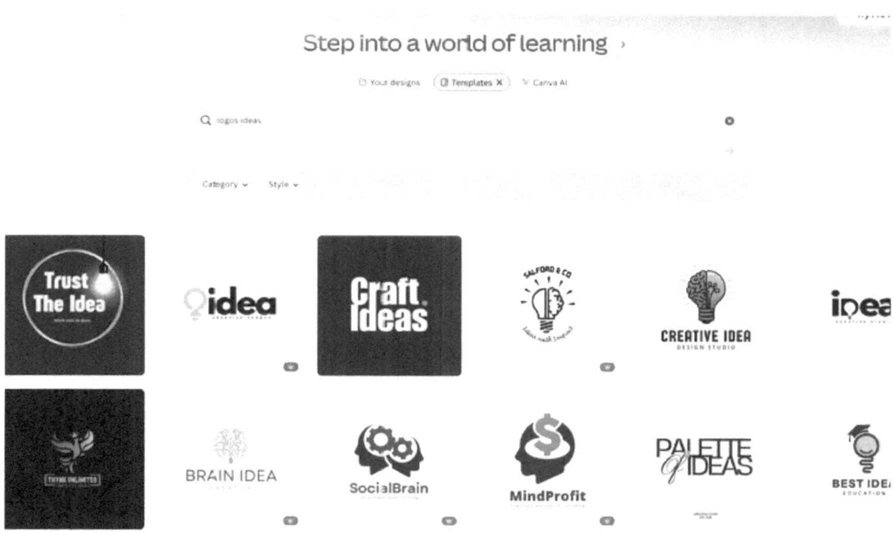

Section 4 — Libraries: Speed by Design

Why this matters.

Creativity isn't fast—systems are. A library means your assets are ready. No more hunting for icons every time. No more uploading the same photo five times.

How to do it.

- **Folders**: Create folders for Photos, Icons, Templates, Overlays.
- **Starred items**: Tag your favorites to appear instantly.
- **Components Page:** One Canva file with reusable CTAs, arrows, overlays, buttons. Copy/paste instead of rebuilding.

Real Scenario — Marketing Team

- **Before**: every team member used random arrows and icons.
- **After**: one Components Page with approved assets. The result? Faster work, and a brand that looked unified.

Pro Tip — Build Once, Reuse Forever

Save commonly used elements (like "Download Now" buttons) as components. Every new design starts 50% done.

Attention — Audit Monthly

Don't let the library grow wild. Every month, delete unused assets. Clutter kills speed.

Mini Exercise — Build Your Warehouse

Create 4 folders. Add 10 assets in each. Build one Components Page with 5 reusable items. You've just built tomorrow's productivity.

Section 5 — Governance: The Rules That Protect Your Brand

Why this matters.

Even the best kit collapses if people ignore it. Governance means rules: who can edit templates, who approves designs, and how to keep consistency intact.

How to implement.

- **Roles**: Decide who edits, who publishes.
- **Rules**: Define logo spacing, font minimums, color usage.
- **Documentation**: Create a 1-page "Brand Rules" doc for quick reference.

Real Scenario — Startup Team

Without governance, interns changed fonts in pitch decks. Investors noticed inconsistency. After governance, only the brand lead could edit masters. The difference was credibility.

Pro Tip — Keep It Light

Governance isn't bureaucracy. One page of rules is enough.

Attention — Don't Overcontrol

Governance is about protecting identity, not killing creativity. Give guidelines, not chains.

Mini Exercise — Write Your Rule Sheet

Draft 1 page: logo rules, font rules, color rules, approval roles. Share with team.

Checklist: Brand Kit & Governance Locked

- If you can answer "yes" to these, your brand is ready:
- Does your palette stay consistent across posts, brochures, and decks?
- Do your fonts sound like one voice, not five?
- Are your logos sharp, transparent, and labeled?
- Do you have a Components Page to speed up design?
- Do you have clear rules on who edits and approves?

Common Mistakes — And How to Fix Them

- Color Chaos: Switching shades every time. Fix: lock palette in Brand Kit.
- Font Addiction: Adding new fonts for "variety." Fix: two fonts max.
- Logo Stretching: Using wrong files. Fix: upload PNGs with transparency.
- Asset Hunting: Wasting hours searching. Fix: build libraries.
- No Rules: Allowing anyone to improvise. Fix: governance sheet.
- Each of these errors isn't catastrophic—but they erode trust piece by piece. Fix them once, and you elevate your entire brand perception.

"Do It Now" Homework — 90 Minutes

1. Palette Build (15 min): Choose 2 primaries, 2 secondaries, 1 neutral. Test on 3 designs.
2. Font Lock (15 min): Pick header/body fonts. Apply to flyer + slide.
3. Logo Audit (15 min): Upload clean versions. Test on backgrounds.
4. Library Setup (25 min): Create 4 folders, add 10 assets each, and a Components Page with 5 CTAs.
5. Governance Sheet (20 min): Draft 1-page doc with roles, rules, approvals. Share or pin for yourself.

QR Bonus (Module Hub):

- Brand Kit Starter Template.
- Palette Builder Worksheet.
- Logo Audit Checklist.
- Governance One-Page.

Closing Thought

Consistency doesn't limit creativity—it amplifies it. With your palette, fonts, logos, libraries, and rules in place, you've built the infrastructure of trust. Canva gives you the tools, but you've provided the discipline. From here on, every brochure, every pitch deck, every social post will feel like it belongs to the same story. That's the difference between looking small and looking professional. And now, with your brand identity locked, you're ready to step onto the stage: presentations that persuade and convert.

Chapter 2

Presentations that Convince: Structure, Rhythm, Slide Master, Notes

Walk into any boardroom, investor meeting, or training session and you'll notice something strange: before you even open your mouth, your slides have already spoken for you. They're saying, "This person is professional," or "This feels amateur." Humans process visuals 60,000 times faster than text, and a presentation is essentially your brand stripped down to images and words on a big screen.

History proves it. Steve Jobs could have stood on stage and simply described the iPhone. **But it was the slides—clean, rhythmic, minimal—that turned his talk into a cultural event.** Airbnb's founders raised millions not just because of their idea, but because their early pitch deck followed a logical structure investors instantly trusted. On the flip side, how many great ideas have died in conference rooms because the presenter buried the audience under unreadable charts and walls of text?

This chapter isn't about making slides "prettier." **It's about turning them into weapons of persuasion.** Canva, with its templates, brand kits, and collaborative features, gives even non-designers the ability to create decks that look like they came from a professional agency. But tools mean nothing without principles. That's why here we go beyond drag-and-drop.

We'll break down the four pillars of a persuasive presentation:

- **Structure**: crafting a logical story arc so your audience never feels lost.
- **Rhythm**: alternating pace and style to keep attention alive.
- **Slide Masters**: enforcing consistency so your deck feels polished, not patchy.
- **Notes**: building your invisible script to speak with confidence.

By the end of this chapter, you'll know how to transform any deck—whether it's a sales pitch, a TED-style keynote, or an internal training—into a story that persuades, motivates, and sticks.

What You'll Do in 10 Minutes (Quick Win)

- Choose a Canva presentation template.
- Strip it to 12 slides. Assign each slide a function: hook, problem, solution, proof, CTA. Apply your brand fonts and colors.
- Add one sentence of speaker notes to the first three slides. Export. In ten minutes, you've turned random slides into a story arc. That's the mindset shift we'll deepen.

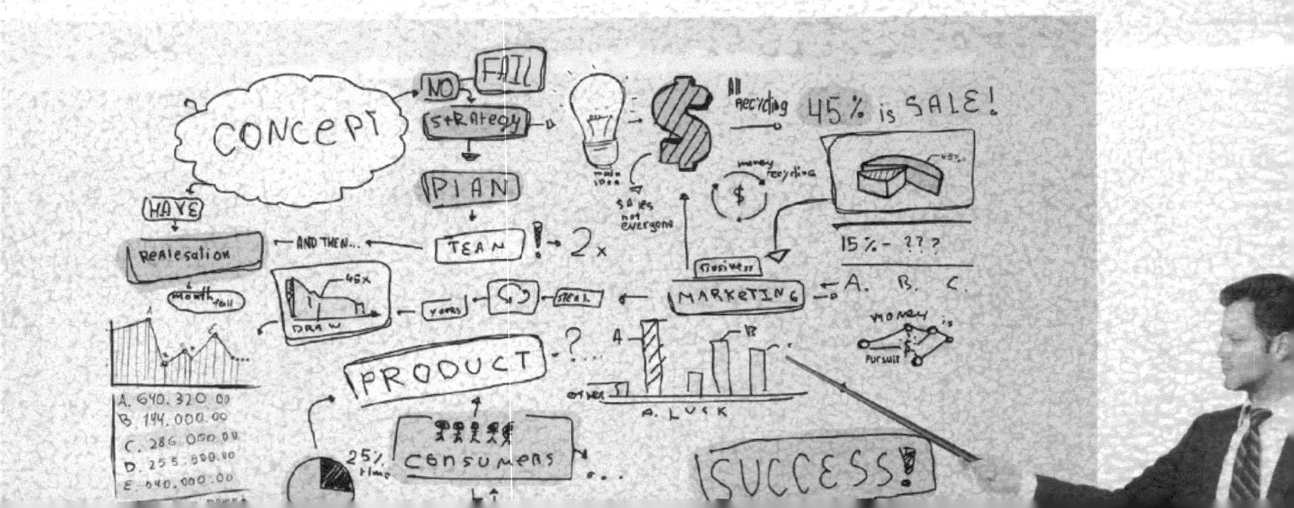

Section 1 — Structure: The Spine of Persuasion

Why structure matters.

Without a skeleton, a body collapses. Without structure, a presentation dissolves into noise. Audiences crave order. They want to know where you're taking them. When you guide them step by step, trust rises.

Two proven structures you can use in Canva:

1. **The Classic Business Arc (Problem → Solution → Proof → CTA)**
    - Problem: Identify a pain point.
    - Solution: Show your product or service.
    - Proof: Use numbers, testimonials, case studies.
    - CTA: End with a clear ask.

1. **The Storytelling Arc (Beginning → Conflict → Resolution)**
    - Beginning: Hook them with a relatable situation.
    - Conflict: Show stakes and challenges.
    - Resolution: Reveal how your idea solves it.

Real Scenario — Nonprofit Pitch

A nonprofit leader once presented 40 slides of scattered data. Donors tuned out. After restructuring into a 3-act story (a child's story → systemic problem → their project as solution), donors leaned forward. Donations rose by 35%.

Pro Tip — Map Before You Design

Spend 15 minutes writing slide titles on paper before opening Canva. If the titles alone tell a story, the structure is right.

Common Pitfall — Kitchen Sink Decks

- Too many beginners cram everything they know.
- Result: audiences remember nothing. The solution is ruthless editing.

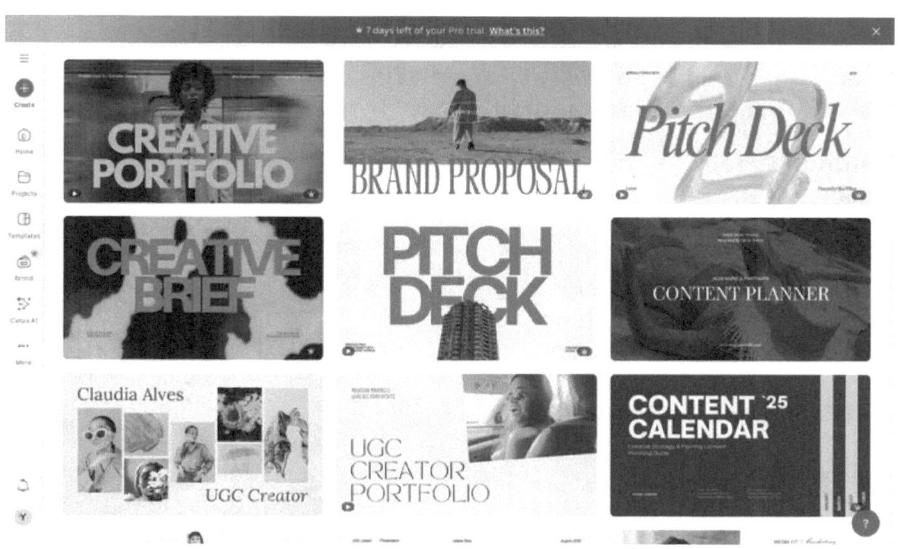

Mini Exercise — Structure Audit

- Take one of your old presentations.
- Write slide titles only.
- Do they form a coherent arc
- If not, cut or reorder until they do.

Section 2 — Rhythm: How to Keep Attention Alive

Why rhythm matters.

Even the best structure dies if rhythm is flat. Presentations are performances, and performance needs pacing. Imagine a song played with one note: unbearable. Rhythm in slides means alternating visual weight, mixing heavy data with simple imagery, balancing logic with emotion.

Practical techniques for rhythm in Canva:

- Insert "breather" slides: one powerful image + two words. In Canva, click Add page → choose a photo layout and write just two or three bold words. These slides act as visual pauses, giving the audience time to absorb the message before moving on.
- Alternate formats: data slide → quote → chart → full photo. You can duplicate your base layout and swap the element type each time. This variation creates motion through structure — not animation.
- Use size for emphasis: big headlines, then smaller context. In Canva, select your headline text box and increase font size dramatically (sometimes 3–4× larger than the supporting text). Big headlines command attention; smaller copy adds rhythm and hierarchy.

Real Scenario — Apple Keynotes

Apple's product launches balance rhythm brilliantly: bold product image, then spec slide, then emotional lifestyle photo, then demo. The alternation keeps energy alive for 90 minutes.

Pro Tip — The 3-Second Rule

A slide should be grasped in three seconds. If it takes longer, simplify.

Attention — Template Whiplash

Switching Canva templates mid-deck destroys rhythm. Stick to one style.

Mini Exercise — Rhythm Pass

Open your last deck. For every two text slides, insert one pure-visual slide. Practice delivery. Does everything feel more alive and with more rhythm? There you go!

Common Pitfall — Kitchen Sink Decks

Too many beginners cram everything they know. Result: audiences remember nothing. The solution is ruthless editing.

Mini Exercise — Structure Audit

Take one of your old presentations. Write slide titles only. Do they form a coherent arc? If not, cut or reorder until they do.

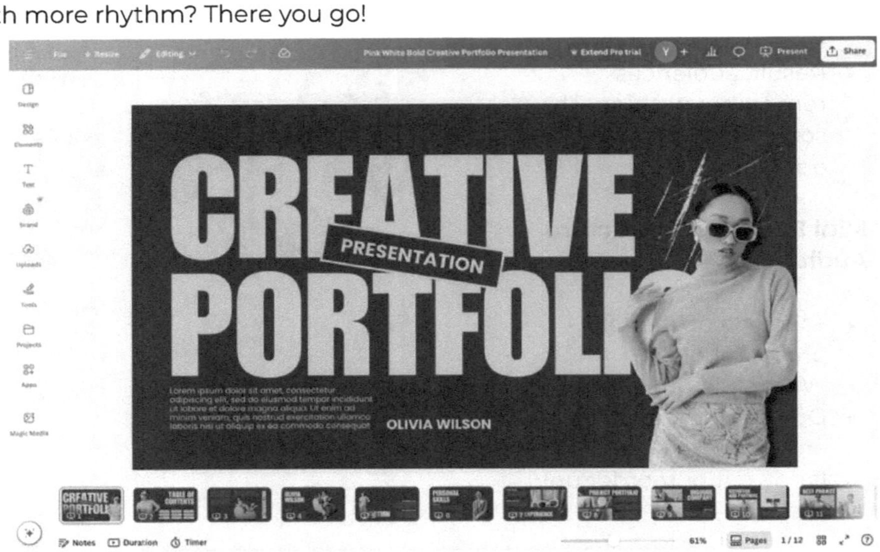

Section 3 — Slide Masters: The Invisible Hand of Professionalism

Why slide masters matter.

Audiences often can't articulate why a deck feels amateur. But they notice when logos jump around, fonts change, or colors shift. Consistency equals credibility. Slide Masters give you that.

How to set them up in Canva:

- Use Brand Kit fonts/colors.
- Design 3 core masters: Title, Content, Quote.
- Lock logos, footers, and background elements.
- Save as a reusable branded template.

Real Scenario — Sales Team Transformation

A B2B company's reps each built their own decks. Prospects complained about inconsistency. After adopting one Canva slide master, their close rate rose 22%—not because of new content, but because of consistent presentation.

Pro Tip — Margins Communicate Authority

Don't cram text to the edges. Wide margins breathe professionalism.

Common Pitfall — Ignoring Screens

A slide that looks fine on a laptop can look unbalanced on a projector. Always preview.

Mini Exercise — Build Your Master

Create 3 layouts in Canva. Lock your logo. Save as a master. Use only this for your next deck.

Section 4 — Speaker Notes: Confidence Without Clutter

Why notes matter.

Slides are for your audience. Notes are for you. Without notes, many presenters cram slides with paragraphs to avoid forgetting. That kills attention. Speaker notes let you strip slides clean while staying confident.

How to use notes effectively:

- Add notes in Canva's editor as cues, not scripts.
- Write keywords: "Tell client story," "Emphasize 20% growth."
- Rehearse delivery so notes jog memory, not replace it.

Real Scenario — Consultant's Breakthrough

A consultant used to fill slides with full paragraphs. Audiences read instead of listening. After switching to visuals + notes, she spoke more freely. Clients reported "engaging" instead of "dense."

Pro Tip — Prompt Yourself, Don't Trap Yourself

Use short cues ("Pause here," "Show enthusiasm") instead of text to read.

Attention — Notes Must Match Timing

Too many notes = rushing. Notes should be concise enough to support your natural rhythm.

Mini Exercise — 5 Slide Test

- Take five slides from one of your designs.
- Now, remove all the text — every headline, every paragraph. Replace each slide with one strong visual that tells the same message on its own.
- Then, beneath each image, write a single one-line note describing its intent (e.g., "Build tension," "Show result," "Invite action").
- Once done, rehearse the flow out loud — as if you were presenting it.
- Does the story still make sense? Does it feel lighter, clearer, more human?

Checklist — Your Presentation System

- Structure follows a logical arc (problem → solution → proof → CTA).
- Rhythm alternates heavy/light, text/visual.
- Slide master enforces consistency.
- Speaker notes guide delivery without clutter.
- If you can say yes, your deck is persuasive.

Common Mistakes — And How to Correct Them

1. **Overstuffed Slides —** More Text ≠ More Impact. Freelancers often feel they have to "prove their worth" by packing every detail of their process onto slides. The result? Overloaded slides that look like pages from a manual. The audience doesn't read—they shut down. A potential client doesn't want to see everything you know; they want to see that you know how to prioritize.

- *The Fix:* Embrace the principle of "one idea, one slide." Take that dense slide with five bullet points and turn it into five clean slides, each with a single takeaway. Suddenly, your message breathes, and your authority grows—because you look like someone who knows what truly matters.

2. Flat Rhythm — Every Slide Looks the Same. Freelancers pitching clients often make the mistake of building slides like invoices: same format, same amount of text, same tone. But when every slide looks identical, attention flatlines. Imagine a song where every note is the same pitch: it becomes unbearable.

- *The Fix:* Introduce rhythm by alternating between heavy slides and light ones. Follow a text slide with a bold image. Balance charts with testimonials. Insert a breather slide: one photo, one phrase. Rhythm signals confidence—you're leading the audience, not drowning them.

3. Design Chaos — Fonts and Colors Gone Rogue. One of the quickest ways freelancers lose credibility is through inconsistent branding. Maybe you use a Canva template that clashes with your website colors, or you swap fonts depending on mood. To a client, it screams "amateur." If your deck doesn't look consistent, why should they trust you with their project?

- *The Fix*: Build and apply a Brand Kit in Canva. Lock in fonts, palettes, and logos. Then set up Slide Masters so every deck looks like it belongs to the same professional brand—you. Consistency isn't boring; it's the foundation of trust.

4. Reading Aloud — Slides Become a Script. Nerves are real, especially for freelancers pitching alone. The temptation is to put your full pitch text onto slides and read it word-for-word. But this kills persuasion instantly. The client reads ahead, tunes out, and thinks, "If I can read it myself, why do I need you?"

- *The Fix*: Use speaker notes as your safety net. Keep slides clean—visuals, headlines, keywords—and put supporting details in notes. Rehearse with them so you speak naturally, not like you're reading instructions. Clients don't buy from slides; they buy from the human behind them.

Why This Matters for Freelancers

Individually, each of these mistakes might seem minor. But stack them together—text overload, monotony, inconsistency, robotic delivery—and you create an invisible wall of mistrust. Clients don't consciously say, "These slides are overstuffed and chaotic."

They just feel you're not ready for bigger opportunities. Correcting these habits moves you from freelancer fighting for scraps to professional trusted with serious projects.

"Do It Now" Homework — 120 Minutes

Presentation isn't learned by theory alone. To become a freelancer who convinces, you need to practice under constraints, with clear goals and time limits. The following two-hour sprint is designed to simulate a real-world client scenario: you've got an upcoming pitch and limited time. By the end, you'll have a lean, persuasive deck—and the confidence that you can build one whenever opportunity knocks.

1. Restructure (≈30 minutes)
Take an old 20-slide deck—maybe one you used for a past client pitch or a workshop proposal. Your task: strip it down to 10–12 slides maximum. Each slide must have a clear role: hook, problem, solution, proof, CTA. The goal here is not to design yet, but to reshape the story.
Why this matters: clients don't remember all your slides—they remember your journey. By forcing yourself to cut, you practice ruthless editing, which signals professionalism.

2. Rhythm Pass (≈30 minutes)
Now, look at your new 10–12 slide deck. Chances are, it still feels flat. Here's where rhythm comes in. Insert at least 3 visual-only slides (photo + headline), 1 testimonial or quote slide, and 1 breather slide (one bold phrase on a clean background).
Why this matters: freelancers often overload decks with text, afraid of leaving silence. Rhythm creates dynamics that keep your audience awake and emotionally engaged.

3. Master Build (≈30 minutes)
Open Canva and create 3 slide master templates:

- Title Slide (for openings and transitions).
- Content Slide (for main points, charts, visuals).
- Quote/Proof Slide (for testimonials, data points).
- Apply your Brand Kit: fonts, colors, logo. Lock footers and logos in place. Save as a reusable template.

Why this matters: freelancers win clients by looking established. A master template means that every future deck already looks branded, even if you're working solo.

4. Notes Draft (≈30 minutes)
For at least half of your slides, write speaker notes. Not full sentences—just prompts: "Tell client X story," "Emphasize 20% growth," "Pause." Then, rehearse once, out loud.
Why this matters: clients don't buy from slides, they buy from you. Notes free your slides from text clutter and free you from panic. You sound natural, but you stay on track.

QR Bonus Assets (for instant leverage)

- 12-Slide Investor Pitch Template → A pre-structured deck you can duplicate and adapt.
- Rhythm & Breather Slide Guide → Visual examples of how to alternate slide types for maximum attention.
- Speaker Notes Prompt Sheet → A simple worksheet to practice turning notes into natural delivery cues.

Closing Thought

Two hours may sound like a lot, but think of it as an investment. As a freelancer, your slides are not decoration—they are your shop window. This sprint not only sharpens your design but also builds a repeatable workflow: cut, balance, brand, rehearse. Do this once, and you'll never again feel unprepared when a client says, "Can you present tomorrow?"

Chapter 3

The Marketing Pack: Brochures, Price Lists, Product Sheets, and Email Headers

Every freelancer and small business owner knows the thrill of a great first call with a client. The energy is high, the interest is real, and you feel like you've won half the battle. But then comes the question that separates the prepared from the improvised: "Can you send me more information?"

This is the moment when the Marketing Pack decides your fate. Some freelancers scramble, typing long emails that drown in text. Others send outdated PDFs with mismatched colors and logos. But professionals —the ones who close contracts—deliver a polished, cohesive pack: a brochure that tells the story, a price list that clarifies, a product sheet that persuades, and an email header that brands every message.

These are not just "extras." They are your silent sales team. They work 24/7 in inboxes, printouts, forwarded attachments. They speak for you when you are not in the room. Canva gives you the power to build this team without an agency or a big budget. But to turn templates into trust, you need principles: clarity, consistency, persuasion.

In this chapter, we'll explore:

- **Brochures**: how to design them as credibility anchors.
- **Price Lists**: how to use structure to inspire trust instead of confusion.
- **Product Sheets**: how to condense persuasion into one irresistible page.
- **Email Headers:** how to brand the inbox and look professional at every touchpoint.

By the end, you will not only know how to design these assets—you'll own a Marketing Pack that makes clients think, "This freelancer is ready for business."

What You'll Do in 10 Minutes (Quick Win)

Pick one brochure template in Canva.
Replace three stock photos with your own, add a logo, and insert one CTA. Export as PDF.
Send it to your own inbox.
In ten minutes, you've created a credibility anchor that is already more professional than what most freelancers send.

Section 1 — Brochures: The Credibility Anchor

Why they matter.

A brochure is more than a pretty PDF. It's often the first tangible piece of your business a client sees. Even in a digital world, a clean brochure is a credibility anchor. It says: "We're real, we're prepared, we've thought about how to present ourselves."

How to build it in Canva.

- Start with bi-fold or tri-fold templates.
- Keep copy minimal: headlines + short text.
- Replace stock visuals with authentic images.
- End with a CTA: "Book a call," "Visit our site."

Real Scenario — The Photographer's Breakthrough

A freelancer used to send long descriptive emails about her packages. Clients ignored them. When she designed a 2-page brochure in Canva with her logo, three services, and sample photos, her bookings jumped. The content didn't change—the format did.

Pro Tip — Evergreen Design

Don't embed details that change monthly (exact prices, promotions). Instead, link to your price list. One brochure can stay valid all year, saving time.

Mini Exercise

In Canva, choose a template. Add logo, three services, and one strong CTA. Export and print. Hold it in your hands. Does it feel like something you'd be proud to hand over to a client?

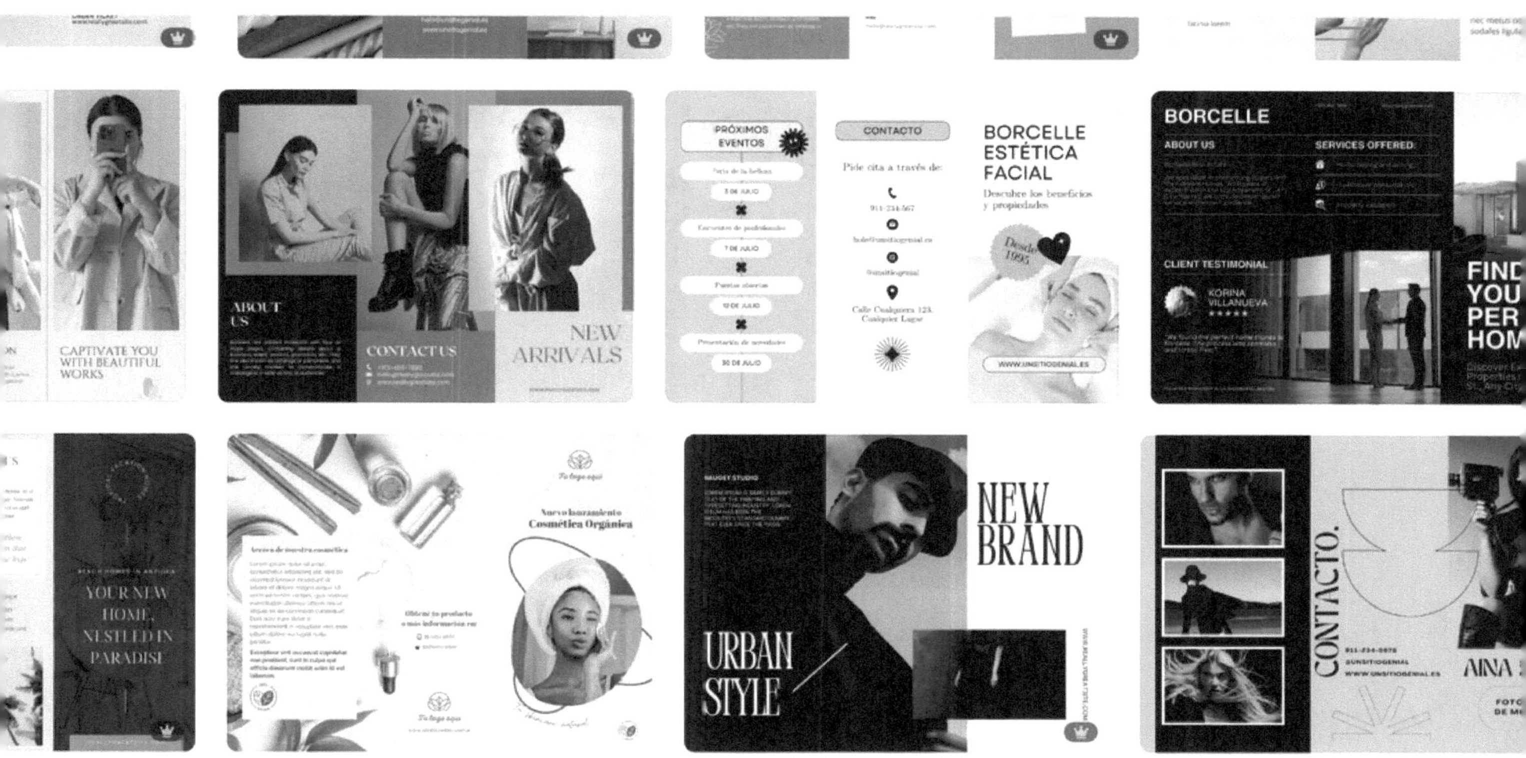

Section 2 — Price Lists: Clarity Builds Trust

Why they matter.

Talking about money makes many freelancers nervous. Some avoid it, hoping to "explain later." But vagueness breeds mistrust. A clear, well-designed price list sends the opposite signal: "I know my worth, and I've packaged it transparently."

How to build in Canva.

- Use simple grids or table templates.
- Offer 3 tiers: Basic, Standard, Premium.
- Add value-driven bullets ("Includes strategy call"), not just tasks.
- Use Brand Kit colors for polish.

Real Scenario — The Copywriter Who Stopped Haggling

A creator used to send long proposals with endless details. Clients nitpicked and negotiated. After designing a 1-page price list with three packages, clean visuals, and clear differences, the haggling stopped. Clients accepted her mid-tier offer without debate.

Pro Tip — Anchor with Tiers

Offer three prices. The low anchors expectations, the premium sets the ceiling, and the middle feels "just right." Design each with distinct visuals in Canva for clarity.

Mini Exercise

Draft a 3-column layout in Canva. Name your packages, list 3 value bullets each, and add pricing. Export and share with a friend. Ask: "Which one feels right to you?"

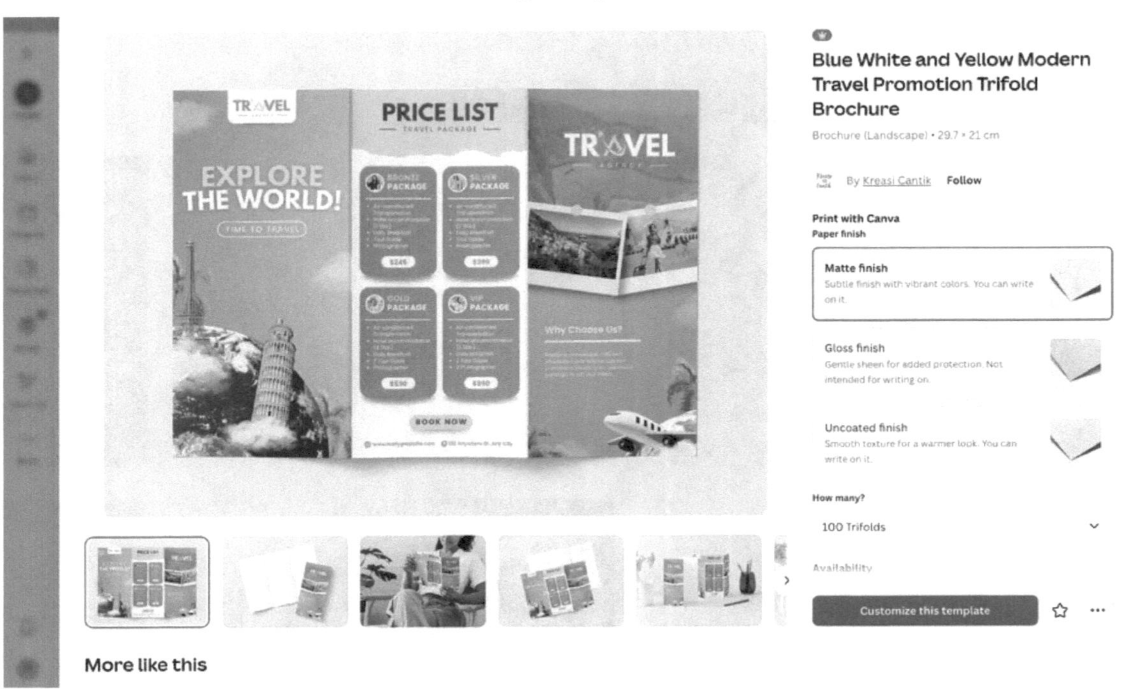

Section 3 — Product Sheets: One Page to Persuade

Why they matter.

While brochures give the overview and price lists give clarity, product sheets persuade. They focus on a single service or product, showing why it matters.

How to build in Canva.

- Use one-page flyer templates.
- Place the product name big and bold.
- List three benefits (not features).
- Add one strong image or mockup.
- End with a CTA.

Real Scenario — The SaaS Consultant

This agency offered audits but explained them only in calls. Prospects didn't get it. When they built a one-page product sheet with "Problem → Solution → Benefits → Next Step," understanding soared. Its close rate doubled.

Pro Tip — Proof Sells

Insert one testimonial, stat, or screenshot. Clients believe what they can see.

Mini Exercise

Pick one service. Create a Canva one-pager with headline, benefits, one image, and a CTA. Export and imagine sending it as an attachment tomorrow.

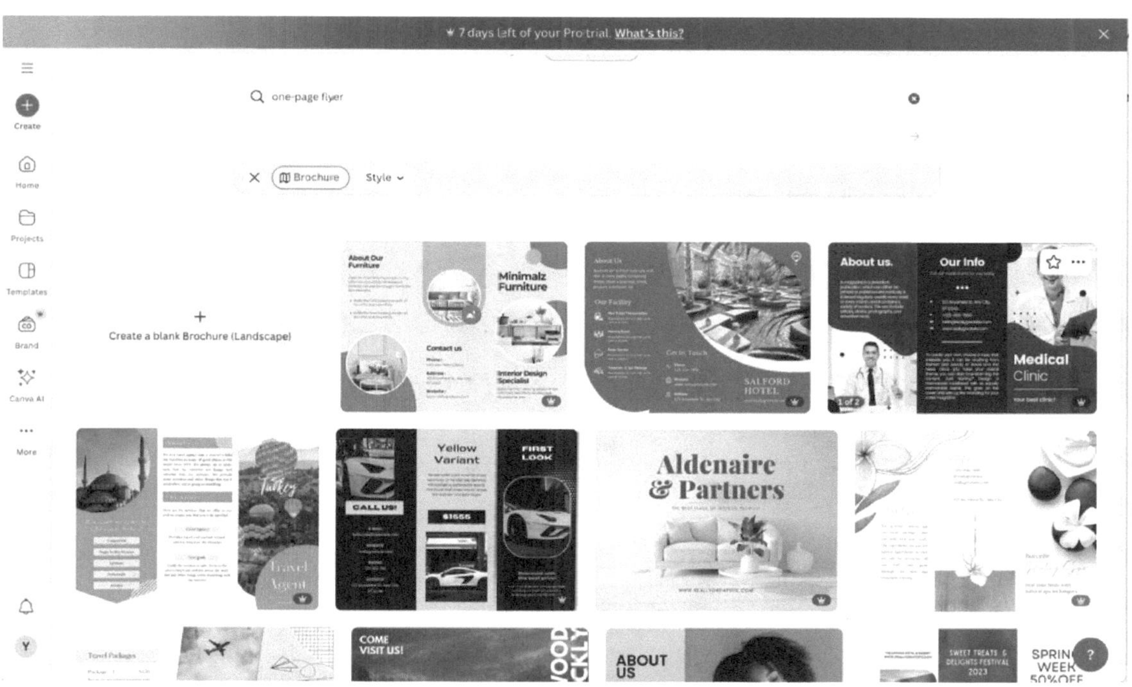

Section 4 — Email Headers: Branding in the Inbox

Why they matter.

Most freelancers forget email branding. Yet every proposal, invoice, and update lands in the inbox. A branded header turns plain messages into professional touchpoints.

How to build in Canva.

- Choose "Email Header" template.
- Add logo + tagline.
- Apply brand colors.
- Keep it minimal—mobile-first.

Real Scenario — The Virtual Assistant

A creator sent plain-text emails for years. When she added a branded header in Canva—logo, tagline, and a booking link—clients perceived her as more serious. Referrals rose.

Pro Tip — Keep It Phone-Friendly

Design at 600px width. Test on your phone. If it feels cluttered, simplify.

Mini Exercise

Design a header with your logo and tagline. Upload to your email platform. Send yourself a test email. Notice how instantly "official" your brand feels.

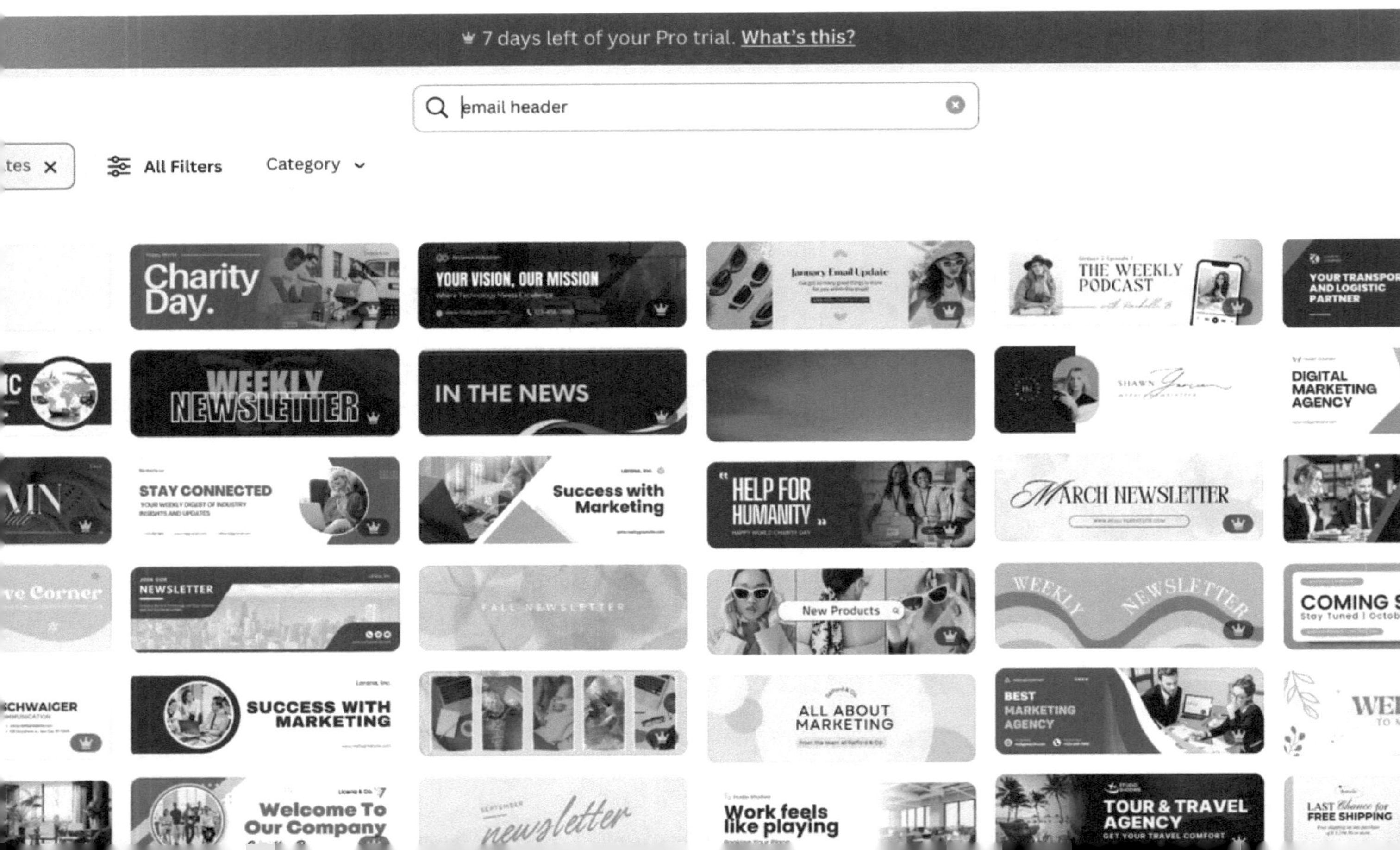

Checklist — Your Marketing Pack Essentials

- Brochure that introduces your brand clearly.
- Price list with 3 tiers for clarity.
- Product sheet with benefits + CTA.
- Email header that brands every message.
- If yes, you now have a Marketing Pack that silently sells for you.

Common Mistakes — And How to Fix Them

1. Overloaded Brochures — The 'Mini-Novel" Trap
Freelancers often treat brochures as proof of expertise, cramming paragraphs of text. Clients skim and tune out.
Fix: Use visuals, bold titles, and short copy. Your brochure is a trailer, not the full story.

2. Confusing Price Lists — Paralysis by Options
A price list with 10 services looks impressive but overwhelms. Clients freeze or haggle.
Fix: Stick to 3 packages. Tier them clearly. Simplicity sells.

3. Product Sheets as Manuals — If your product sheet looks like a technical spec, you've lost persuasion.
Fix: Focus on 3 benefits, one strong image, and a CTA. Keep it visual.

4. Messy Email Headers — Cluttered and Distracting
Headers with slogans, multiple logos, or stock photos scream "amateur."
Fix: Keep it clean: logo, tagline, color. Always test mobile.

Why this matters.
Together, these mistakes kill trust. Individually they seem small—but a client who sees them thinks: "This freelancer isn't ready for serious projects." Correct them, and suddenly your brand radiates confidence.

"Do It Now" Homework — 120 Minutes

This sprint is designed to simulate a real scenario: a prospect just asked for materials. In two hours, you'll have a Marketing Pack draft you can send.

1. Brochure Draft (30 min)
Pick a Canva template. Add logo, 3 services, 3 images, and a CTA. Export as PDF.
Why: A brochure is your credibility anchor. Even a simple draft elevates you.

2. Price List (30 min)
Create 3 packages: Basic, Standard, Premium. Add 2–3 bullets each. Apply Brand Kit.
Why: A clear price list signals transparency and confidence.

3. Product Sheet (30 min)
Build a one-page flyer for your main service. Add headline, 3 benefits, image, CTA.
Why: A product sheet persuades when words alone fail.

4. Email Header (30 min)
Design a branded header in Canva. Upload to your email platform. Send a test.
Why: Every email becomes a professional touchpoint.

QR Bonus (Module Hub):

- Brochure Starter Template.
- Price List 3-Tier Layout.
- Product Sheet Framework.
- Email Header Pack.

Closing Thought

A Marketing Pack is not about decoration—it's about trust. Brochures, price lists, product sheets, and headers are silent salespeople. They present you as prepared, credible, professional. With Canva, you can create them in hours. The next time a client asks for "more information," you won't scramble. You'll send a pack that makes them think: "This is the freelancer I want to hire."

Chapter 4

Websites with Canva: One-Page, CTAs, Domains, and SEO Basics

Once upon a time, the first thing a client asked for was a business card. Today, **the first thing they do is Google you**. If nothing shows up—or worse, if they land on an outdated or clumsy site—you lose authority instantly. In the digital world, your website isn't a "bonus"—it's the foundation of your credibility.

Freelancers and small businesses often resist creating websites because they think it requires coding, agencies, or thousands in budget. **But Canva has quietly changed the game**. With its Website builder, you can launch a clean, branded one-page site in hours, not months. No code, no plugins, no hidden costs. The challenge is not building—it's building well.

A Canva site is not meant to compete with a 200-page e-commerce platform. It's not for everyone, but for freelancers, coaches, consultants, small shops, and service providers, **a well-designed one-page site can do 90% of the job:**

- Showcase your offer.
- Guide visitors to a clear Call to Action (CTA).
- Present your brand consistently.
- Help you appear in search results.

In this chapter, we'll learn how to:

- Design a one-page site that works like a focused sales funnel.
- Craft effective CTAs that convert interest into action.
- Connect your site to a custom domain so you look professional.
- Apply SEO basics so clients can actually find you.

By the end, you'll walk away with a functioning, branded website that sells your story while you sleep.

What You'll Do in 10 Minutes (Quick Win)

Open Canva → Websites → choose a one-page template. Replace headline with your name or service. Add one CTA button ("Book a Call" or "Get a Quote"). Publish with a free Canva domain. In 10 minutes, you've gone from invisible to searchable. That's momentum.

Section 1 — One-Page Websites: Why Less Is More

Why one-page works.

Attention spans are shorter than ever. Prospects don't want to dig through 10 tabs to understand what you do. A one-page site forces clarity: who you are, what you offer, why it matters, and how to take action.

Structure of a high-converting one-page site:

1. **Hero section**: name, tagline, and CTA.
2. **About section**: who you are, why you're credible.
3. **Services/Offer:** what you provide, 3–4 items max.
4. **Proof**: testimonials, logos, case study.
5. **CTA again**: reinforced at the end.
6. **Publish as a one-page site:** when your deck or portfolio is finished, click Share → More → Website. Choose the Scrolling / One-page option and click Open website to preview. Canva instantly hosts your deck online under a shareable link — no coding needed.

Real Scenario — The Coach Without a Site

A freelance coach kept relying on Instagram DMs. Clients asked, "Do you have a website?" She didn't. Prospects disappeared. When she launched a Canva one-pager—headline, her photo, 3 services, testimonials, and a booking link—her pipeline doubled. The site itself didn't "sell," but it signaled professionalism.

Pro Tip — Start Simple, Scale Later

Your Canva site doesn't need 20 sections. Launch lean. You can always expand with more content later.

Mini Exercise — One-Page Draft

Choose a Canva template. Create sections: Hero, About, Services, Proof, CTA. Even with placeholder text, you'll see your offer take shape visually.

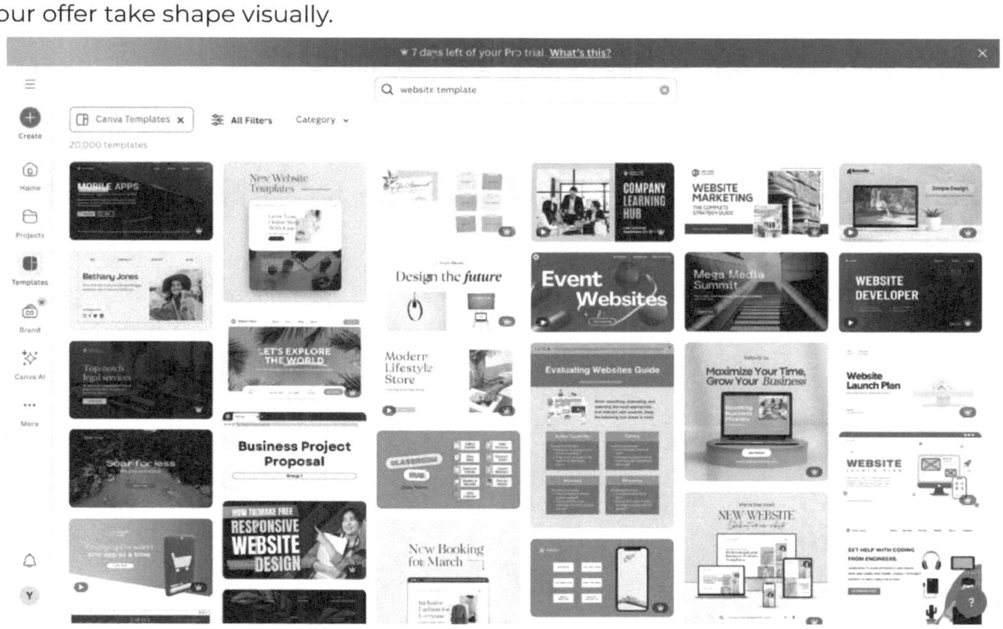

Section 2 — CTAs: Turning Visitors Into Clients

Why CTAs matter.

A site without a CTA is like a store without a checkout. Visitors may admire your design, but they'll leave without action.

What makes a CTA effective:

- **Clear**: "Book a Call," "Download Guide," "Get a Quote", or "Shop Now."
- **Visible**: buttons in contrasting brand colors.
- **Repeated**: at least twice (top and bottom).
- **Urgent but honest:** "Spots Open for March" feels stronger than "Contact Me."

Real Scenario — The Designer's Fix

A freelance designer had a site with gorgeous visuals but no clear CTA. Visitors admired her work, then left. She added two CTAs—"Book Discovery Call" in the header, and "Work With Me" at the bottom. Conversion tripled.

Attention — Avoid Weak CTAs

"Learn more" is safe, but forgettable. It tells people what to do, not why to care.
Empathetic or community-style CTAs work better because they speak to belonging, curiosity, and shared progress. They make the audience feel invited — not sold to. A strong CTA isn't a command; it's a continuation of the story. **Examples?** "Join 1,000 designers already testing this workflow." / "Save this for the day you finally start your project." /"See how others in our community are using this idea."

Pro Tip — Use Canva Buttons

In Canva, you can hyperlink text or shapes. Use branded buttons with strong verbs.

Mini Exercise — CTA Test

Write three possible CTAs for your service. Place them on a mockup button in Canva. Which one feels irresistible? That's your winner.

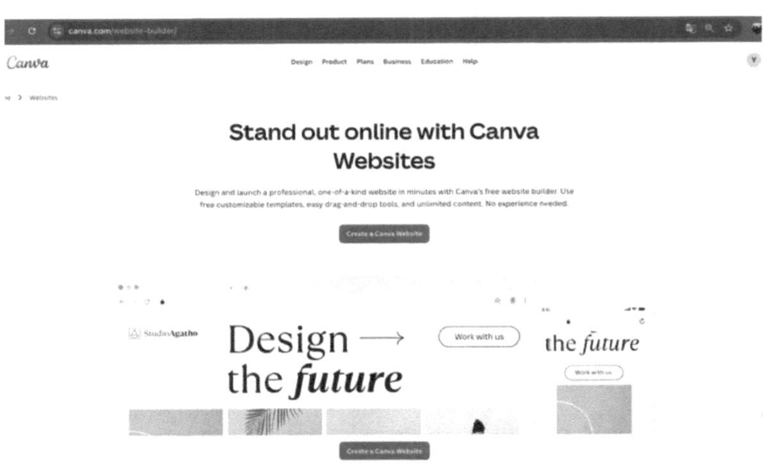

Section 3 — Domains: From Free to Professional

Why domains matter.

Clients notice details. Sending a Canva free link (yourname.my.canva.site) is better than nothing—but attaching your own domain (yourname.com) transforms perception instantly. It says: "I invest in my business."

How to connect:

- Purchase a domain via Canva or registrars like Namecheap/GoDaddy.
- In Canva, go to Website → Publish → Use Custom Domain.
- Follow simple DNS instructions (Canva guides you step by step).

Real Scenario — The Agency That Upgraded

A small agency used a free Canva link for a year When they upgraded to a custom domain, clients started forwarding the link confidently. Same site, different perception—contracts increased.

Pro Tip — Keep It Simple

Shorter is better. Avoid hyphens and long names. Clients must type it easily.

Mini Exercise — Domain Brainstorm

Write 5 possible domains for your brand. Check availability. Buy one and connect it to your Canva site. In one step, you move from hobbyist to pro.

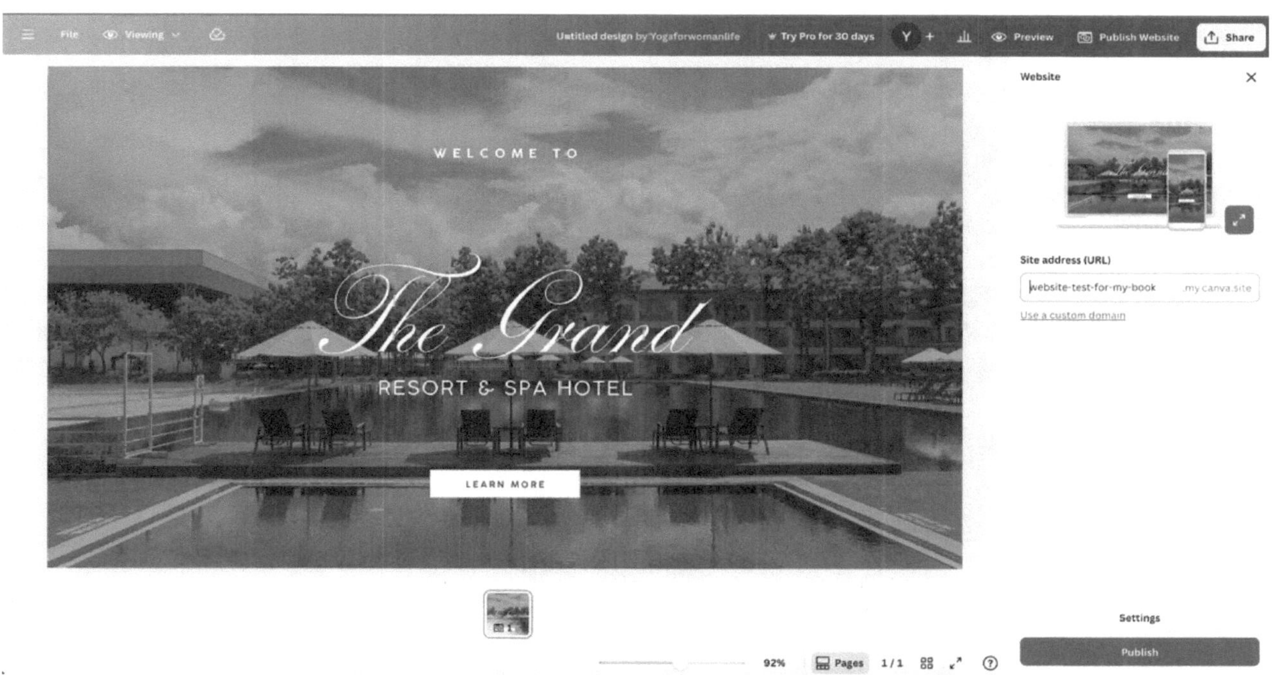

Section 4 — SEO Basics: Being Found, Not Just Seen

Why SEO matters.

A site that looks good but can't be found is invisible. SEO (Search Engine Optimization) helps you appear in Google when clients search for services like yours. Canva doesn't replace advanced SEO tools, but it covers essentials.

Essentials in Canva:

- **Title & Description:** edit under "Website Settings." Include keywords (e.g., "Freelance Graphic Designer in Madrid").
- **Image Alt Text:** describe images so Google understands them.
- **Mobile-Friendly Design:** Canva sites are responsive—test on your phone.
- **Content Simplicity:** use clear headlines with client-focused words.

Real Scenario — The Local Yoga Teacher

This teacher built a Canva site but left "Untitled Website" as the title. No one found it. After adding "Yoga Classes Barcelona | Teacher [Name]" in settings, she appeared on page one for local searches. Students increased.

Pro Tip — Think Like Your Client

What would they type into Google to find you? Use that phrase in your title and headings.

Common Pitfall — Keyword Stuffing

Don't repeat the same phrase unnaturally. Google penalizes it. Write for humans, optimize for search.

Mini Exercise — SEO Setup

- In Canva, go to Website Settings.
- Write a title, meta description, and set alt text for three images.
- Then search for yourself after a few days—you may already appear.

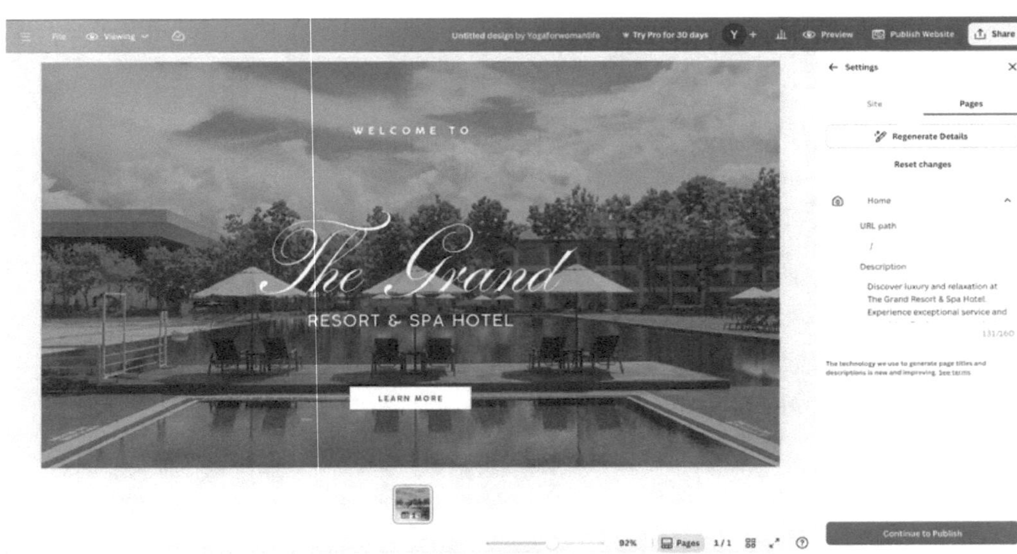

Checklist — Website Essentials

- One-page structure: Hero, About, Services, Proof, CTA.
- At least two strong CTAs.
- Custom domain connected.
- SEO basics applied (title, description, alt text).
- If yes, you don't just have a site—you have a professional storefront online.

Common Mistakes — And How to Fix Them

1. The "Brochure Site" with No CTA. Many freelancers treat their site as a static brochure. Visitors admire, then leave.
Fix: Always add CTA buttons—top and bottom.

2**. Too Much, Too Soon.** New freelancers often overload: 10 sections, too much text. Clients get lost.
Fix: Keep it one page, focused. Simplicity persuades.

3**. Free Link Forever.** A Canva subdomain is fine at first—but sticking with it signals amateurism.
Fix: Invest in a custom domain early.

4. Ignoring SEO. Without a title and meta description, your site is invisible.
Fix: Fill Canva's Website Settings with keywords your client would search.

Why This Matters for Freelancers

Each mistake signals inexperience. Together, they cost trust. Correcting them shifts perception: from "beginner experimenting with Canva" to "professional worth hiring."

"Do It Now" Homework — 90 Minutes

Your assignment: simulate a client scenario. They ask, "Do you have a website?" In 90 minutes, you'll build one.

1. One-Page Draft (30 min): Create a site with Hero, About, Services, Proof, CTA. Publish on a free Canva domain.
2. CTA Build (15 min): Add at least 2 buttons—top and bottom.
3. Domain Connect (20 min): Brainstorm and buy a domain. Connect it.
4. SEO Setup (25 min): Add title, description, and alt text for 3 images.

By the end, you'll have a live, professional site that can be shared today.

QR Bonus (Module Hub):

- One-Page Site Template.
- CTA Button Pack.
- SEO Quick Checklist.
- Domain Connection Guide.

Closing Thought

Your website is not a luxury—it's the digital handshake every client expects. With Canva, you no longer have excuses. A one-page site with clear CTAs, a connected domain, and basic SEO can transform you from invisible to professional in a single afternoon. The sooner you publish, the sooner you exist in your clients' world.

Chapter 5

Make Money with Canva: Digital Products, Platforms, Pricing, and Delivery

Most freelancers and small businesses learn Canva to support their own projects: social posts, presentations, brochures. But few realize that Canva can also be turned into a source of direct revenue. You're not just creating assets for yourself—**you can create templates, mini-ebooks, or digital packs that others will pay for. Yes, you can earn money using Canva!**

This isn't about "getting rich quick." Forget the clickbait videos promising thousands overnight. This is about practical, repeatable ways to monetize the design systems you already know. Think of it as a side income that can grow into a significant revenue stream. With Canva, the entry barriers are low: you don't need complex software, you don't need a design degree, and you don't need a warehouse. You need ideas, clarity, and a platform to sell on.

In this chapter, we'll cover:

- **Digital products you can create with Canva:** templates, mini-ebooks, planners.
- **Platforms to sell them**: Etsy, Gumroad, and beyond.
- **Pricing strategies** that make your work accessible but profitable.
- **Delivery systems** that automate the process.

By the end, you'll see Canva not just as a tool, but as a potential business model.

What You'll Do in 10 Minutes (Quick Win)

Create a simple 5-page Canva template pack (e.g., Instagram posts). Export as PDF or share as "Template Link." Upload it to Gumroad with a price of $5. Even if no one buys today, you've just launched your first product—and felt how simple the process can be.

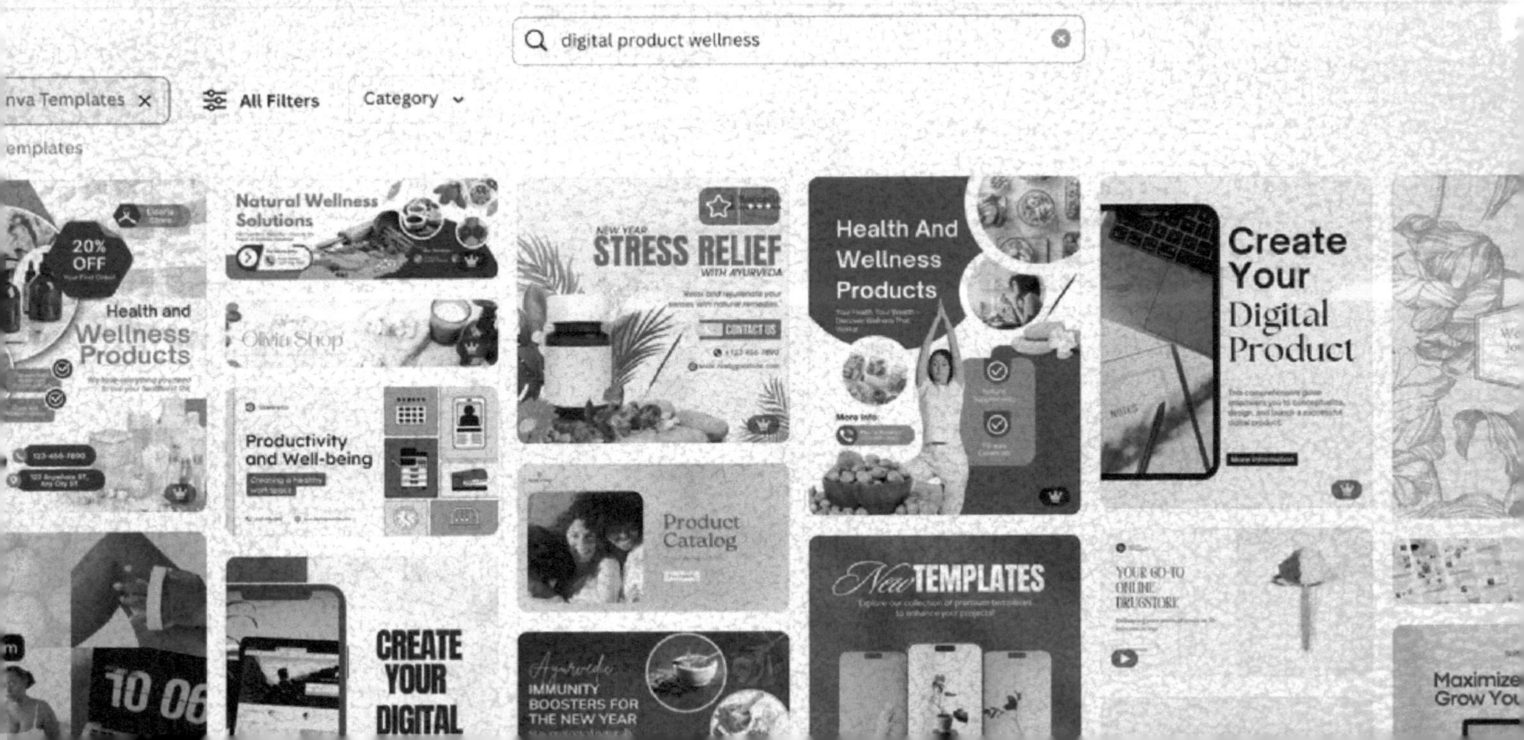

Section 1 — Digital Products: From Canva to Cash

Why digital products work.

Unlike client projects (which trade time for money), digital products scale. You design once, and you can sell infinite copies. They're lightweight, cheap to produce, and in constant demand.

Examples of products that sell well:

- **Templates**: social media packs, pitch decks, resumes, CVs, planners.
- **Mini-ebooks**: guides (e.g., "30 Instagram Ideas for Coaches"), workbooks, checklists.
- **Printables**: calendars, journals, invitations.

Real Scenario — The Planner Designer

A freelancer in New York built a Canva planner, uploaded it to Etsy, and sold 50 copies in her first month at €10 each. That's €500 from one weekend's work—without managing a single client.

Pro Tip — Niches Beat General

Don't create a "social media pack for everyone." Create "social media pack for yoga teachers" or "proposal template for wedding planners." Specific sells. Always!

Mini Exercise — Your First Product Idea

Write down 3 problems your audience faces. Now, design a Canva product that solves one (e.g., "too busy to design posts" → a 20-template Instagram pack).

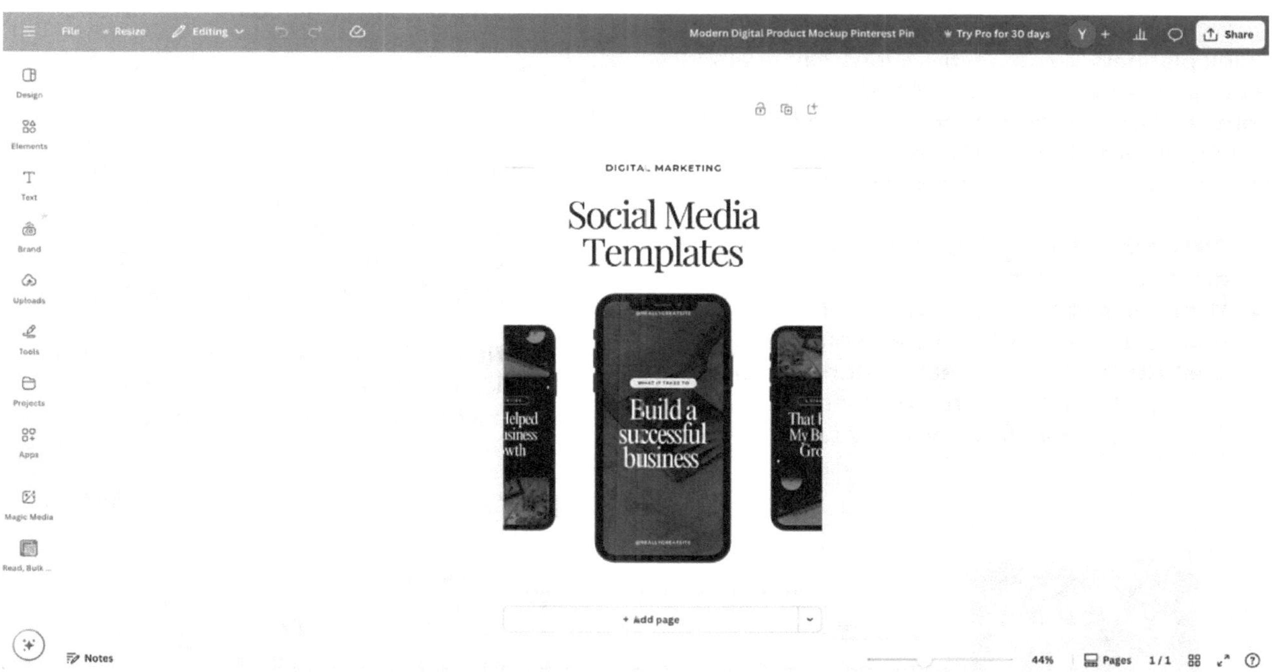

Section 2 — Platforms: Where to Sell

Why platforms matter.

Designing a Canva product is only half the battle. The other half is distribution: getting your work in front of people who want it and making the transaction smooth. You could, in theory, build your own store from scratch—buy a domain, install software, connect payment gateways—but that's time, money, and technical work that most freelancers don't have.

Platforms like Etsy and Gumroad exist to remove those barriers. They provide three things instantly:

1. Traffic — buyers are already searching there.
2. Trust — platforms handle payments securely.
3. Systems — delivery and refunds are automated.

Instead of worrying about the tech, focus on what matters: creating good products and learning what sells.

Etsy: The Marketplace for Creative Printables

Etsy is ideal if your Canva products lean toward lifestyle, printables, or visually appealing assets.

Think planners, wedding invitations, calendars, journals, resume templates, or wall art. Buyers come to Etsy already in a creative mood, ready to purchase something that looks beautiful and solves a personal or professional need.

- **Strengths:** Huge organic traffic, buyer trust, discovery via search.
- **Weaknesses:** Competition is intense; you must stand out with niche and branding.
- **Best fit:** Freelancers creating printable or semi-customizable Canva designs (planners for teachers, wedding packs, CV templates).

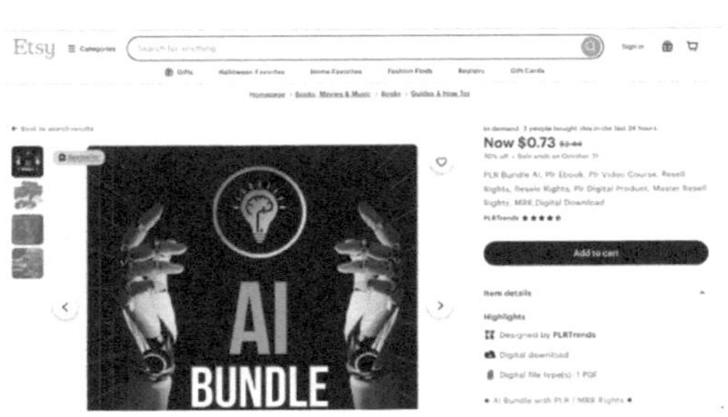

Gumroad: The Digital-First Platform

If Etsy is like a bustling market, Gumroad is like a clean digital storefront. It's best for templates, ebooks, courses, or any purely digital product.

Gumroad makes setup incredibly fast: upload your product, set a price, and share your link. That's it. It's global, simple, and highly trusted among creators.

- **Strengths**: Extremely easy to set up; supports pay-what-you-want pricing; integrates instantly with social links.
- **Weaknesses**: Doesn't bring you much organic traffic—you'll need to market your link.
- **Best fit:** Freelancers who want speed and simplicity, or those already active on social media who can drive their own audience.

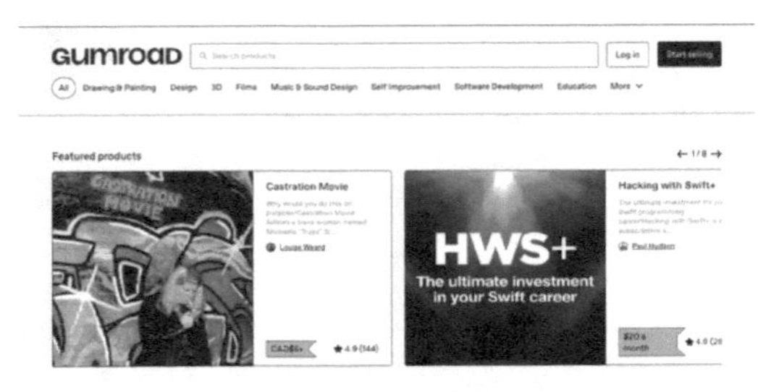

Your Own Site: The Long-Term Play

As you grow, nothing beats selling from your own website. With Canva's one-page website builder, you can embed Gumroad links, buttons, or even full product previews directly on your branded page. This way, **you control the look, the branding, and the relationship with the customer.**

- **Strengths**: 100% control of branding, no marketplace competition, better margins.
- **Weaknesses**: Requires you to bring your own traffic; no built-in discovery.
- **Best fit:** Freelancers with an audience (newsletter, LinkedIn, Instagram) who want to look established and keep buyers inside their ecosystem.

Real Scenario — Resume Templates on Etsy

A freelance designer uploaded 10 Canva-based CV templates on Etsy. She didn't have an audience, no website, no email list. Within 6 months, she was earning a steady side income. Why? Because Etsy buyers were already there searching for "modern resume template." She simply put her designs where the traffic was.

Attention — Platform Fees Exist

Both Etsy and Gumroad take a cut from your sales. It's easy to see this as a loss, but think of it as rent in a prime location. Without them, you'd have no store, no customers, no secure payment gateway. Accept the fee as the cost of exposure and professionalism.

Pro Tip — Focus Before You Expand

Don't make the rookie mistake of uploading one product on five platforms. Each platform has its culture, its audience, its quirks. Start with one. Learn what sells. Optimize your listing. Then, once you have proof of traction, expand. Depth beats breadth.

Mini Exercise — Open Your First Shop

Choose the platform that best fits your product: Etsy for printables and lifestyle designs, Gumroad for pure digital, or your own Canva one-pager if you already have traffic. Create your shop profile: upload your logo, write a short description, and add your first product. Then share the link with one friend or on one social channel. That's it—you've gone from "thinking about selling" to actually being in business.

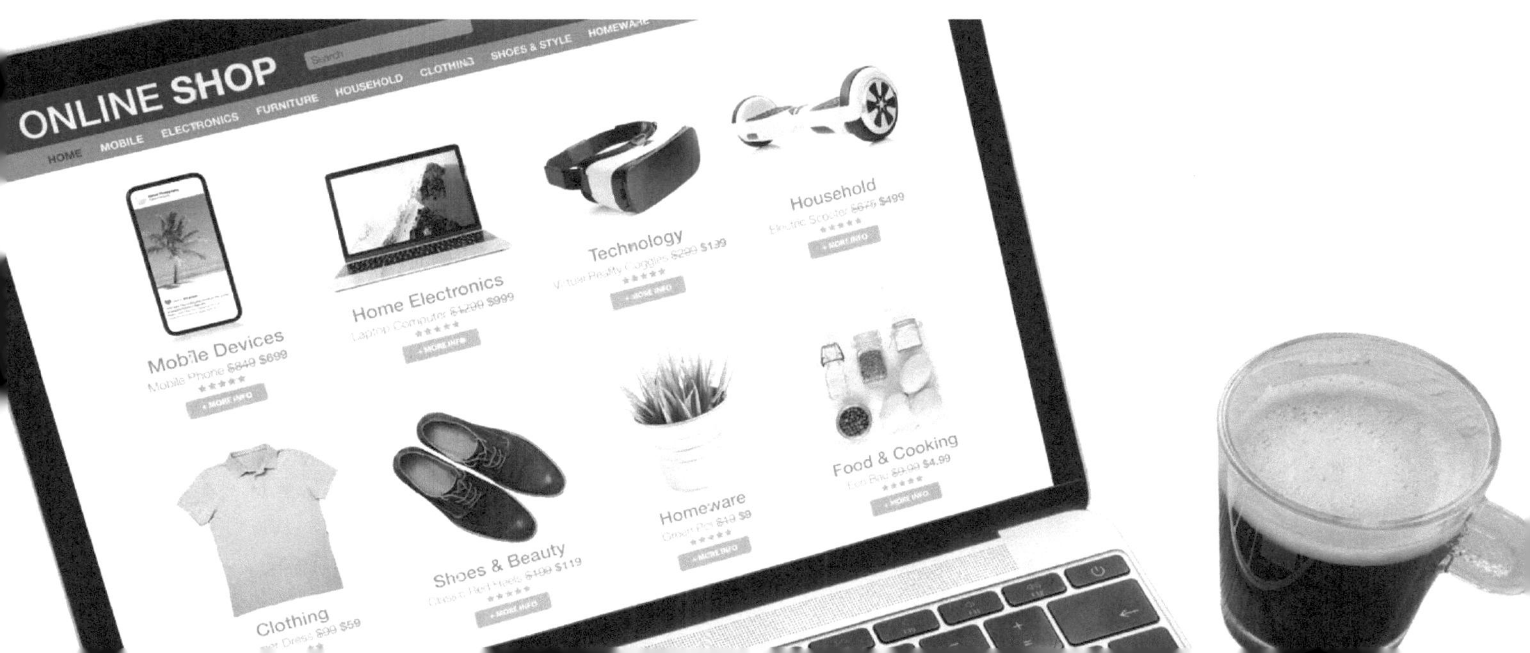

Section 3 — Pricing: Balancing Accessibility and Profit

Why pricing matters.

Many freelancers underprice, thinking "cheap sells." In reality, too-low pricing signals poor quality. On the flip side, overpricing without brand trust scares buyers.

How to approach pricing:

- **Templates**: $5–$30, depending on size and complexity.
- **Mini-ebooks**: $7–$25, depending on depth.
- **Bundles:** $20–$100 for packs of templates, guides, or resources.

Real Scenario — The Underpriced Template Pack

A freelancer launched 20 Instagram templates for $2. Sales came in, but buyers didn't value them—and left average reviews. When she raised price to $12 and improved branding, reviews improved and revenue grew.

Pro Tip — The Bundle Effect

People love feeling they're getting a deal. Sell a $10 template, but offer a $25 bundle of three. Most will choose the bundle.

Common Pitfall — Copying Competitors Blindly

Just because another seller charges $50 doesn't mean you should. Start with modest pricing, then increase as reviews and credibility grow.

Mini Exercise — Price Your Product

- Decide price for your first Canva product.
- Write down why it's fair—for both you and your buyer.

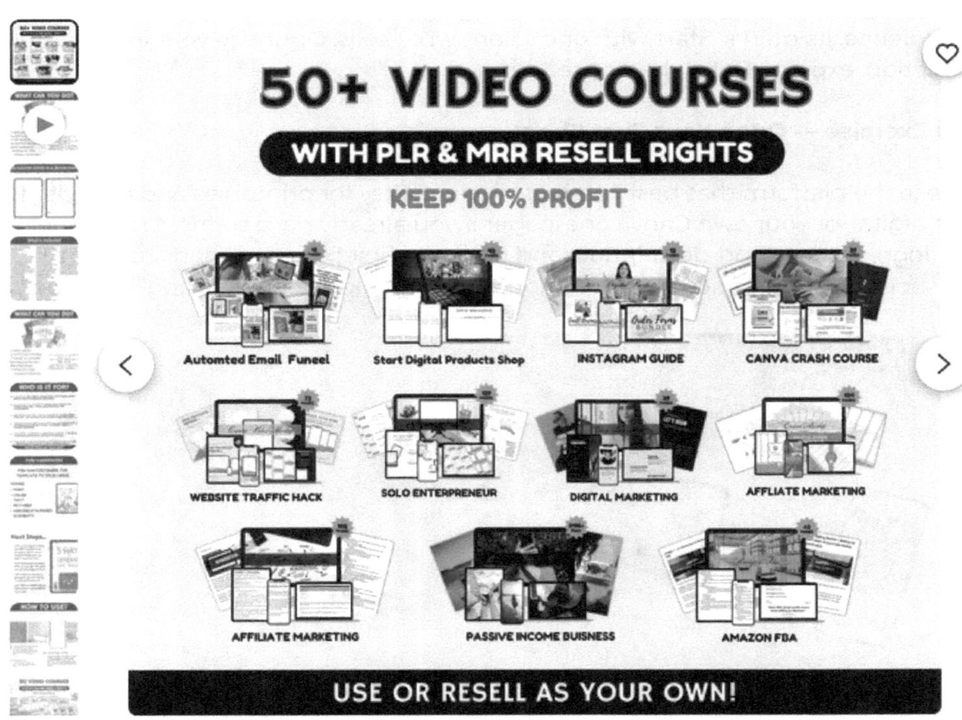

Section 4 — Delivery: Automating Success

Why delivery matters.

Clients want instant access. If you make them wait, trust dies. Canva makes delivery easy: you can share Template Links or downloadable PDFs instantly.

Options for delivery:

- **Gumroad**: automatically emails files or links after purchase.
- **Etsy**: lets you upload PDFs; inside, you can place the Canva template link.
- **Direct**: email the link after PayPal/Stripe payment.

Real Scenario — The Ebook Launch

A health coach sold a Canva-designed mini-ebook through Gumroad. Buyers received a PDF instantly after payment, with a personalized welcome email. She never had to lift a finger.

Pro Tip — Add Instructions

If you're selling templates, include a simple PDF guide: "How to use this template." Saves support emails.

Mini Exercise — Create Your Delivery File

Export one Canva template as "Template Link." Add a short PDF with instructions. Upload both to Gumroad/Etsy. Test buying it yourself.

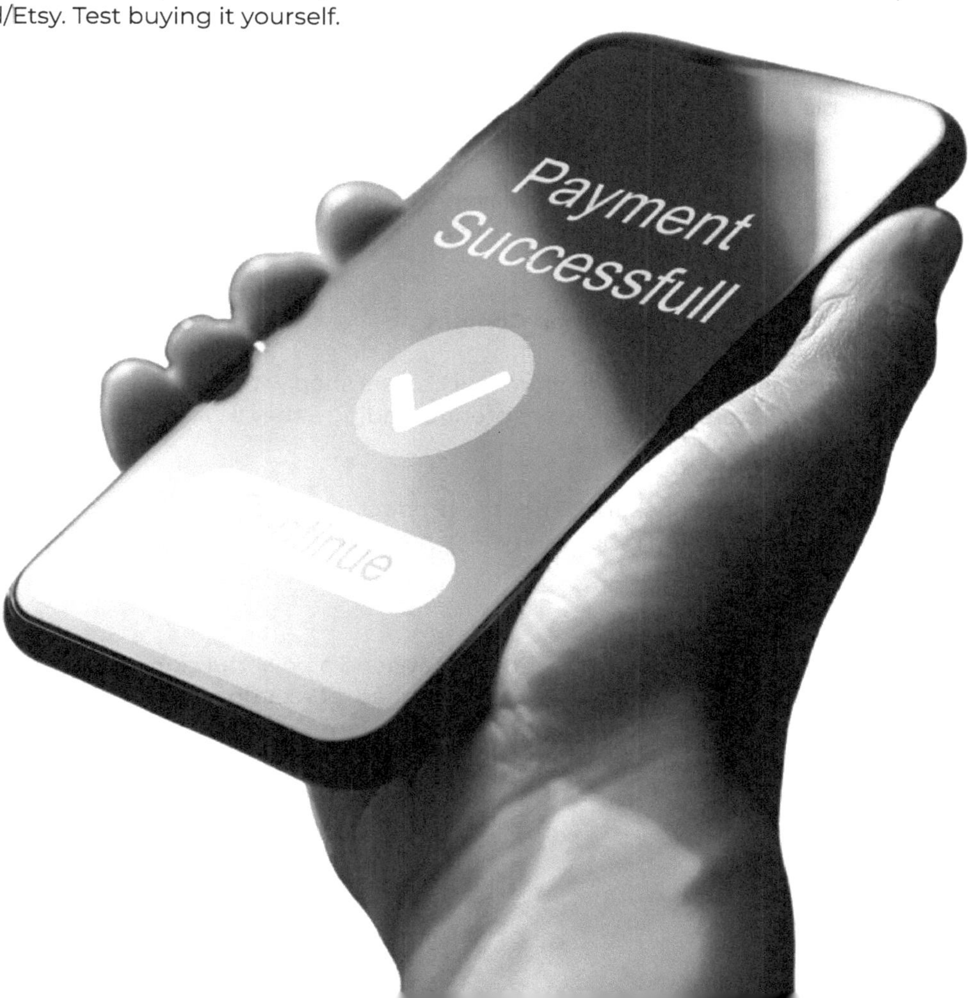

Checklist — Make Money System

A checklist isn't just a summary—it's a mirror. If you can tick each of these boxes honestly, you don't just "know" about monetizing Canva, you're actually doing it.

1. Too Generic Products — Trying to Please Everyone. The fastest way to kill sales is to create something for "everyone." A generic social media pack doesn't resonate with anyone in particular. Buyers look for products that feel made just for them.

The Fix: Narrow down. Instead of "Instagram Templates," create "Instagram Templates for Real Estate Agents" or "Proposal Deck for Wedding Planners." The more specific, the more buyers feel, "This is exactly what I need."

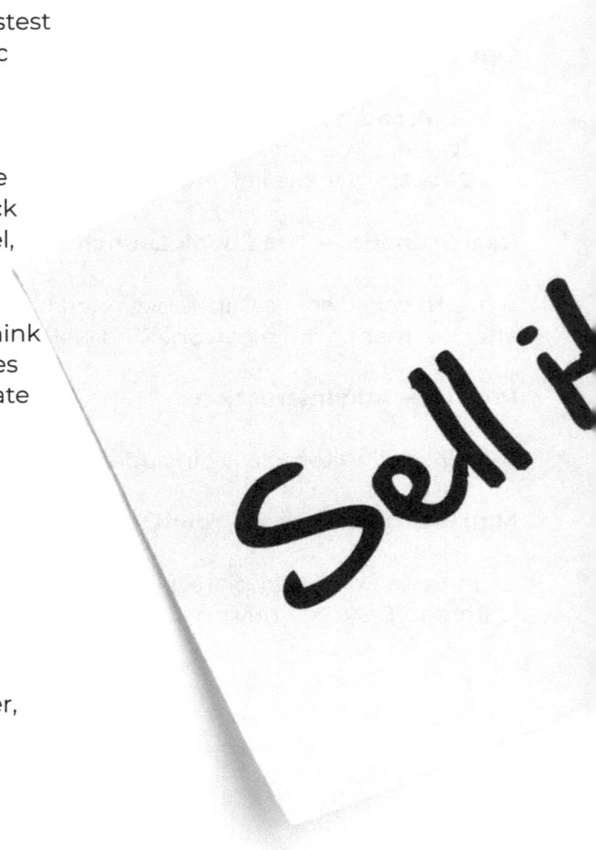

2. Underpricing — Cheap Signals Cheap. Freelancers often think setting a low price will drive sales. In reality, underpricing makes products look low-quality, even if they're excellent. A $2 template doesn't say "bargain"—it says "throwaway."

The Fix: Start at a reasonable price point (e.g., $10–$15 for a template pack). As reviews and credibility build, you can raise prices. Buyers are happy to pay more for perceived value and professional presentation.

3. Manual Delivery — Burning Time, Losing Trust. Some freelancers still send files manually via email after each PayPal transfer. This is unsustainable. One mistake—forgetting a buyer, sending the wrong file—and your credibility vanishes.

The Fix: Use automation. Etsy and Gumroad handle delivery instantly. Buyers expect to receive their product in seconds. Meeting that expectation builds trust; failing it kills it.

4. Ignoring Presentation — Covers Sell More Than Content

A brilliant template hidden behind an ugly cover won't sell. Buyers shop with their eyes first. If your product listing looks sloppy—bad screenshots, inconsistent branding—they'll click away, no matter how good the product is.

The Fix: Use Canva to design polished mockups. Show the product in action: a planner open on a desk, a template shown on a phone. Presentation is not vanity—it's persuasion.

Why This Matters for Freelancers

Individually, each mistake might look small. But together, they send a powerful signal: "This seller isn't professional." And in the crowded marketplace of Etsy or Gumroad, perception is everything. Correcting these errors transforms you from "someone experimenting with Canva" into a real business owner who can be trusted with money. The sooner you fix them, the sooner buyers stop hesitating—and start buying.

"Do It Now" Homework — 90 Minutes

A business isn't built by theory, it's built by execution. Reading about digital products is safe—but money only appears when you ship something into the world. That's why this sprint matters. In 90 focused minutes, you'll not only create your first monetizable Canva product, you'll also experience the full arc: design, list, price, deliver. Think of it as your rehearsal for a real business day.

Here's how to spend that hour and a half:

1. Design (≈25 minutes). Open Canva and create a tangible product: either a 5-template Instagram pack or a 5-page mini-ebook. Don't overthink design perfection—this is about shipping version 1.0.
Why this matters: Until you have a product, you're not in the game. Even a small pack is enough to test demand, gather feedback, and prove to yourself that you can create sellable assets.

2. Platform Setup (≈20 minutes). Choose Etsy or Gumroad, depending on your product type. Open a shop, upload your design, add a cover image and short description. Even if you only have one product, your store is officially live.
Why this matters: A product that only exists on your laptop is worthless. Uploading makes it real. From now on, anyone in the world can, in theory, buy from you. That's a psychological shift.

3. Pricing (≈20 minutes). Set a fair, confident price. For a template pack, $10–$15 is a strong start; for a mini-ebook, $7–$12 works well. Add a note to yourself about a potential bundle idea—e.g., "3 packs for $25"—so you're already thinking in scalable systems.
Why this matters: Pricing is positioning. The number you choose communicates value before a client ever downloads your work. Undervaluing yourself hurts more than overpricing.

4. Delivery (≈25 minutes). Export your Canva file, create a clean PDF instruction sheet ("How to use this template"), and upload both to your platform. Test the buyer experience by "purchasing" yourself. Make sure the product arrives instantly and looks polished.
Why this matters: Automated delivery is the invisible trust builder. If clients get their product in seconds, your brand feels professional—even if you're a one-person shop.

At the end of these 90 minutes, you won't just have a product—you'll have proof that you can design, sell, and deliver in a single sitting. That's the muscle of entrepreneurship.

QR Bonus Assets

To accelerate, scan the QR codes in this module and duplicate the assets into your own account. Use them, and your launch will feel smoother, faster, and far more professional.

- Template Shop Starter Kit → Ready-to-customize Canva storefront materials.
- Etsy Product Listing Checklist → Step-by-step guide to optimize titles, tags, and photos.
- Gumroad Delivery Guide → Screenshots and instructions to automate instant delivery.
- Canva Mockup Pack → Polished mockups to showcase your product like a pro.

Chapter 6

Implementation: Approval Flows, File Naming, and Version Control

Every freelancer or small business dreams of being remembered for bold ideas, fresh visuals, and creative spark. But ask any client, and you'll hear a different truth: what earns lasting trust isn't only creativity, it's reliability. It's the feeling that when they open your files, everything is clear, organized, and professional.

Think about it. You can design the most brilliant presentation, but if the client receives a PDF named "deck_final_v3_REALFINAL.pdf", their confidence takes a hit. Or you might create a stunning brochure, but without clear approval checkpoints, you'll find yourself stuck in endless revision loops. Implementation—the hidden system of approvals, naming, and versioning—is the backstage work that makes the show credible.

Great creatives lose clients because of sloppy systems. Average creatives win them because they deliver predictably. This chapter is about making sure you don't sabotage your own work. With Canva, the tools are already there: collaborative comments, sharable links, simple duplication for versions. The key is not the tool itself, but the discipline to use it consistently.

By the end of this chapter, you'll know how to:

- Set up clear approval flows that cut revision cycles in half.
- Build a file naming system that communicates professionalism.
- Manage versions so you never lose track—or lose trust.

What You'll Do in 10 Minutes (Quick Win)

- Pick one of your active Canva projects.
- Rename it with a clear convention (Client_Project_Type_Date_v1).
- Share the file with a colleague or friend using comment access only, and ask them to leave two notes.
- Duplicate the file and label it v2. In ten minutes, you've practiced approval flow, naming, and versioning all at once.

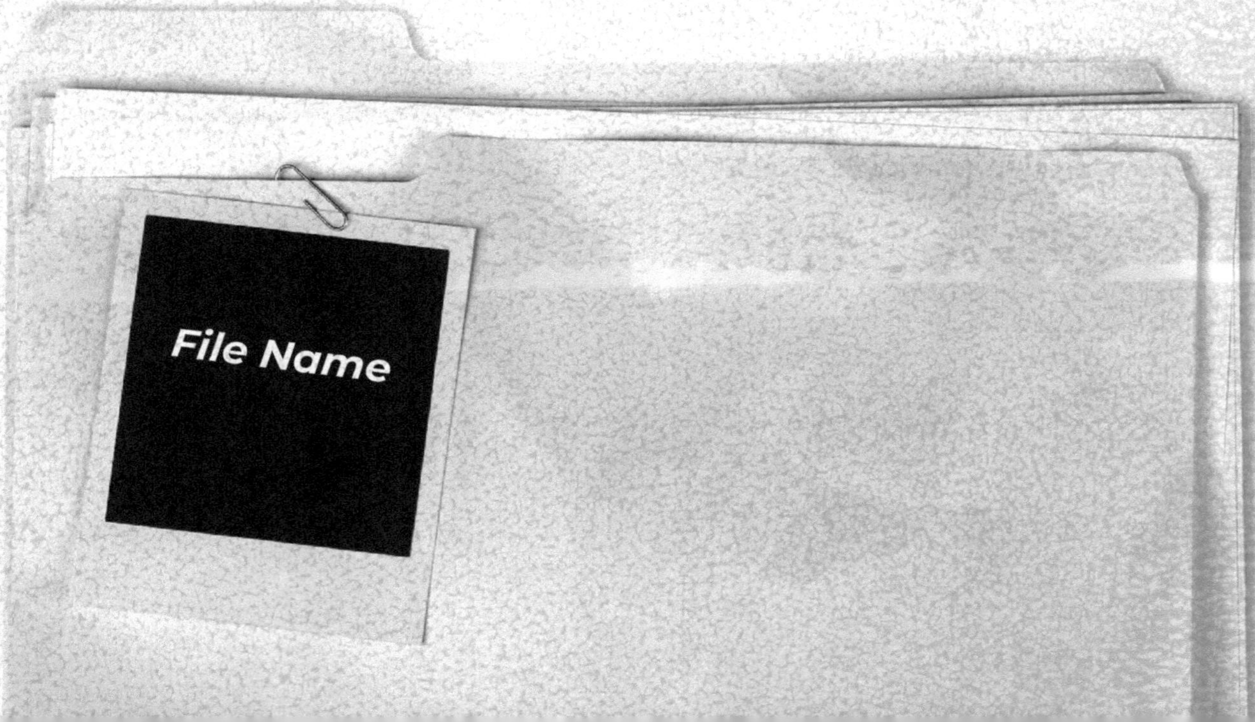

Section 1 — Approval Flows: Controlling Chaos Before It Starts

Why approval flows matter.

One of the biggest frustrations in client work isn't design—it's revisions. Without a structured flow, projects drag endlessly. Clients give fragmented feedback by email, WhatsApp, or even voice notes. You lose track, corrections overlap, and deadlines stretch. A broken approval flow doesn't just cost time, it erodes authority.

How to fix it.

With Canva, you can control feedback instead of drowning in it. Share the design with "comment only" access, so clients can leave notes directly on the page. Establish checkpoints from the start: draft → review → final. Communicate clearly: "I'll deliver the draft Tuesday, collect all feedback in Canva by Thursday, and deliver final Friday." This sets boundaries that protect you and reassure them.

Real Scenario — The Endless Brochure Loop

A freelancer once delivered a product brochure The client replied with five different emails, each from a different team member, each with conflicting notes. The result? Three wasted weeks. The solution came when she switched to Canva comments: one link, all feedback centralized, deadlines enforced. Suddenly, revisions went from six rounds to two.

Pro Tip — Lead the Process

Don't wait for clients to improvise. Tell them how to review: "Please use the comment feature in Canva. Add all notes by Thursday. Consolidate as a team first." It positions you not as a task-taker, but as a professional guiding the workflow.

Attention — The "Invisible Deadline" Trap

If you don't set review deadlines, clients wil send feedback whenever they feel like it. Days, weeks, even months later. Protect yourself by attaching timelines to approvals.

Mini Exercise — Build Your Approval Flow

- Choose one active or past project. Write down three stages: Draft, Review, Final.
- Decide how long each stage should last.
- Share your Canva link with comment-only access and practice receiving feedback in one place.

Section 2 — File Naming: The Silent Mark of Professionalism

Why names matter.

It sounds trivial, but filenames speak louder than you think. A client may never comment on your typography, but they will instantly notice if your files are labeled “final-final-USETHIS.pdf.” To them, messy naming means messy thinking. To you, it means wasted time searching for the right file.

The system - Adopt a consistent structure:

- Client_Project_Type_Date_v#
- Example: AcmeCo_PitchDeck_Aug2025_v1.pdf

This instantly communicates order. It also ensures that if your file is forwarded internally (and it will be), you look professional at every stage.

Real Scenario — The Wrong Price Sheet

A freelancer sent a client a file named “brochurefinal.pdf.” Unfortunately, it wasn’t the final version—it had outdated pricing. The client printed 1,000 copies with the wrong numbers. The cost: hundreds of euros and lost trust. After implementing naming conventions, the problem never repeated.

Pro Tip — Date First for Large Projects

If you manage big campaigns, start filenames with YYYYMMDD (e.g., 20250920_Client_Project_v1). That way, files sort chronologically.

Attention — Keep Names Human

Naming should be structured, not cryptic. Don’t overload with codes. Aim for clarity: the filename should explain itself to someone new on the project.

Mini Exercise — Rename Your Last 5 Files

- Open your project folder.
- Rename your last five Canva exports using the system.
- Notice how much cleaner your folder looks—and how quickly you can identify the latest version.

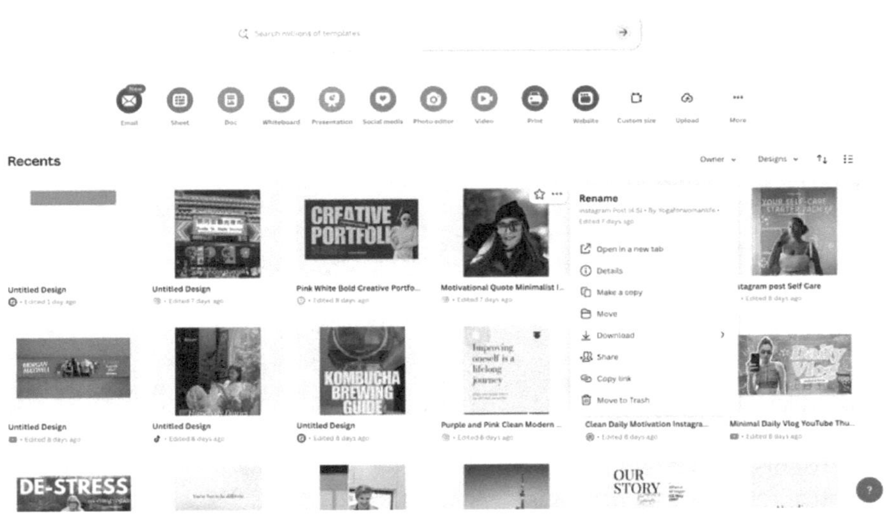

Section 3 — Version Control: Protecting Yourself From Yourself

Why versioning matters.

Design is iterative. You tweak layouts, adjust colors, replace images. But without version control, those iterations blur together. You risk sending the wrong draft or losing track of client-approved edits. Worse, in disputes, you have no record of what changed and when.

The method.

- Keep one clean "master file."
- Duplicate for each new version: v1, v2, v3.
- Maintain a simple changelog: one line per version describing edits.

Real Scenario — The Pitch Deck Disaster

A small agency worked on a startup's investor deck. Two designers overwrote each other's changes. The result was a Frankenstein file: old slides mixed with new edits. The investor meeting collapsed. The fix came when they implemented strict version control: every major edit required a duplicate file with a version number.

Pro Tip — Archive Aggressively

Don't let 20 old versions clutter your space. Archive them in a "History" folder. Keep only the latest two or three visible. Clarity beats clutter.

Common Pitfall — Relying on Memory

Telling yourself "I'll remember the changes" is wishful thinking. After a week, details blur. Write version notes—it takes 30 seconds, and it saves hours.

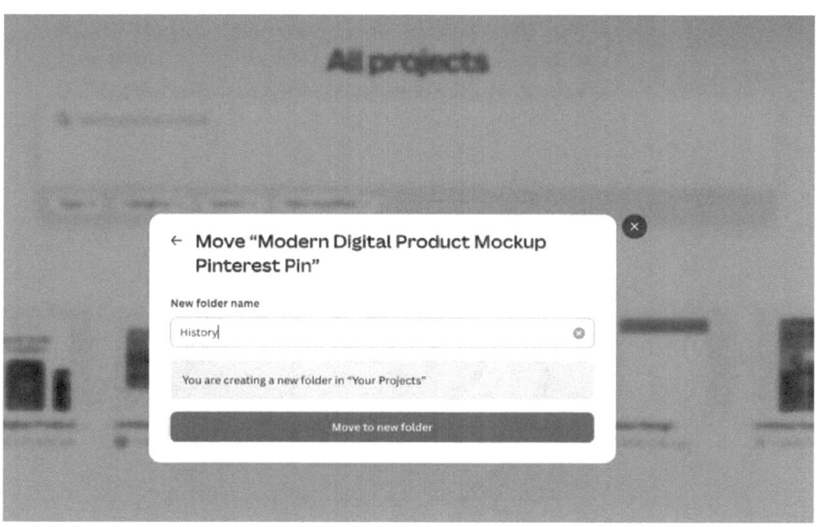

Mini Exercise — Version Log

- Pick a current project.
- Create v1, v2, v3 files in Canva. In a separate doc, write one sentence describing changes in each.
- This is your first version log.

Checklist — Implementation Locked

If you can check all of these, you've moved from chaotic creative to structured professional:

- You share files with clients using clear approval flows and deadlines.
- Your file naming convention communicates order, not panic.
- You track versions, archive old drafts, and can prove what changed when.

That's not just organization—it's insurance for your reputation.

Common Mistakes — And How to Fix Them

1. Feedback by Chaos
Accepting feedback through random emails, screenshots, or messages multiplies confusion.
Fix: Channel all notes through Canva comments or one central doc.

2. The "Final-Final" Syndrome
Every freelancer has sent a "FINAL_v3_REALLYFINAL.pdf." It's unprofessional and dangerous.
Fix: Use structured, date-stamped filenames.

3. No Version History
Without a log, you forget what's been approved. Clients repeat old requests, and you waste hours.
Fix: Keep a one-line changelog for each version.

Why this matters for freelancers.

Individually, these mistakes look small. Together, they erode trust. Clients rarely say, "Your filenames are messy." They simply decide not to hire you again. Clean systems silently say, "I'm reliable. You can trust me."

"Do It Now" Homework — 45 Minutes

Imagine a real client calls tomorrow and asks for version 2 of a pitch deck you delivered last week. Would you be ready—or would you panic? This exercise ensures you'll be ready.

1. **Approval Flow (15 min)**: Open a Canva project, invite a peer, and practice collecting feedback via comment mode. Notice how much simpler it feels than scattered emails.
2. **File Naming (15 min):** Choose 10 of your most recent files. Rename them with the Client_Project_Type_Date_v# system.
3. **Version Log (15 min):** Take your most recent project. Write a one-sentence note about what changed from v1 to v2. Archive old drafts.

This is not busywork. It's rehearsal for real client situations. Tomorrow, when someone asks for "the latest version," you'll deliver instantly.

Closing Thought

Implementation isn't glamorous, but it's power. Creative brilliance gets attention, but structured systems win loyalty. Clients can forgive a design tweak; they won't forgive lost files, wrong versions, or endless revisions.
By mastering approval flows, file naming, and version control, you separate yourself from the crowd of freelancers improvising their way through projects. You show that you're not just creative—you're dependable. And in business, dependability is what gets you called again.

Module 4 – Canva Advanced + AI (Magic Studio & Hacks)

From Designer to Director of Systems

Until now, Canva has helped you master the fundamentals: layouts, typography, social posts, and business kits. But in today's fast-moving digital world, speed is not just an advantage—it's survival. Teams must produce dozens of assets in hours. Freelancers must deliver fast enough to stay competitive without burning out. This is where Canva's Magic Studio and advanced workflows come in.

AI is not about replacing creativity—it's about multiplying it. Magic Write helps you kill the blank page. Magic Edit and Eraser give you Photoshop-level control in seconds. Magic Switch transforms one idea into multiple formats instantly. Bulk Create lets you scale from one design to fifty variations with a single CSV file. Together, these tools move you from being a "Canva user" to becoming a creative systems operator—someone who directs, scales, and optimizes output like a full agency, even if you're working solo.

But let's be clear: AI is not a magic wand. Used blindly, it produces generic, forgettable work. Used strategically, it doubles your productivity, maintains brand consistency, and frees your time for higher-level thinking. The difference lies in understanding prompts, setting up workflows, and combining tools with discipline.

This module is about showing you how to use Canva's advanced features and AI not as toys, but as weapons of efficiency. You'll learn not only the buttons to click, but the mindset to adopt: think in systems, design in batches, automate the repeatable, and polish the details that machines can't.

What You'll Do in This Module (and why it matters)

By the end of this module, you will:

- Use Magic Write, Magic Edit, Magic Eraser, Magic Expand, and Magic Switch with precision.
- Create and apply prompts that generate usable, high-quality outputs.
- Scale designs with Bulk Create, integrations, and smart duplications.
- Maintain brand quality while producing assets at speed.
- Complete a Rebrand Sprint: refreshing a logo and rolling out 20 coordinated assets in just a few hours.

This is the point where Canva stops being a design tool and becomes a creative engine.

Chapter 1

Magic Overview & Prompt Principles

Creativity has always been a blend of skill, time, and tools. In the past, the biggest limitation for freelancers and marketing teams wasn't imagination—it was bandwidth. A single social media campaign could take weeks to draft, design, and adapt across formats. Presentations consumed entire afternoons. Rebrands stretched into months. The work was rewarding, but the pace was unsustainable.

Enter AI. Suddenly, we live in a world where a blank slide is no longer a threat but an opportunity. With Canva Magic Studio, you can draft a headline in seconds, erase unwanted objects from a photo without Photoshop, convert a blog post into slides instantly, or produce a batch of fifty designs from a single spreadsheet. **The AI promise is speed. But speed without direction is chaos.**

That's why this chapter exists. It's not enough to "know" that Canva has AI features. You need to learn how to prompt them, how to control them, and how to combine them into workflows that multiply your output without diluting your voice. AI is not a substitute for taste or vision—it's a force multiplier for both.

The aim here is simple: to move you from curiosity to control. By the end of this chapter, you'll know the principles of prompting, the real strengths and weaknesses of Magic Studio, and the mindset shift required to treat AI not as a toy but as a trusted assistant. You won't just "play" with Magic Write—you'll direct it. You won't just erase backgrounds—you'll design images with intention. You won't just switch formats—you'll orchestrate them strategically.

What You'll Do in 10 Minutes (Quick Win)

To feel the difference before diving deep:

- Open Canva Docs and use Magic Write to draft a 100-word LinkedIn post.
- Use Magic Edit on a photo to replace a background element with something new.
- Try Magic Switch to convert a short text into a three-slide presentation.
- Review outputs critically: what worked, what felt generic, what surprised you.

This quick sprint is your first taste: AI is fast, but only as good as the instructions you give it.

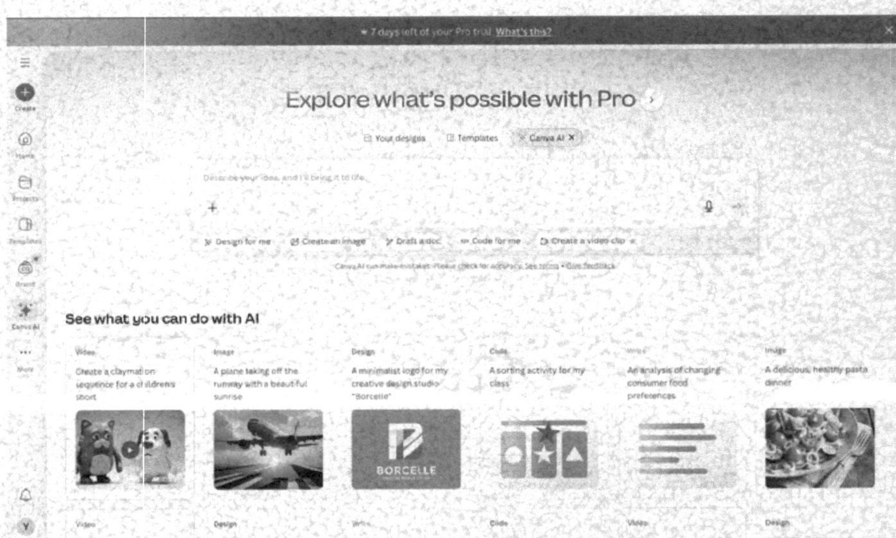

Section 1 — The DNA of Prompts: Why Words Shape Output

Why prompts matter.

AI is like a hyper-efficient assistant: it doesn't think, it executes. Your words are the blueprint. A vague prompt produces vague results. A sharp, contextual prompt produces targeted, useful material. The quality of your prompt is directly proportional to the quality of the output.

Principles of strong prompting:

- **Clarity beats cleverness.** "Write 5 playful Instagram captions for a summer café promotion" is better than "write something fun."
- **Context frames style.** "For LinkedIn" vs "for TikTok" radically alters tone and length.
- **Constraints create focus**. Word counts, audience types, brand adjectives—all sharpen results.

Real Scenario — The Forgettable Poster

A small gym asked Magic Write for "a catchy tagline." The AI suggested generic lines like "Get Fit Today!" Nothing stood out. When the prompt was reframed—"Write 5 taglines for a gym poster targeting young professionals, maximum 6 words, tone: energetic but premium"—the output included "Strength Meets Your Schedule" and "Train Smart, Live Stronger." Suddenly, the AI wasn't guessing, it was aiming.

Pro Tip — Layer Instructions

Don't dump everything in one sentence. Use structure: "Act as [role]. Create [output]. For [audience]. In [style]. With [length]." This scaffolding guides AI like GPS coordinates.

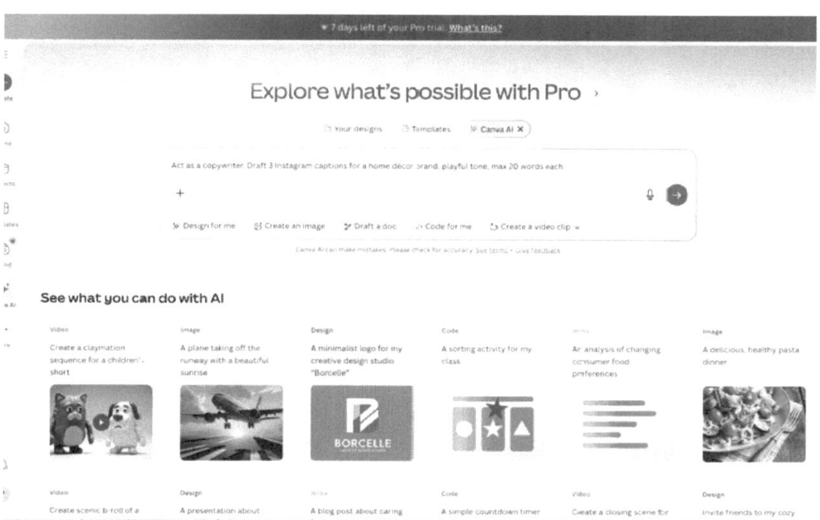

Mini Exercise — Prompt Refinement

- Write a vague prompt: "Create a social media post for my service."
- Then rewrite it with specifics: role, audience, tone, format, and length.
- Run both in Magic Write. Compare outputs. Which is closer to what you actually need?

Section 2 — Magic Write: Breaking the Blank Page

Why Magic Write is powerful.

Blank screens paralyze even seasoned creators. Magic Write transforms hesitation into momentum. In Canva Docs, you can generate blog outlines, captions, ad copy, or even email intros with a single command.

How to use it effectively:

1. Open Canva Docs.
2. Type "/" and select Magic Write.
3. Enter a structured prompt. Example: "Act as a copywriter. Draft 3 Instagram captions for a home décor brand, playful tone, max 20 words each."
4. Review outputs critically. Keep what sparks, cut clichés, refine with your brand voice.

Attention — First Draft, Not Final Draft

The biggest mistake is copy-pasting AI text untouched. Magic Write is the assistant, not the author. Use it to break inertia, then inject your voice and your personal touch.

Real Scenario — The Frozen Freelancer

A freelancer needed to write a LinkedIn post about a new service. Staring at the cursor for an hour led nowhere. Magic Write produced three options instantly. They weren't perfect—but they sparked ideas. Within 15 minutes, she had a polished, authentic post.

Pro Tip — Prompt for Variations

Ask for multiple takes: "Write 5 variations." The first idea is rarely the best; the gold is often in version three or four.

Mini Exercise — 15-Minute Caption Sprint

- Pick a service or product.
- Use Magic Write to generate 10 captions.
- Highlight 3 you like.
- Rewrite them in your own style. Now you have a mini library for future posts.

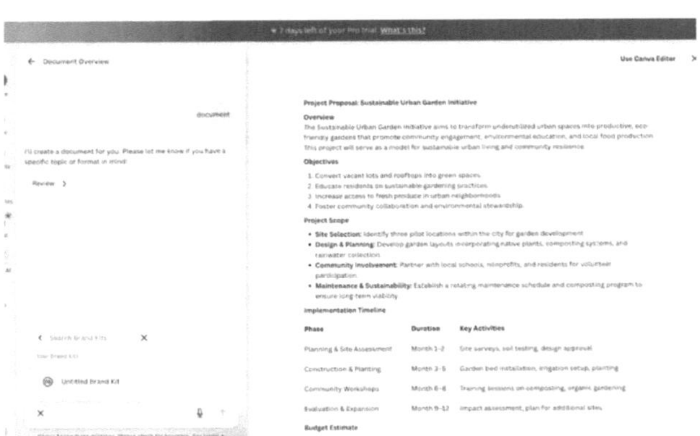

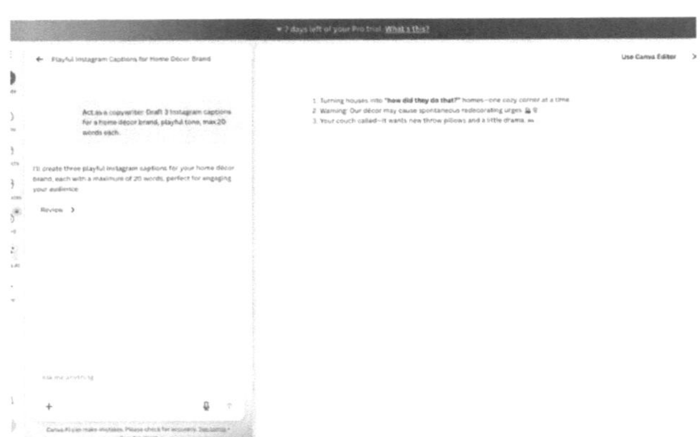

Section 3 — Magic Edit, Eraser, and Expand: Visual AI for Non-Designers

Why these tools matter.

In traditional workflows, removing a background object, replacing details, or extending an image required Photoshop-level skills. With Canva's Magic tools, anyone can do it in seconds. The result? Cleaner product shots, flexible visuals, and saved hours.

- **Magic Edit**: Select part of an image, replace with something else.
- **Magic Eraser**: Remove unwanted elements.
- **Magic Expand:** Extend canvas beyond original photo edges.

Real Scenario — The Café Ad Rescue

A café had a great latte photo—but a messy spoon ruined the vibe. With Magic Eraser, the spoon vanished. With Magic Edit, they added a small croissant on the side. Suddenly the image felt intentional, premium, and ad-ready.

Common Pitfall — Overuse

Just because you can replace everything doesn't mean you should. Subtlety is what makes edits feel professional.

Pro Tip — Keep Brand Consistency

When editing, think: does this align with my brand visuals? A random AI-inserted object might break consistency.

Mini Exercise — One Edit, One Erase

- Upload a photo.
- Erase one distraction.
- Edit one object.
- Export both before/after. Notice how minor tweaks elevate credibility.

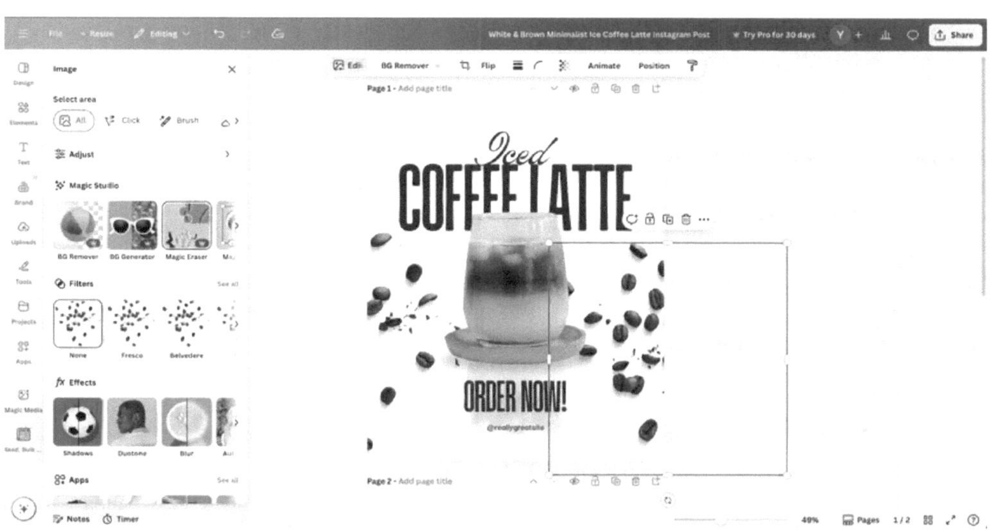

Section 4 — Magic Switch: From Idea to Multi-Format

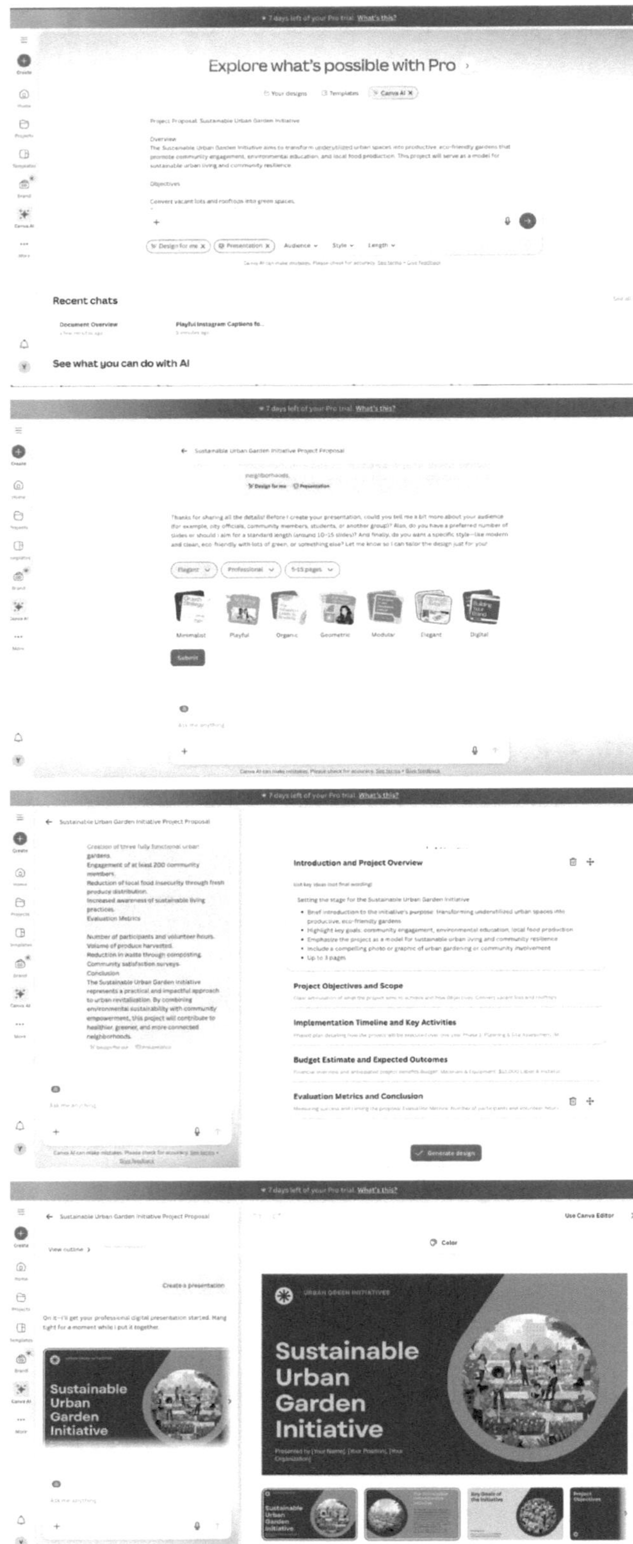

Why Magic Switch matters.

Marketing isn't about one post—it's about repurposing across formats. Magic Switch lets you turn a LinkedIn post into a slide deck, a blog into a PDF guide, or a caption into a poster.

Workflow:

1. Create or paste text into Canva Docs.
2. Select your Magic Switch "Design for me" → Presentation (or another format).
3. Review slides, apply Brand Kit, refine layouts.

Real Scenario — The Batch Creator

A startup founder needed a pitch deck and a one-pager, but had only a blog draft. With Magic Switch, he converted the blog into a 10-slide deck. After polishing design, he had both assets ready in under an hour.

Attention — Raw Doesn't Mean Ready

Outputs are starting points. They need human polish. A raw Switch deck often looks generic until you refine.

Pro Tip — Systemize Repurposing

Use Magic Switch weekly: one idea → blog, slide deck, carousel, PDF. Content multiplies without burnout.

Mini Exercise — One Idea, Three Formats

Write a 100-word post. Switch it to a presentation. Then to a PDF. Refine both. In 20 minutes, you've created three assets from one thought.

Checklist — Magic Studio Basics Locked

If you can say yes to these, you're ready to scale:

- I can write prompts that are specific, role-based, and contextual.
- I use Magic Write to create drafts, then refine them into my own voice.
- I can edit photos with Magic Edit/Eraser/Expand for clean, on-b

Common Mistakes — And How to Fix Them

Even with great tools and templates, many creators fall into the same traps. These small errors don't just affect results — they reveal a lack of process. Here's what to watch for, and how to fix it fast.

1. Vague Prompts = Vague Results. Typing "write caption" or "make post" gives the AI nothing to work with — so it gives you nothing worth keeping. The output ends up generic, robotic, and disconnected from your brand.

Fix: Always provide context. Tell the AI who you're speaking to, how you want to sound, what format you're using, and how long it should be.
Example: "Write a 2-line Instagram caption for busy small-business owners, in a confident, minimal tone." Specificity doesn't limit creativity — it directs it.

2. Copy-Pasting AI Text. Publishing raw AI output without editing is like serving uncooked dough — it might have the ingredients, but it's not ready to eat. It signals laziness and instantly flattens your brand voice.

Fix: Use AI as your assistant, not your ghostwriter.
Take the draft it gives you, then refine it: inject your tone, rhythm, and phrasing. Edit as if you were speaking to your audience directly. The best AI-generated content still sounds human — because you touched it.

3. Overediting Visuals. One click too far, and your photo goes from professional to plastic. Over-smoothing faces, changing every color, or swapping entire backgrounds breaks trust. People can sense when something feels off.

Fix: Edit with restraint. Enhance lighting, adjust tones, clean up distractions — but keep the soul of the image intact. Good design doesn't shout "edited"; it whispers "intentional." Subtle tweaks amplify credibility.

4. Treating "Magic Switch" as Final. AI tools can create decks, posts, or carousels in seconds — but exporting them as-is is a rookie mistake. Raw outputs rarely match your brand's finesse or attention to detail.

Fix: Treat AI results as first drafts, not final products. Polish layouts, refine typography, align spacing, and ensure the message feels cohesive with your visual identity. Automation saves time — craftsmanship earns trust.

Closing Thought

Magic Studio isn't about replacing you—it's about multiplying you. The freelancer who learns to prompt with precision and edit with restraint can outpace entire teams still doing everything manually. The real skill isn't clicking the button—it's knowing what to ask, how to refine, and when to stop. AI is the engine. You are the driver. And with the right commands, you'll reach destinations faster than ever before.

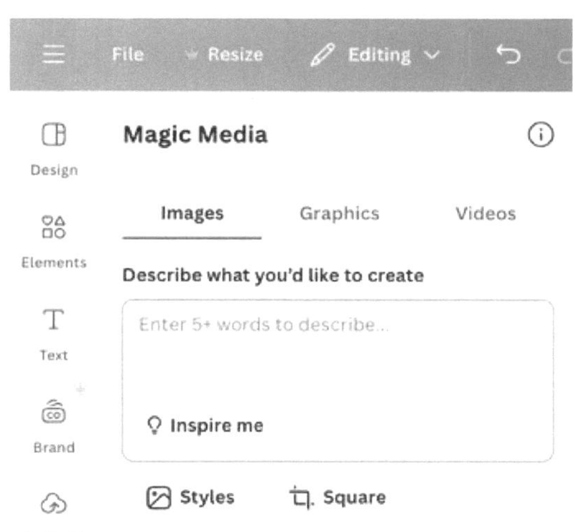

Chapter 2

Quick Images: Magic Edit, Eraser, Expand, Background Removal, and Styles

Every campaign, brand kit, or product launch stands on the shoulders of visuals. Words can persuade, but it is images that stop the scroll, set the tone, and create the first impression. And here's the truth: in the age of endless content, a mediocre image is invisible. But creating polished visuals used to require a designer's toolbox—Photoshop for background removal, Lightroom for retouching, and hours of practice for believable edits.

Not anymore. With Canva's AI-powered features like Magic Edit, Magic Eraser, Magic Expand, Background Remover, and Style Transfer, **you now have pro-level control inside the same dashboard where you're building your designs**. That means you can take an average stock photo or a quick smartphone snapshot and elevate it into a professional-grade asset—without leaving Canva and without external software.

This chapter is about speed without compromise. It's about cleaning distractions, enhancing focus, adapting visuals to multiple contexts, and experimenting with style—all within minutes. You'll see how a single photo can transform into three different assets, each tailored to a platform or audience. You'll also learn the limits of these tools and why restraint is as important as creativity.

By the end of this chapter, you won't just "use" Magic Edit or Eraser—you'll direct visuals intentionally, removing noise, adding detail, expanding frames, and keeping consistency across a full set of assets. You'll step from "Canva user" to someone who can control imagery like a seasoned creative director, even if you're working solo.

What You'll Do in 10 Minutes (Quick Win)

- Upload a photo of your product, workspace, or yourself.
- Use Magic Eraser to remove one distracting object.
- Apply Magic Edit to add one relevant element that enriches the story.
- Try Magic Expand to reframe the photo, leaving room for text overlay.
- Export both the original and the edited version. Compare: which one tells your brand story better?

Section 1 — Magic Edit: Adding What Was Missing

Why It Matters

Even a great photo can feel incomplete — the table looks empty, the background too plain, or the concept is almost there but missing a final touch.
Magic Edit lets you select part of an image and replace it with something new: an object, a texture, or an element that completes the visual story.

How It Works in Practice

- Open your photo in Canva.
- Click "Edit Photo" → "Magic Edit."
- Brush over the area you want to change or improve.
- Type your prompt — for example: "Add a latte in a white ceramic cup" or "Replace background with a minimalist office" or "Add a cat beside the person."
- Generate and choose the best version.

Canva automatically blends the new element into your photo for a natural, professional look.

Real Scenario — From Bland to Branded

A wellness coach had a flat-lay photo of a notebook and pen. It looked clean, but generic. Using Magic Edit, she added a branded coffee mug and a sprig of lavender. The image instantly transformed — from a notebook to her notebook, part of a personal, recognizable brand aesthetic.

Pro Tip — Edit for Story, Not Decoration

Before editing, ask yourself: "What story should this image tell?"
Add only what reinforces that story. Every random object weakens credibility. The best edits are subtle — they clarify meaning without stealing attention.

Mini Exercise — Story Add-On

Pick a photo from your gallery. Use Magic Edit to add one meaningful element — a product, a symbol, or a tool from your work.
Then export and review: Does the addition make the message stronger, or just busier? Good visual storytelling is about adding purpose, not clutter.

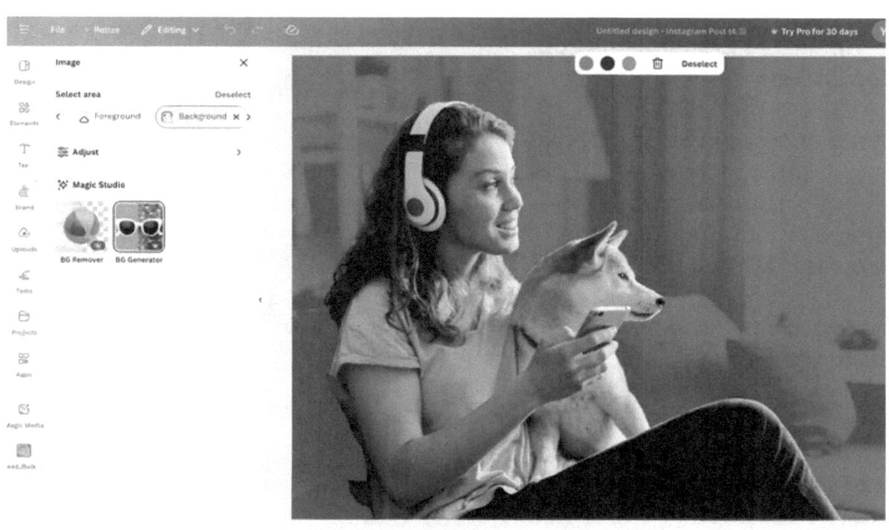

Section 2 — Magic Eraser: Clearing the Noise

Why it matters.

The best photos are often ruined by the smallest distractions: a messy bag on the floor, a stranger in the background, a logo you don't own the rights to. Magic Eraser solves this instantly, letting you clean the frame and keep only what matters.

How it works in practice.

- To start, select your photo inside Canva and click on "Edit Photo." This opens the editing tools in the left-hand panel.
- From there, choose "Magic Eraser." Your cursor will turn into a soft brush.
- Next, carefully brush over the object or area you want to remove. As you do, Canva will highlight the selection with a light overlay. Take your time here — the cleaner your selection, the more natural the final result will look. You can also adjust the brush size using the slider at the top of the screen to control how detailed your edit is.
- Once the unwanted element is completely covered, release the mouse. Canva will automatically regenerate the missing area, matching the color, lighting, and texture of the surrounding image for a seamless finish.
- Finally, review the edit. If it looks natural, click "Done." If something feels off, press "Undo" and try again with a smaller brush or a more precise coverage.

Real Scenario — The Product Rescue

An artisan jewelry maker had a beautiful necklace photo, but a busy café background made it unusable. With Magic Eraser, the clutter vanished, leaving only the jewelry against a soft backdrop. The piece suddenly looked premium, catalog-ready.

Attention — Don't Over-Clean

Removing everything makes images sterile. Some context adds authenticity: a desk with a laptop feels real, while a floating coffee cup in a void looks odd.

Pro Tip — Use Eraser as a Crop Alternative

Instead of cropping tightly, erase background clutter while keeping composition wide. This preserves breathing room for text overlays.

Mini Exercise — The One-Minute Clean

Take a casual photo. Erase one distracting object. Compare: is the photo calmer, more focused, more professional?

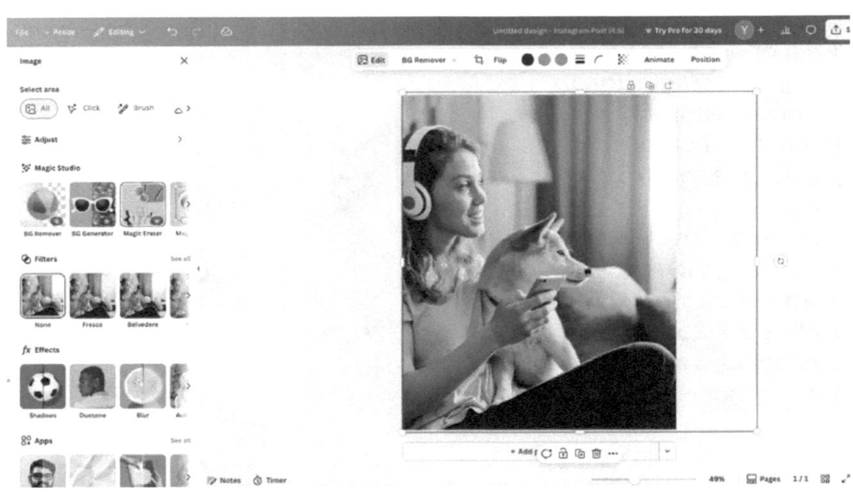

Section 3 — Magic Expand: Reframing Your Story

Why it matters.

Not every photo fits every format. An Instagram post might need square; a YouTube thumbnail needs wide; a Pinterest pin demands vertical. Magic Expand solves the frustration of "wrong aspect ratio" by generating extra canvas around your photo.

How it works in practice.

Open photo → click Magic Expand → drag crop handles to new dimensions (square, vertical, or wide). Canva fills in edges intelligently.

Real Scenario — The LinkedIn Fix

A coach had a perfect headshot—cropped too tightly. For LinkedIn banners, it looked awkward. With Magic Expand, the image gained clean space around the subject, enough for a tagline and contact info. The same photo now worked across LinkedIn, Instagram, and her website.

Common Pitfall — Unrealistic Expansions

Expanding too far can create "AI mush"—weird patterns, repeated textures. Subtle expansions (10–30% frame) look natural; extreme expansions rarely do.

Pro Tip — Expand for Text Zones

When designing ads, leave space for copy. Expanding a photo to create a "blank" side is often better than squeezing text over the subject.

Mini Exercise — The Format Shuffle

- Take one image. Expand it to square, vertical, and wide.
- Place the same headline in each.
- Notice how composition affects storytelling.

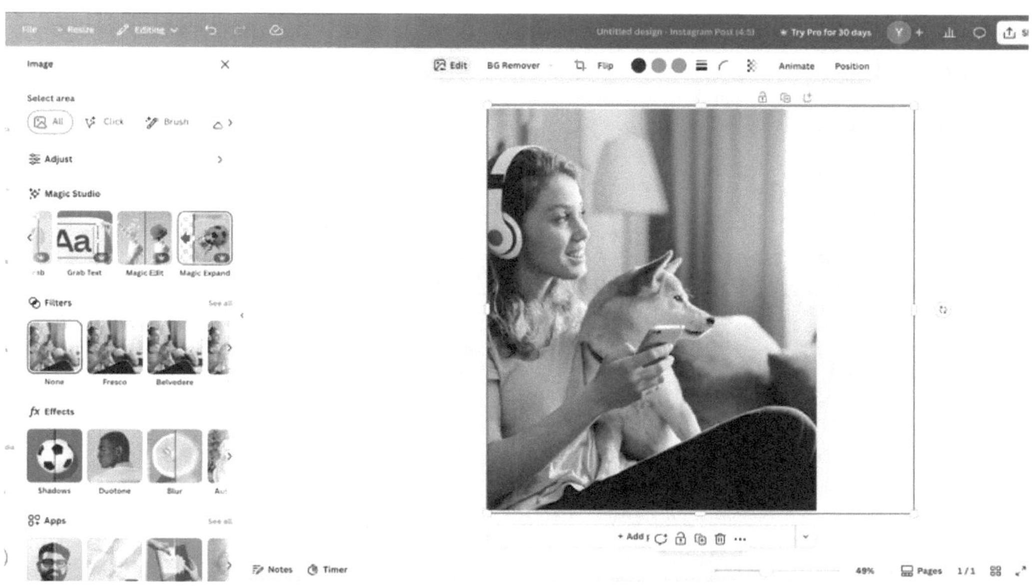

Section 4 — Background Removal & Styles: Context Is a Choice

Why it matters.

A clean background can make your product pop. But sometimes a styled background sells better: a candle against a cozy living room, not a white void. Canva gives both: instant background removal and AI-generated style applications.

How it works in practice.

Upload photo → click Remove Background → choose either transparent, solid color, or apply a generated scene.

Real Scenario — The Etsy Seller Upgrade

An Etsy seller listed handmade mugs. Original photos were against a kitchen table—cluttered and uneven lighting. With Background Remover, mugs appeared on crisp, branded-colored backdrops. Sales increased, not because the mugs changed, but because presentation screamed professional.

Attention — Style Consistency Matters

Switching from "tropical beach" to "minimalist studio" to "urban loft" within the same carousel confuses audiences. Pick one vibe and stick with it across a series.

Pro Tip — Save Styled Backgrounds

If one generated background works well, duplicate it. Build a consistent series (all product shots in the same environment).

Mini Exercise — Three Contexts

Take a product photo. Remove background. Place it on:

1. White background.
2. Brand color background.
3. Styled AI-generated scene.
4. Which one feels most on-brand?

Checklist — Image AI Mastery Locked

1. Magic Edit as Storytelling, Not Decoration

You're no longer dropping random objects into photos just because you can. With Magic Edit, every added element has a purpose: a product on a desk, a prop that clarifies context, a visual that strengthens the story you want to tell. If the edit helps the viewer understand faster, you've used the tool professionally.

2. Magic Eraser for Clean Focus

Distractions—like a trash can in the corner or a stranger walking behind your subject—don't belong in your final design. With Magic Eraser, you remove them without leaving awkward gaps. The image feels authentic, not manipulated, because the absence doesn't call attention to itself.

3. Magic Expand for Platform Agility

Instead of cropping one photo a dozen different ways and losing quality, you use Magic Expand to extend the frame intelligently. That single portrait now adapts to Instagram square, TikTok vertical, and LinkedIn banner—all while maintaining composition. Your content stretches without breaking.

4. Backgrounds That Serve the Brand

Every brand has a mood. Some demand clean white, others prefer textured gradients or branded patterns. By mastering background removal and replacement, you ensure every image sits inside a style that reinforces identity. It's no longer about "removing the background"—it's about replacing it with one that amplifies your message.

Common Mistakes — And How to Correct Them

1. Over-Editing into Unrealism
Adding too many elements creates surreal, unbelievable photos.
Fix: Limit edits to one or two meaningful changes.

2. Sterile Background Removal
Removing all context makes products feel lifeless.
Fix: Keep or add subtle context that fits your brand.

3. Overexpansion Artifacts
Stretching photos too far creates distorted AI fills.
Fix: Expand modestly; frame strategically.

4. Inconsistent Styles
Switching backgrounds between posts breaks cohesion.
Fix: Choose one style and replicate it across assets.

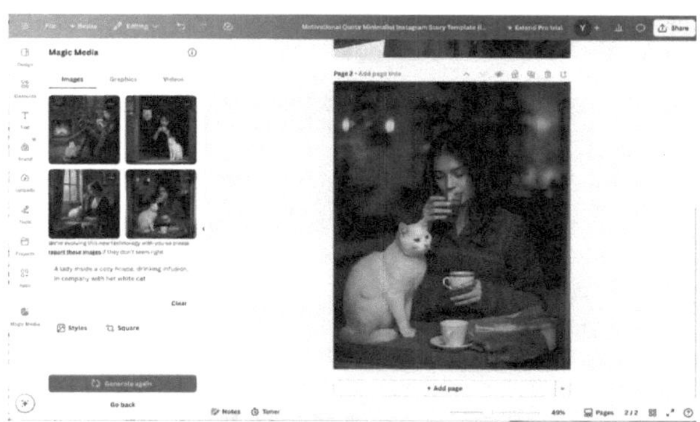

Closing Thought

Images are no longer static—they're adaptable, editable, expandable, and style-shiftable. But the true professional is not the one who edits most, but the one who edits with intention. With these AI tools, you can turn casual photos into polished brand visuals in minutes. Used well, they don't just clean pictures—they tell stories. In the next chapter, we'll move from images to text and documents, exploring how Magic Write, Docs, and Switch can make you a publishing powerhouse.

Chapter 3

Text & Documents: Magic Write, Docs, and Switch (Post → Slide → PDF)

In every brand journey, words are as important as images. They persuade, inform, and invite action. But writing takes time—drafting a blog, creating captions, converting posts into slides, turning slides into PDFs. Each step traditionally meant starting over. That's why so many freelancers dread content: not because they can't write, but because they can't keep up.

Canva's Magic Write, Docs, and Magic Switch change this dynamic completely. Instead of reinventing the wheel, you can draft, refine, and repurpose inside a single ecosystem. A LinkedIn post becomes a slide deck in minutes. A blog draft turns into a polished PDF guide. Captions multiply with variations. Suddenly, you're not just writing—you're orchestrating.

This chapter will show you how to:

- Use Magic Write to break the blank page.
- Build longer-form pieces in Docs that flow into presentations and PDFs.
- Repurpose content across formats with Magic Switch, so one idea becomes many assets.

The outcome? You stop being a "writer who drowns in drafts" and **start being a content systems director** —someone who creates once and leverages forever.

What You'll Do in 10 Minutes (Quick Win)

- Open Canva Docs and ask Magic Write for a 200-word article draft.
- Use Magic Switch to turn it into a 6-slide presentation.
- Export that presentation as a PDF handout.
- Compare: you've just created 3 deliverables in under 10 minutes.

Section 1 — Magic Write: The Blank Page Killer

Why this matters.

Every professional has felt the paralysis of starting from scratch. Magic Write replaces hesitation with a draft. It won't give you brilliance, but it gives you momentum.

How to use it.

1. Open Canva Docs, from the general Dashboard.
2. Type "/Magic Write."
3. Prompt with clarity: "Write a 3-paragraph introduction to a fitness guide, tone: inspiring but practical."
4. Review results. Cut filler. Refine tone. Keep what sparks.

Real Scenario — The Stalled Freelancer

A social media manager froze writing captions for a new product launch. Magic Write gave her 10 draft options in 15 seconds. She rewrote two into polished captions that matched the brand. What would have taken hours took 20 minutes.

Pro Tip — Prompt for Roles

Frame prompts as "Act as a copywriter," "Act as a coach," "Act as a CEO." Role-based prompts sharpen results.

Common Pitfall — Publishing Raw AI Text

Clients spot generic tone instantly. Always rewrite in your own voice.

Mini Exercise — Caption Sprint

Prompt Magic Write: "Write 5 Instagram captions for a handmade jewelry brand, playful but elegant tone." Edit into your own words. Save the top 3 as your caption library.

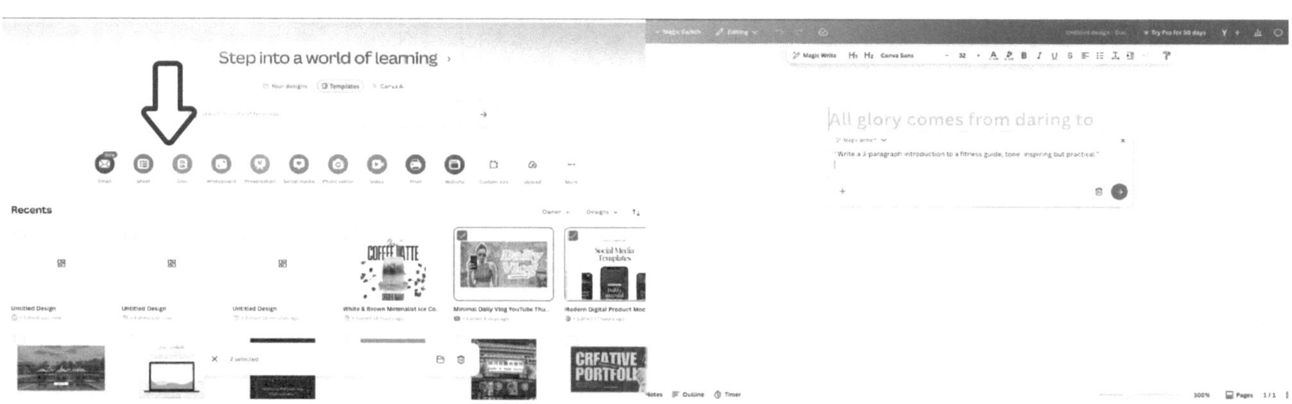

Section 2 — Docs: Long-Form with Flexibility

Why Docs matter.

Social media needs brevity, but businesses need long-form: proposals, blog posts, reports. Canva Docs combine text-first writing with embedded visuals. Unlike Google Docs or Word, you can directly integrate photos, charts, and design assets.

How to use it.

- In Canva, open a Doc from the homepage and start writing (as seen in Section 1)
- To insert a design, click the "+" icon on a new line, then select "Designs."
- A side panel will appear with your recent projects — scroll or search by name to find the one you want.
- Click on it once, and Canva automatically embeds a scrollable, live-linked design directly into your document.
- Collaborate with comments, just like Google Docs.

Real Scenario — The Mini-Ebook

A coach wanted a lead magnet: a 10-page PDF ebook. Using Canva Docs, she drafted chapters with Magic Write, embedded branded visuals, and exported directly to PDF. No InDesign, no outsourcing.

Attention — Docs Are Not Just Text

If you use Docs only as a writing pad, you miss the point. Docs are hybrid: writing + design + collaboration.

Pro Tip — Embed, Don't Attach

Instead of linking a chart as an external file, embed it directly into Docs. Clients see context, not clutter.

Mini Exercise — Lead Magnet Draft

In Canva Docs, draft 3 pages of a guide (topic of your choice). Add one image per page. Export to PDF. You just built the skeleton of a lead magnet.

Section 3 — Magic Switch: One Idea, Many Assets

Why it matters.

A blog should not die as a blog. A caption should not stay a caption. Magic Switch multiplies ideas across formats, saving time and amplifying reach.

How to use it.

- Write text in Docs.
- Select Magic Switch → Presentation / Post / PDF.
- Review auto-generated layouts. Apply Brand Kit.
- Refine slides or posts to align with strategy.

Real Scenario — The Startup Pitch

A founder wrote a 2-page business concept in Docs. With Magic Switch, it became a 12-slide deck in seconds. After polish, she presented it to investors. Same content, three formats: doc, deck, and PDF.

Attention — Raw Output ≠ Ready Output

Switched assets often look generic. Always refine typography, spacing, and visuals.

Pro Tip — Systemize Your Conversions

Every week, pick one long-form piece. Switch into a carousel, slide deck, and PDF. Multiply content without new drafts.

Mini Exercise — Triple Format Test

Draft a 200-word blog intro.

Switch to:

1. Presentation (6 slides).
2. Instagram carousel.
3. PDF handout.
4. Edit each. Which version feels strongest?

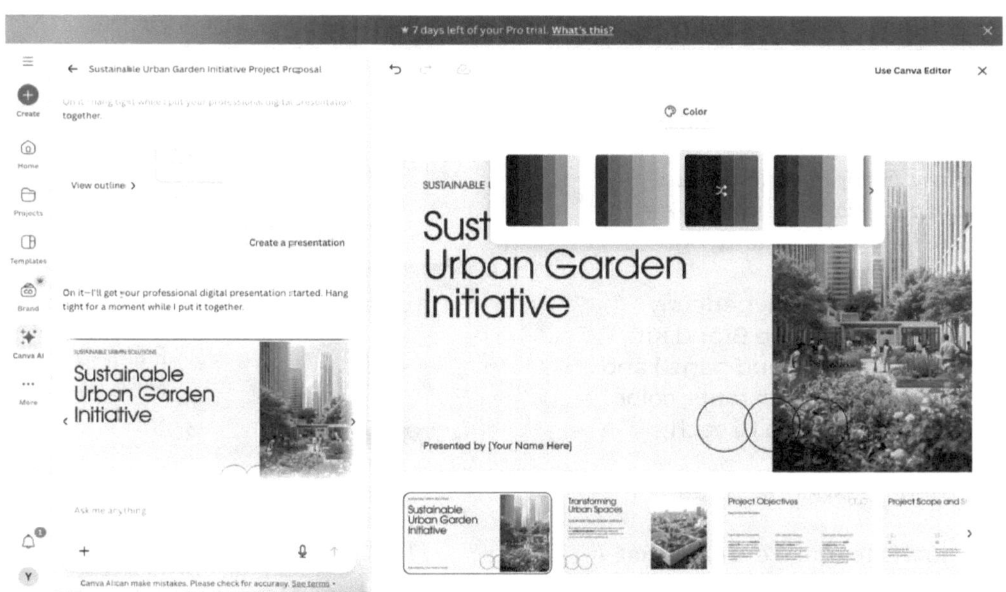

Section 4 — Integration of Text & Visual: Why Hybrid Wins

Why this matters.

The strength of Canva AI is not just text generation, but text-visual synergy. Docs + Magic Write + Magic Switch allow words and visuals to live in the same workflow. This makes repurposing natural, not forced.

Real Scenario — The Content Team

A marketing team built a full campaign in one week: blog (Docs), captions (Magic Write), deck (Magic Switch), and one-pager PDF. Because all formats lived in Canva, design stayed consistent across platforms.

Common Pitfall — Treating Formats Separately

When Docs, Slides, and PDFs look unrelated, your brand loses coherence. Canva solves this if you align them inside one workflow.

Pro Tip — Use Brand Kit Across Formats

Always apply logos, fonts, and palettes before exporting. This ensures consistency across switched assets.

Mini Exercise — Triple Format Test

- Choose one piece of content you've already created — for example, a blog post, a presentation, or a one-pager.
- In Canva Docs, use Magic Switch to convert it into two additional formats (for instance, a presentation and a PDF).
- Now, compare the three outputs side by side: look at the fonts, colors, and logo placement.
- If they don't look perfectly aligned, open the Brand Kit (from the left-hand panel) and apply your official fonts, color palette, and logo to each version.
- Then re-export all three.

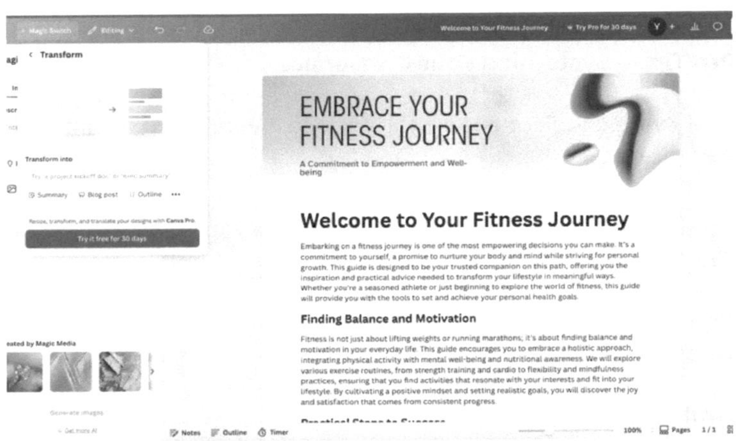

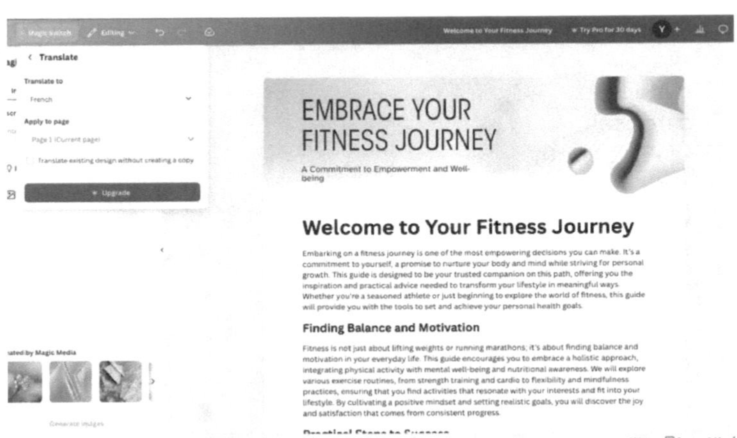

The goal is to make every format — Docs, Decks, and PDFs — feel like part of the same visual system. A unified brand identity across formats builds instant recognition and trust.

Checklist — Implementation Locked

If you can genuinely affirm each of these points, you are not just using Magic Write, Docs, and Switch—you are directing them like an advanced operator.

- **I can draft in Magic Write without freezing.** The blank page no longer intimidates me. I know how to break inertia by prompting Magic Write with clarity, then shaping its draft into my authentic voice. What once took an hour of hesitation now takes minutes of decisive editing.

- **I can use Docs to combine text and visuals for longer content.** My documents are no longer walls of text. I integrate charts, photos, and branded elements directly into Canva Docs so that every page communicates visually as well as verbally. I can design a lead magnet, proposal, or blog draft that looks like a finished product, not just a draft file.

- **I can repurpose with Magic Switch into at least 3 formats.** One idea is no longer locked in one form. I know how to turn a blog into a slide deck, a slide deck into a carousel, or a post into a PDF—multiplying my reach without multiplying my effort. My workflow has moved from "linear" to "exponential."

- **I can maintain consistency with Brand Kit across outputs**. Whether I'm exporting a PDF, a carousel, or a deck, my fonts, colors, and logos remain identical. I no longer worry about brand dilution, because Canva's Brand Kit applies the same identity across all my switched formats. This consistency is what makes a freelancer look like an established agency.

Common Mistakes — And How to Fix Them

Even with the best tools, professionals fall into predictable traps. They're not signs of failure—they're milestones on the learning curve. What matters is how quickly you identify and correct them.

1. Vague Prompts in Magic Write. Result: generic, lifeless text that could belong to anyone. When you type "write a caption" without context, the AI delivers a filler line that convinces no one.
Fix: Always add role, audience, tone, and length. Instead of "write a caption," try: "Act as a social media copywriter. Draft 3 Instagram captions for a sustainable fashion brand, playful but premium tone, max 15 words each." Suddenly, your results are sharper, more usable, and tailored to your context.

2. Treating Docs as WordPad. Result: a document that looks like a school essay, not a professional asset. If you only use Docs as a text pad, you miss Canva's hybrid power.
Fix: Embed visuals inline. Add charts, images, and branded headers. A lead magnet with visuals feels premium; a plain-text version feels amateur. Use Docs as a design-capable canvas, not a typewriter.

3. Exporting Raw Switch Assets. Result: decks and carousels that look generic, sloppy, or "cookie-cutter." Magic Switch is powerful, but its first draft is rarely client-ready.
Fix: Always refine after switching. Apply your Brand Kit, adjust layouts, trim redundant slides, and polish flow. Treat Switch outputs as scaffolding, not as a finished building.

4. Inconsistent Voice Across Formats. Result: your blog sounds formal, but your carousel sounds casual; your deck feels corporate, but your PDF feels playful. This inconsistency breaks trust.
Fix: After switching, rewrite copy to unify tone. Keep one editorial guideline for all formats. Remember: audiences notice tone shifts even more than design shifts.

Chapter 4

Automations: Bulk Create, Integrations, and Smart Duplications

For beginners, the hardest part of design is making one good-looking post. For advanced users, the hardest part is different: making fifty good-looking posts that all feel on-brand, consistent, and ready on time. A freelancer might need to deliver a month of social content to a client. A marketing team might have to prepare variations for five markets at once. The work is not about creativity anymore—it's about scale.

That's where automation comes in. Canva's Bulk Create, integrations with apps and data, and smart duplication systems are not gimmicks. They are lifelines. They turn the grind of "manual copy-paste" into the flow of "set once, generate many." **If you've ever felt the fatigue of building similar designs one by one, this chapter will change how you work forever**.

We'll explore:

- Bulk Create with CSV: how one spreadsheet can generate dozens of unique designs.
- App integrations: bringing data, content, and assets into Canva automatically.
- Smart duplications: systems for reusing layouts without starting over.

By the end of this chapter, you'll stop thinking like a solo designer and start thinking like an automation architect. You'll know how to design once and scale infinitely, saving hours while maintaining brand control.

What You'll Do in 10 Minutes (Quick Win)

- Prepare a simple spreadsheet with 10 rows of text (e.g., quotes, product names, or event dates).
- Import it into Canva using Bulk Create.
- Apply it to a single template.
- Watch as Canva generates 10 ready-to-export designs automatically.

Congratulations—you just experienced the leap from "manual" to "scaled."

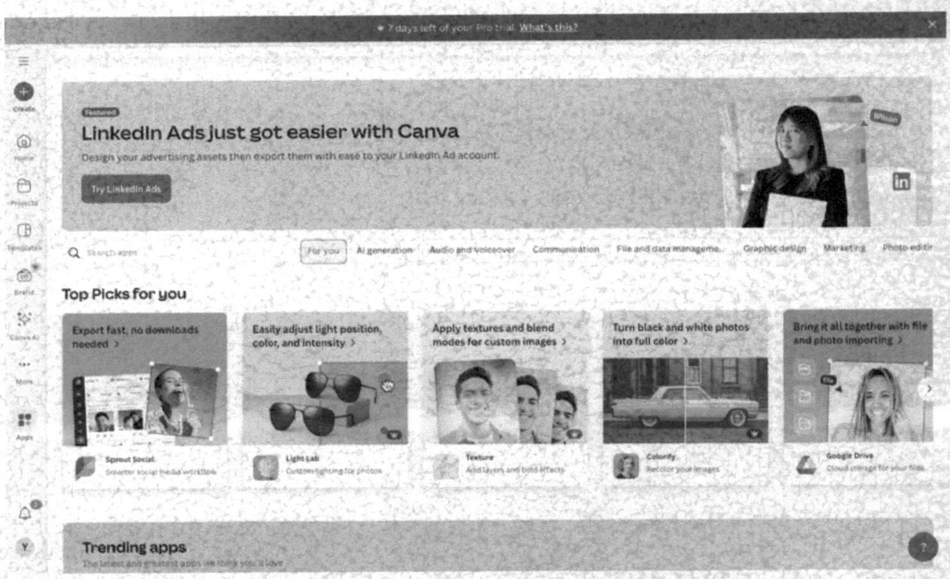

Section 1 — Bulk Create with CSV: Designing at Scale

Why it matters.

Imagine you have to create 50 Instagram posts with different quotes. Doing it one by one would take all night. With Bulk Create, one spreadsheet does the heavy lifting: Canva swaps content into your design template automatically.

How it works.

1. Open a design template.
2. In the toolbar, click Apps → Bulk Create.
3. Upload your CSV (spreadsheet file).
4. Map each column (e.g., “Quote,” “Author”) to placeholders in your design.
5. Generate multiple versions in seconds.

Real Scenario — The Quote Marketer

A life coach needed 30 motivational posts for her feed. Instead of building them manually, she created a spreadsheet with 30 quotes and 30 author names. Bulk Create filled her template automatically. In under an hour, she exported a full month of branded content.

Pro Tip — Keep Your CSV Clean

Use short, clear text. Long strings break layouts. Test 2–3 rows before generating the full batch.

Mini Exercise — The 10-Row Test

Build a CSV with 10 quotes. Apply to a Canva post template. Export all versions. Notice how automation saves you from repetitive work.

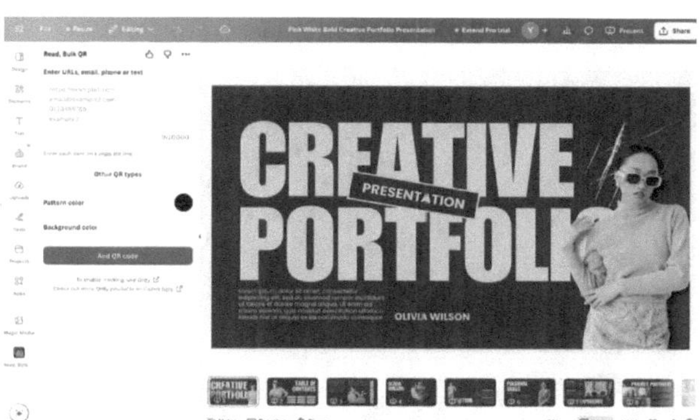

Section 2 — App Integrations: Bringing Data into Canva

Why it matters.

Your content doesn't live in isolation. It comes from Google Sheets, Dropbox, Google Drive, or even apps like Typeform. Integrating them with Canva saves you from endless copy-paste cycles.

How it works.

- Google Sheets → Canva: connect your sheet to Bulk Create directly.
- Dropbox/Drive → Canva: import image libraries straight into your workspace.
- Other apps: pull in logos, brand assets, or data dynamically.

Real Scenario — The Event Manager

An event agency ran 12 workshops across Europe. Instead of redesigning flyers each time, they connected a Google Sheet with event details (date, location, speaker). Canva auto-generated 12 flyers, one for each city. Updates in the sheet updated the designs.

Attention — Integrations Save Time, Not Thinking

Automation doesn't fix bad strategy. If your spreadsheet is messy, your designs will be messy faster.

Pro Tip — Build "Master Sheets"

Keep one Google Sheet as the source of truth. Feed Canva from that. Any update cascades across designs.

Mini Exercise — Event Batch

Create a Google Sheet with 5 events (title, date, location). Connect to Canva Bulk Create. Generate flyers automatically.

Section 3 — Smart Duplications: Scaling Without Losing Quality

Why it matters.

Not every automation requires a CSV. Sometimes the fastest way to scale is to duplicate a design smartly—keeping structure but changing content. This is where Canva's folders, Brand Kit, and duplication tools become powerful.

How to do it.

- Create one "Master Design."
- Duplicate for each variation.
- Use Brand Kit and "Styles" to swap colors/fonts instantly.
- Keep components reusable in a "Components" page.

Real Scenario — The Agency Carousel

A digital agency needed 4 variations of the same carousel for different niches. Instead of redesigning, they duplicated one master file, swapped colors and examples, and exported in an hour.

Common Pitfall — Blind Duplication

If you duplicate without organizing, you create chaos: dozens of files, no naming convention, no version control.

Pro Tip — Name Files Intentionally

Use naming like "Client_Aug2025_Carousel_V1." Clear labels avoid confusion later.

Mini Exercise — Smart Duplication

Design one Instagram carousel. Duplicate into 3 versions (different colors/texts). Apply Brand Kit. Export. Time saved = hours.

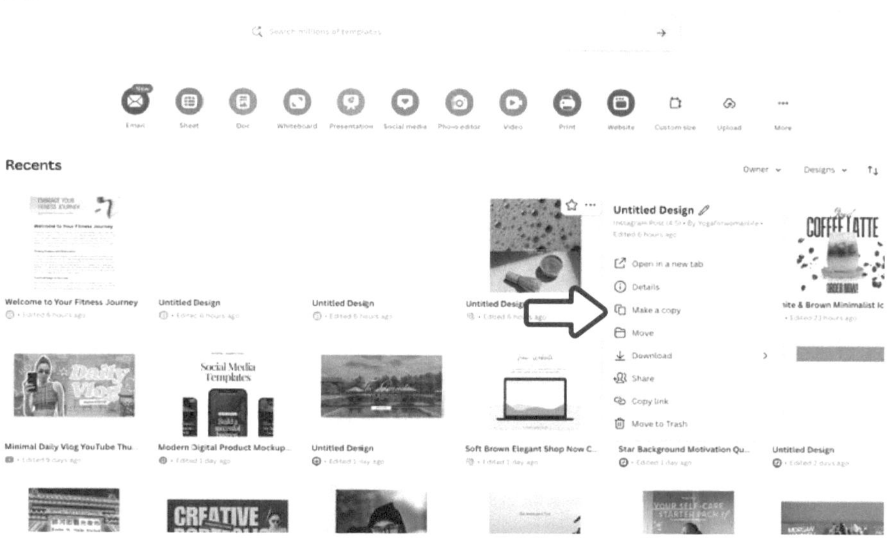

Section 4 — Building Automation Systems: From Solo to Team

Why it matters.

Automation is not just about saving minutes—it's about scaling your identity across time. A freelancer who automates becomes a one-person agency. A small business that automates looks like a big one.

How to build a simple system.

- In Canva, open your chosen template and click Apps → Bulk Create.
- Connect your spreadsheet or paste your data directly into the table.
- Then, map each column (e.g., "Title," "Price," "Image") to the corresponding text or image placeholder in your design.
- Once connected, click Generate — Canva will automatically duplicate and populate each version for you.
- The output layer is where you polish and distribute. Review the generated designs, apply your Brand Kit to ensure colors and fonts are consistent, and export in the required formats (PDF, MP4, PNG).
- Finally, maintain a feedback loop. Once a month, review your folder structure, remove unused assets, and refine your templates. Each cycle makes the system leaner, faster, and more scalable — turning repetition into effortless consistency.

Real Scenario — The Monthly Content Factory

A startup founder built a "Content Engine" in Canva: one spreadsheet, 5 templates, one monthly duplication workflow. Each month, she generated 60 posts in 3 hours. Her competitors still hired external agencies.

Attention — Automation Without Oversight

Scaling fast is useless if quality drops. Always build a review step before publishing.

Mini Exercise — Your First Workflow

Choose one recurring content type (quotes, promos, events). Create one master design + spreadsheet. Automate once. Document the process in 5 steps. That's your new SOP (Standard Operating Procedure).

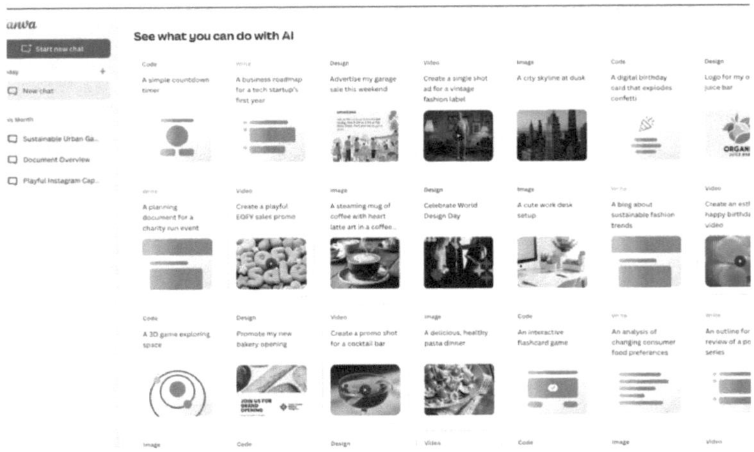

Checklist — Automation Mastery Locked

Check if the following is true: "I am ready if:"

- I can generate multiple designs with Bulk Create using a clean CSV.
- This means I no longer fear high volumes of content. If a client asks for 50 quote posts or an e-commerce catalog with 100 product cards, I don't panic. I prepare a spreadsheet, map fields correctly, and let Canva handle the heavy lifting. The difference is radical: what once felt impossible is now an afternoon's work.
- I can connect external apps (Sheets, Drive, Dropbox) to feed Canva directly.
- Instead of juggling copy-paste chaos, my Canva designs pull data straight from the source. Product details in Google Sheets, images in Drive, or logos in Dropbox sync directly into my workspace. This integration means fewer mistakes, less wasted time, and a creative process that feels fluid instead of fragmented.
- I can duplicate designs smartly with Brand Kit consistency.
- I don't just hit "duplicate" randomly. I duplicate with intention, making sure every variation inherits my fonts, colors, and logo placements. My carousels, flyers, and presentations all look like they belong to the same brand family—even when I'm producing dozens of them. Consistency is no longer something I chase; it's something I build into the system.
- I have built at least one repeatable workflow (SOP) for recurring content.
- I no longer reinvent the wheel every week. If I need to produce social posts, event flyers, or product sheets, I already have a documented process: one master template, one spreadsheet or folder system, one review step. This SOP saves me hours each month and gives me peace of mind—because I know my future self won't be scrambling.

If you can confidently tick all four of these boxes, you've crossed the line from "Canva user" to automation operator. You are no longer working harder—you are working at scale, with systems that save you time and elevate your professionalism.

Common Mistakes — And How to Fix Them

1. **Messy Spreadsheets —** Garbage In, Garbage Out
Bulk Create is only as good as your CSV. If it's full of typos or missing fields, Canva will multiply the errors. The result? Dozens of bad designs and wasted time.
Fix: Test with three rows before scaling. Check formatting, clean the data, then rerun. A clean CSV keeps the engine running smooth.

2. **Ignoring the Brand Kit —** The Killer of Consistency
Bulk Create works fast, but without your Brand Kit, results look random — mismatched fonts, colors, logos. Inconsistency kills trust.
Fix: Apply your fonts, palette, and logo before generating. Consistency is the mark of a professional, not a detail.

3. **Blind Duplication —** Chaos in Disguise
Duplication saves time but breeds confusion. "Copy of Copy (Final V3)" means lost files and frustration.
Fix: Use clear names like. Client_Campaign_Month_V1 and keep folders tidy. A few seconds of order save hours later.

4. **Over-Automation Without Review**
Speed without control is dangerous. One typo or off-brand color replicated 50 times ruins credibility.
Fix: Always review before export. Check spacing, tone, and alignment. Automation should scale quality, not mistakes.

Why This Matters

Small errors compound fast — messy data, missing logos, chaotic folders. Cleaning them up isn't perfectionism; it's brand protection.

When your systems run clean, every output says the same thing: this is pro work.

Chapter 5

Hacks & Quality: Brand Control, Consistency, and Common Errors

In the rush to produce content at scale, it is easy to believe that speed is the only measure of success. But speed without quality is a trap. A single sloppy post—a logo cropped incorrectly, a headline unreadable on mobile, or a mismatched color palette—can erode trust built over months. Your audience may never articulate why your designs feel "off," but they will sense inconsistency. And in a digital marketplace overflowing with choices, inconsistency is the quickest way to lose credibility.

Think about the brands you admire. Apple, Nike, Airbnb—their campaigns are not just fast, they are flawless. Every color, font, and placement feels intentional. That polish is not an accident. It comes from systems: checklists, locked templates, brand kits, and disciplined review processes. The difference between a freelancer who struggles and a freelancer who scales is not creativity alone—**it is the ability to maintain quality at speed.**

This chapter is your quality insurance policy. You will learn how to lock your brand identity into Canva so it never drifts, how to build consistency across dozens of assets, which hacks elevate design instantly, and how to avoid the most common errors professionals make when working fast. By the end, you won't just move quickly—you'll move confidently, knowing that every asset leaving Canva represents you at your best.

What You'll Do in 10 Minutes (Quick Win)

- Open your Brand Kit and confirm: fonts, colors, and logos are correct and updated.
- Export three recent designs side by side. Look for mismatched fonts, inconsistent spacing, or color shifts.
- Apply one hack: lock a logo in a template, use "Copy Style" across slides, or add alt text to an image.

In 10 minutes, you'll feel the difference: your system is already more controlled, and your designs more trustworthy.

What You'll Do in 10 Minutes (Quick Win)

- Prepare a simple spreadsheet with 10 rows of text (e.g., quotes, product names, or event dates).
- Import it into Canva using Bulk Create.
- Apply it to a single template.
- Watch as Canva generates 10 ready-to-export designs automatically.

Congratulations—you just experienced the leap from "manual" to "scaled."

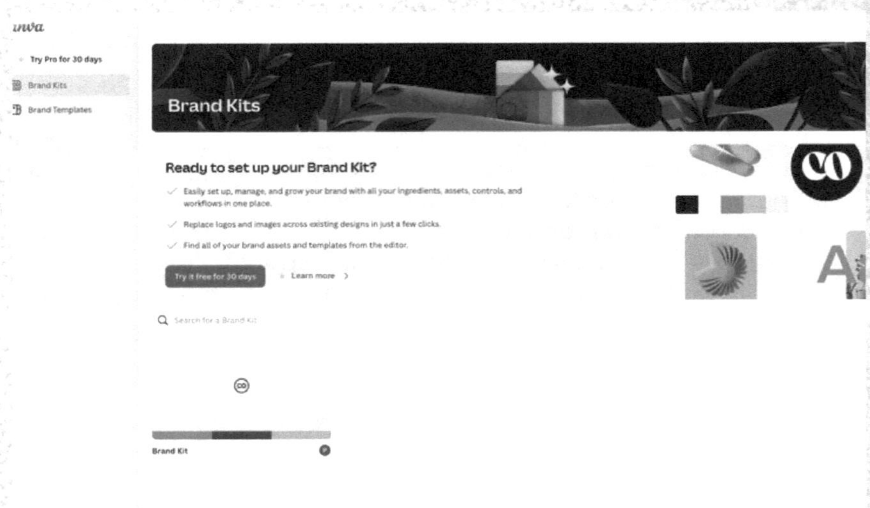

Section 1 — Brand Controls: Protecting Your Visual DNA

Why it matters.

A brand is more than a logo—it is a promise of consistency. Every post, brochure, or slide is part of your visual DNA. If your Instagram stories look playful but your website looks corporate, the audience experiences cognitive dissonance. Canva's Brand Kit is designed to prevent this drift.

How to implement it.

- Upload all logos (primary, secondary, monochrome) into the Brand Kit.
- Define exact HEX codes for colors—never rely on "close enough."
- Set font hierarchies: heading, subheading, body.
- Apply these defaults before generating assets with Bulk Create or Magic Switch.

Real Scenario — The Professional Leap

A freelance social media manager used random templates, tweaking colors "by eye." Posts looked decent individually but chaotic as a feed. After implementing a strict Brand Kit, engagement rose—not because the content changed, but because the brand felt stable

Pro Tip — Lock the Fundamentals

In templates, lock the placement of your logo and footer margins. This ensures that, even if you duplicate or bulk generate, your identity never shifts out of place.

Mini Exercise — Brand Audit

Open your Brand Kit and test: do all templates inherit your chosen fonts and colors automatically? If not, adjust. Export one design and compare it to your website—do they look like family?

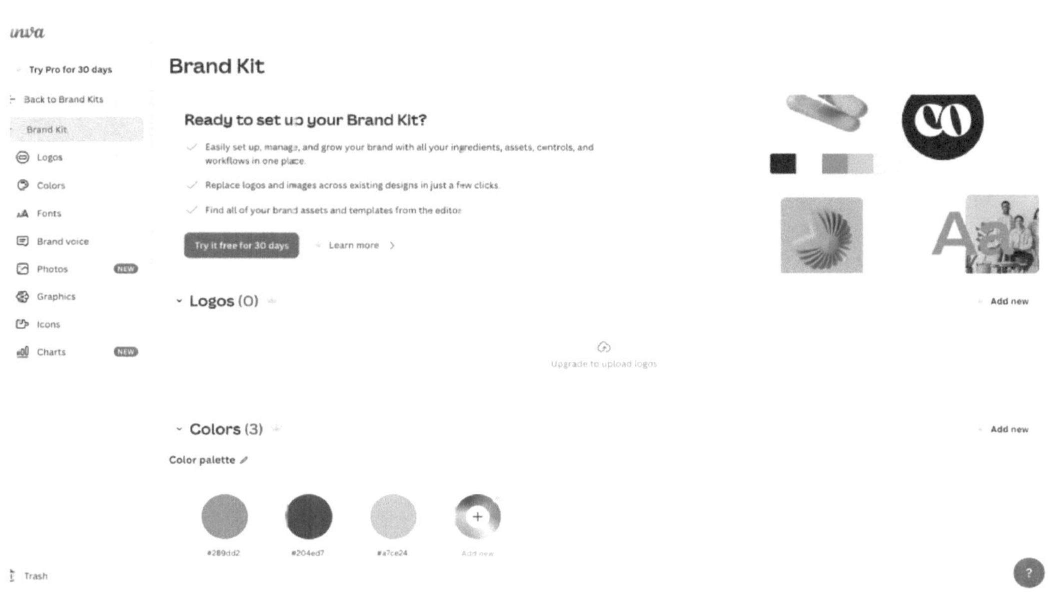

Section 2 — Building Consistency Systems

Why it matters.

A single polished post can impress, but trust is built through repetition. Consistency is what makes a brand recognizable even without the logo. In Canva, consistency comes from deliberate systems: templates, reusable components, and disciplined file management.

How to enforce it.

- Open any design and go to Styles (from the left panel or Apps → Styles).
- Apply your Brand Kit fonts and colors to all pages with one click to keep visuals consistent.
- Create a separate Components Page where you store reusable elements — buttons, overlays, dividers — ready to copy into new projects.
- In Projects, name files systematically (e.g., Client_Campaign_Month_V1) and organize them into folders.
- This keeps your entire workflow clean, aligned, and scalable.

Real Scenario — The Startup Engine

A founder produced 60 posts per month. Initially, each one felt disconnected. After creating one master carousel template and a set of reusable overlays, the feed looked cohesive. Followers commented: “Your posts are instantly recognizable.”

Attention — Template Whiplash

Jumping between too many templates breaks rhythm. Pick 2–3 core templates and adapt them; don’t start from scratch every time.

Mini Exercise — Consistency Check

Line up 5 exported designs. Do they look like a set? If not, note which details break rhythm (spacing, fonts, colors). Correct them by applying Brand Kit + Styles.

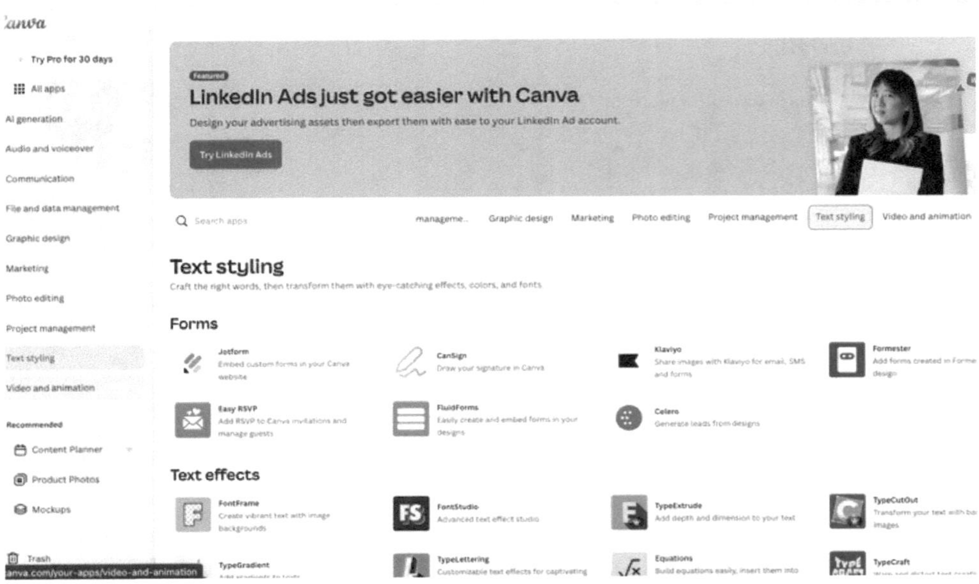

Section 3 — Quality Hacks: Two-Minute Fixes with Huge Impact

Why hacks matter.

Sometimes the difference between "good enough" and "professional" is not a redesign—it's a two-minute tweak. Canva hides several features that, when used consistently, elevate your work dramatically.

Hacks to adopt:

1. Guides & Rulers

- Click: File (top-left corner) → View settings → Show rulers and Show guides.
- Then drag a guide from the ruler along the edge of your canvas to align text and elements precisely.
- Shortcuts: Shift + R (toggle rulers), Shift + G (toggle guides). For extra layout control, you can also turn on Margins or Print bleed in the same menu.

2. Copy Style (Paint Roller)

- Click: select the element with the style you want → click the Paint Roller (Copy style) icon in the top toolbar → then click on other text boxes or shapes to apply it.
- Shortcuts: Cmd/Ctrl + Alt + C to copy style → Cmd/Ctrl + Alt + V to paste style. This ensures consistent fonts, colors, and sizes across all slides.

3. Alt Text (Accessibility & SEO)

- Click: select an image → click the three dots (...) in the mini toolbar → choose Alt text → write a short, clear description → click Done.
- Alternatively, right-click the image → Alt text. This improves accessibility for PDFs and helps search engines understand your visuals.

4. Mobile Preview

- Click: Share (top-right) → Download → choose PNG or JPG → set Width: 1080 px → Download. Open the file on your phone to check text readability and spacing.
- If anything feels cramped or too small, adjust font size and layout back in Canva.

Real Scenario — The Thumbnail Rescue

A YouTube creator's thumbnails looked fine on desktop but unreadable on mobile. After previewing in phone size, he enlarged fonts, added overlays, and improved spacing. CTR doubled—not because of clickbait, but because viewers could actually read the title.

Pro Tip — Save Your Overlays

Create a "Components" design with your preferred overlays, CTA buttons, and frames. Copy-paste from there instead of rebuilding. This cuts hours and ensures consistency.

Mini Exercise — Hack Pass

- Take one of your designs and turn on Rulers and Guides to align every element with precision.
- Use the Copy Style tool to match fonts and colors across all subheads, then add Alt Text to each image for accessibility and SEO.
- Finally, export your file and compare it with the original — the layout now feels cleaner, sharper, and unmistakably professional.

Section 4 — Common Errors That Break Trust

If you can affirm each of these points honestly, you have crossed a threshold. You are no longer "using Canva to make designs." You are running a quality-controlled creative system. That system is what separates the hobbyist from the professional, and the rushed freelancer from the trusted brand-builder.

- **My Brand Kit is active and consistent across all projects**. I no longer rely on memory to pick colors or fonts. Every design begins with a locked system: fonts, palettes, and logos are preloaded, guaranteeing that whether I'm creating one Instagram post or a 30-slide deck, my brand identity never drifts. Consistency is no longer an afterthought—it is automatic.

- **My designs share fonts, colors, and spacing that make them instantly recognizable.** When I line up my assets, they look like members of the same family. The typography speaks with one voice, the colors resonate with the same tone, and the spacing breathes with balance. To my audience, this cohesion translates into reliability. They don't need to see my logo to know it's mine—they recognize the style at a glance.

- **I use at least three Canva hacks (guides, copy style, alt text) to elevate polish**. I've gone beyond templates. I turn on guides to align with precision, I use "Copy Style" to spread consistency in seconds, and I add alt text for accessibility and SEO. These are not fancy tricks—they are the finishing touches that make my work look as if a professional design studio produced it.

- **I run a review pass (alignment, spelling, export format) before publishing.** I don't let speed blind me. Before I release anything, I check margins, proofread text, and confirm the correct export format. Social posts go out as crisp PNGs, photos as JPGs, print assets as PDFs. This habit ensures my final product is not just done quickly—it is done right.

Closing Thought

Speed is seductive. But without quality control, speed becomes reckless. True professionals are not just fast—they are disciplined, consistent, and intentional. Canva's AI and automation tools give you the power to produce at scale. This chapter gives you the filters to ensure that scale doesn't erode your identity.
When you master both—automation + polish—you unlock a new level of leverage. Your output grows, your brand strengthens, and your audience sees you not as a "fast designer," but as a trusted professional whose work is both efficient and flawless.

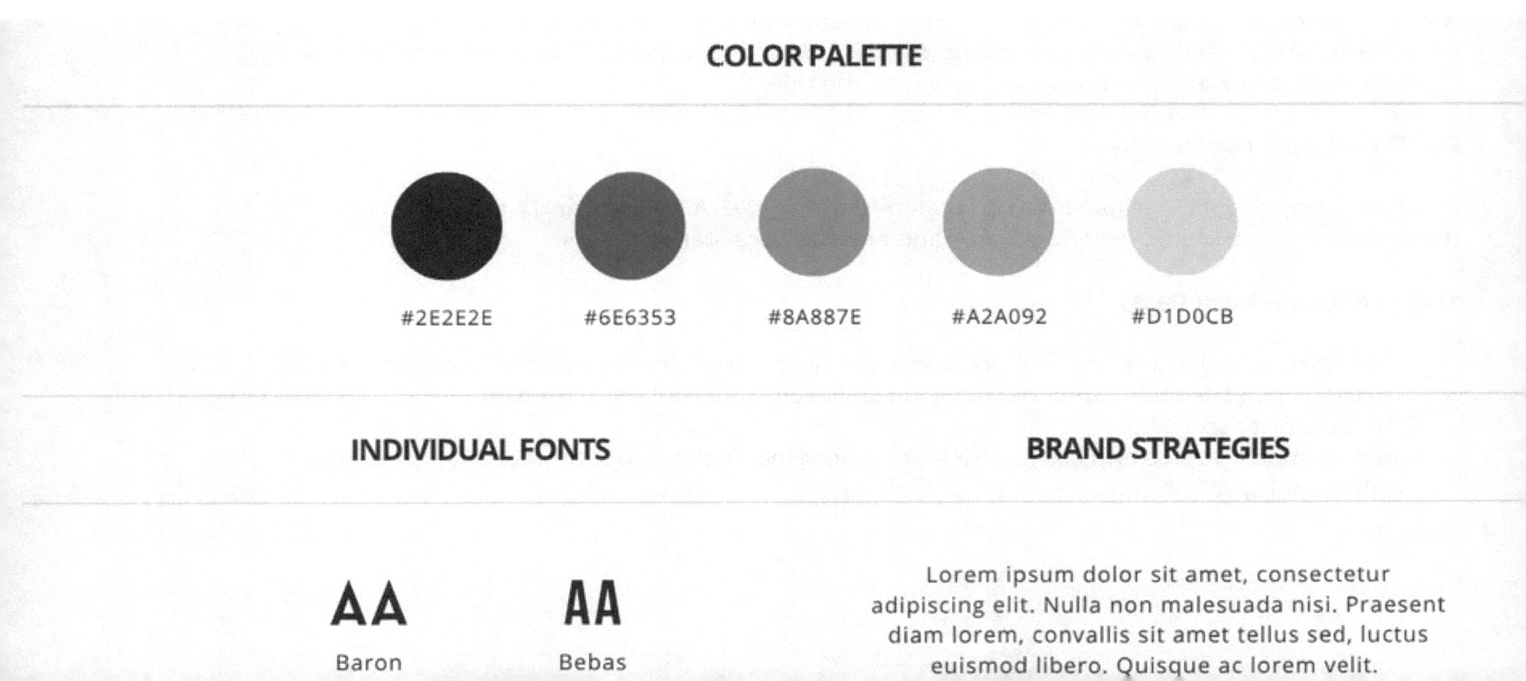

Module 5 – Canva for Video Editing

From Static to Motion

Once, mastering video editing meant investing in heavy software, high-end machines, and hours of tutorials filled with jargon about codecs, rendering, and multi-cam setups. For most creators, freelancers, and small businesses, video felt out of reach—a professional-only playground. But the truth today is very different. **Video is no longer optional, and Canva has lowered the barriers so that anyone with a message can bring it to life in motion.**

Why does this matter? Because the world scrolls faster than it reads. Social feeds prioritize video. Algorithms push Reels, Shorts, and TikToks to the top. Your audience expects to see you move, not just read your words. The brand that only posts static graphics looks dated; the one that pairs visuals with video feels alive, timely, and human.

This module is not about becoming a Hollywood editor. It's about giving you the practical ability to create short, sharp, brand-aligned videos that grab attention in seconds and deliver value without wasting time. Canva's video editor isn't Final Cut Pro—but that's the point. It's faster, friendlier, and built for the platforms that matter most right now.

In this final stage of the journey, you'll learn how to:

- Use Canva's video editor like a professional—understanding timelines, layers, keyframes, and audio assets.
- Master vertical video, the king format of 2025: crafting hooks in the first 3 seconds, pacing rhythm, layering B-roll.
- Design titles, captions, and transitions that carry your brand identity while staying legible on mobile.
- Export with confidence, choosing the right bitrate, FPS, and file size for each platform (Instagram, YouTube, TikTok, LinkedIn).
- Build reusable templates so you're not reinventing the wheel every time, but scaling campaigns systematically.

By the end, you'll be able to deliver a mini-campaign of five coordinated short videos—designed, edited, branded, and ready for publishing. That's not just a technical skill. It's a business asset. Because the freelancer or small business that can launch consistent video content has an edge over competitors stuck in static posts. Think of this module as your graduation project: we started with templates and simple posts, but now you'll stand in the world's most competitive content arena—short-form video—and deliver work that looks like it came from a full creative team. Except it's just you, Canva, and a smart system.

What You'll Do in 10 Minutes (Quick Win)

- Open Canva's video editor and start a 9:16 vertical design.
- Drop in a 5-second B-roll clip (from stock or your phone).
- Add a bold title for the first 3 seconds (your hook).
- Layer auto-captions with one click.
- Export and preview on your phone.

In 10 minutes, you've made your first short video. It may not be perfect, but it proves the point: you don't need Hollywood—just a clear message and the right workflow.

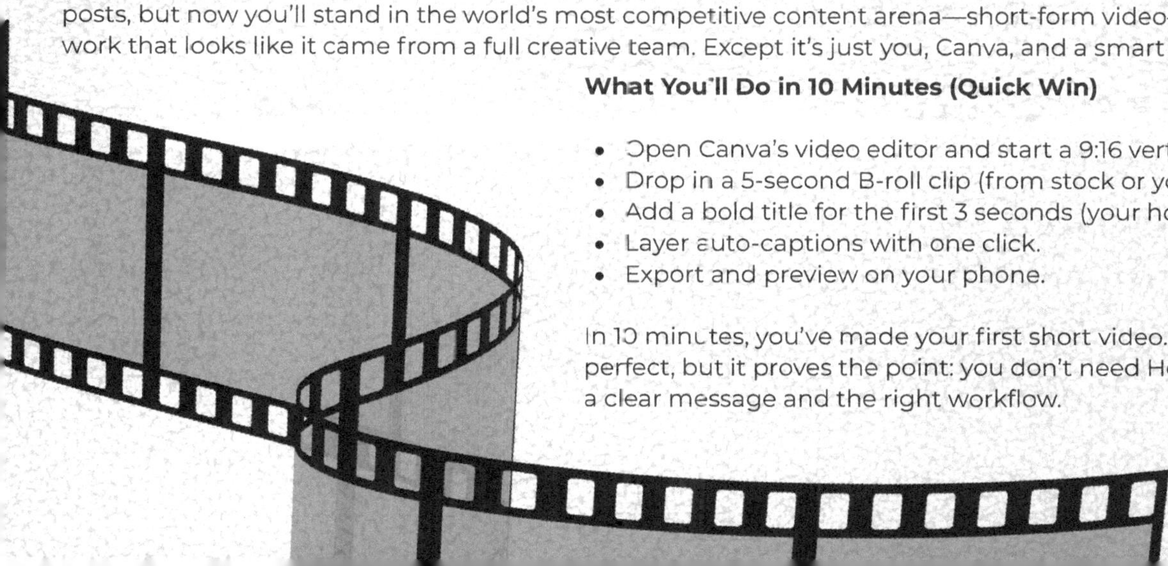

Chapter 1

Mastering Canva's Video Editor: Timeline, Layers, Keyframes, and Audio

If design is how your brand looks, editing is how it feels. You can shoot great footage, write clever captions, even have a strong hook, but if the edit falls flat—if timing drags, if music jars, if captions arrive too late—the story collapses. Video editing is where ideas transform into experiences.

For years, this was the intimidating wall between amateurs and professionals. Editing required mastering software like Premiere Pro, Final Cut, or DaVinci Resolve. Each came with steep learning curves, technical jargon (bitrate, codecs, frame interpolation), and machines powerful enough to handle 4K rendering. Small businesses, solo creators, and freelancers were locked out—not by creativity, but by complexity. **Canva changes this dynamic.**
Its video editor takes the intimidating complexity of timelines and keyframes and distills them into a tool you can learn in an afternoon, yet still wield with the intention of a professional. It doesn't replace Hollywood editing software—but it doesn't need to. For 90% of the content that drives engagement in today's digital economy—Reels, Shorts, Stories, LinkedIn explainers—Canva is more than enough.

Why does this matter for you? Because platforms no longer reward those who "just post." They reward those who can stop the scroll. And scroll-stopping video is rarely about expensive cameras—it's about smart editing. The first 3 seconds are cut sharp, the captions land perfectly, the rhythm matches the beat, and transitions feel invisible. Viewers don't notice the edit when it works; they only notice when it doesn't.

This chapter is your crash course in turning Canva's editor from a toy into a toolkit. We'll slow down and cover:

- Timeline mastery: how to structure your story second by second.
- Layer control: organizing text, graphics, and B-roll so nothing clashes.
- Keyframes: subtle animations that create professional polish without gimmicks.
- Audio: because half of video is sound—music, voice, and clarity.

By the end, you'll know how to direct attention, balance emotion, and export a video that feels deliberate—not accidental. And once you feel that control, you'll never see a rough edit the same way again.

What You'll Do in 10 Minutes (Quick Win)

Before diving into theory, let's get your hands dirty:

1. Open Canva and select "Video (9:16)" format.
2. Import a 10-second stock clip (e.g., coffee pouring).
3. Trim the clip in the timeline to 6 seconds.
4. Add a text layer: "Your Morning Routine, Upgraded."
5. Drop background music, lower its volume to 25%.
6. Export and preview on your phone.

In under 10 minutes, you've touched timeline, layers, and audio. The product isn't polished, but it proves the point: you don't need complex software to make motion that feels alive.

Section 1 — The Timeline: Story in Seconds

Why the timeline matters.

A video without a timeline is chaos. Clips pile randomly, moments stretch too long, energy dips. The timeline is the skeleton—each block of footage is a bone, and how you trim and place them determines whether your video runs, limps, or collapses.
In Canva, the timeline runs horizontally at the bottom of the editor. Each clip, audio track, text block, or effect appears as a rectangular segment. By trimming, splitting, and arranging, you decide the rhythm of your story.

How to use it well.

- **Trim with purpose:** Don't show 4 seconds of someone opening a door if 1.5 seconds is enough. In social media world, attention is currency.
- **Sequence logically:** Hook → Context → Payoff → CTA. This arc works across shorts, ads, or explainers.
- **Split strategically**: Use the scissors tool to break long clips into beats.

Real Scenario — From Flat to Snappy

A yoga instructor filmed a 45-second clip demonstrating a pose. Raw, it dragged. By trimming each step into 3-second beats (setup, execution, payoff), and cutting dead air, she created a 15-second reel. Views tripled.

Pro Tip — Think Like Music

Edits land better when cuts match natural beats: a gesture, a head turn, a lyric change. Watch your footage with sound on and cut where energy shifts.

Mini Exercise

Take a 30-second raw clip. Trim it to 12 seconds, focusing only on highlights. Export both and compare. Which one keeps you watching?

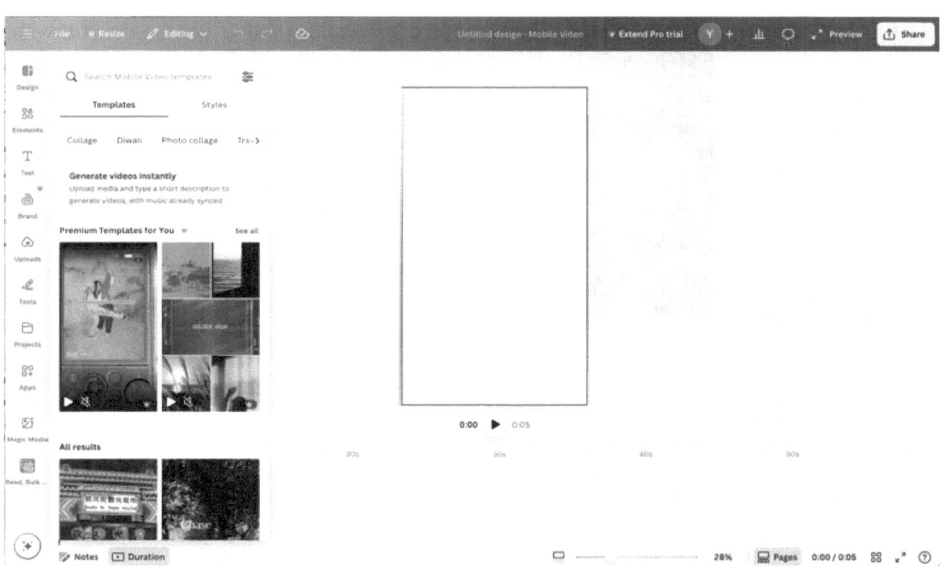

Section 2 — Layers: Organizing Chaos into Clarity

Why layers matter.

Video is not flat—it's stacked. A main clip, a caption, a callout arrow, background music—all of these must coexist without stepping on each other. Layers are how professionals separate, control, and balance these elements.
In Canva, layers appear as horizontal (violet) strips in the timeline. You can drag them above or below each other, just like Photoshop. Top layers are visible; bottom ones sit behind.

Practical uses:

- **Captions**: Add auto-captions on a separate text layer.
- **Shapes**: Place semi-transparent rectangles behind captions for readability.
- **Logos/Watermarks:** Keep in a consistent corner across the whole video.
- **B-roll**: Layer secondary footage above main narration to add texture.

Real Scenario — Saving a Coaching Reel

A business coach recorded advice in her office. Captions blended into the books behind her. By adding a black 40% opacity rectangle behind the captions (layer below text, above video), readability shot up. Her watch time increased because people could follow every word.

Attention — Hierarchy Rules

If text disappears, it's likely hidden behind video. Drag it to the top.

Pro Tip — Keep Layers Tidy

Name them: “Main Clip,” “Captions,” “B-roll 1,” “Music.” A messy timeline kills efficiency.

Mini Exercise

- Build a 3-layer stack: one main video, one caption, one overlay shape. Export.
- Compare with a flat version.
- Notice the difference in clarity.

Section 3 — Keyframes: Motion with Intention

Why keyframes matter.

Static visuals feel dead. Movement keeps attention alive. But too much motion looks cheap. Keyframes give you control—setting a start and end point so Canva animates between them. Done well, they guide the eye.

How to use keyframes in Canva:

- Select element (text, image, logo).
- Click "Animate" → "Custom."
- Place first keyframe (start position).
- Place second keyframe (end position).
- Canva interpolates the movement.

Use cases:

- Zoom subtly on a product shot (100% → 115%).
- Slide a headline in from the left.
- Fade in a logo at the end.

Real Scenario — Dessert with Drama

A bakery shot a wide tray of cupcakes. By zooming in with keyframes on one frosted cupcake, they created cinematic focus. Sales from that post? +22% in one week.

Attention — Less is More

Wild spins, bounces, and zooms scream amateur. Professional motion is subtle: slow pans, soft fades, gentle slides.

Pro Tip — Use Emotion

Zoom in to emphasize pride, zoom out to give perspective. Movement isn't decoration—it's storytelling.

Mini Exercise:

- Add a product image.
- Create a zoom from 100% → 120% over 5 seconds.
- Export.
- Compare static vs animated.

Section 4 — Audio: The Other Half of the Story

Why audio matters.

Viewers forgive shaky visuals. They do not forgive bad audio. Silent reels flop; music that's too loud kills comprehension; un-synced captions break trust. Audio carries emotion, rhythm, and clarity.

In Canva, you can:

- Import music (Canva library or upload).
- Trim to fit cuts.
- Record voiceover directly.
- Add sound effects (swipes, pops, ambient).

Balance is key:

- Voice at 100% → Music at 20–30%.
- Captions on for muted autoplay.
- SFX only where it adds clarity.

Real Scenario — From Ghosted to Viral

A fitness trainer posted silent demos. Nobody engaged. Adding upbeat tracks and auto-captions increased views 5×. Same visuals, new sound = new impact.

Attention — Licensing

Not all Canva tracks are free for commercial use. Always check rights if using for ads.

Pro Tip — Match BPM

Pick music whose beats per minute align with your cut speed. Fast song = fast cuts. Slow track = longer shots.

Mini Exercise

- Layer voiceover, music, and SFX. Adjust volumes until the mix feels natural.
- Export and replay on your phone.

Checklist — Editor Mastery

You know you've locked in the fundamentals of Canva's video editor when you can confidently check off these skills:

1. Trimming, Splitting, and Sequencing with Purpose. You're no longer dragging clips randomly—you cut deliberately. Every trim removes dead air, every split creates rhythm, and every sequence builds a clear story arc from hook to call-to-action.

2. Organizing Layers for Clarity. Your timeline isn't chaos. Text sits above shapes for readability, B-roll supports main footage, and logos stay anchored in place. Layers aren't accidents; they're tools for hierarchy, balance, and visual order.

3. Applying Keyframes with Professional Subtlety. You understand that motion isn't gimmickry. A slow zoom on a product, a gentle fade on a logo, or a headline sliding in at the right moment adds polish without distraction. Keyframes are now part of your visual language.

4. Balancing Audio for Emotion and Readability. Your videos don't fight the viewer's ears. Music supports but doesn't overwhelm, voiceovers are clear, and captions sync with speech. Audio isn't background noise—it's half the experience, tuned to keep attention alive.

When you can nod "yes" to each of these, you're not just using Canva's editor—you're directing with it. Your edits carry intention, your layers carry clarity, your motion carries focus, and your audio carries emotion.

One More Thing: Editing isn't about software. It's about intention. Canva gives you a simple stage—but when you master timeline, layers, keyframes and audio, you become more than a user. You become a storyteller. And in an era where attention is scarce, storytellers win.

Common Mistakes — And How to Fix Them

Each mistake alone won't kill you. Together, they scream "beginner." Correcting them signals professionalism.

- Overstuffed Timeline. New editors drop 10 clips in a row. Viewers lose focus. Fix: Ruthlessly trim. Three clips done well beat ten sloppy.
- Text Lost in Background. Captions over busy visuals disappear. Fix: Always add a shape layer or outline.
- Motion Overkill. Too many spins and zooms look amateur. Fix: One subtle movement per element.
- Audio Imbalance. Music drowns voice. Fix: Reduce music volume; preview with headphones.

"Do It Now" Homework — 90 Minutes

- Trim & Sequence (20 min): Cut raw 30s clip into 12s story.
- Layer Build (20 min): Add captions, overlays, and watermark.
- Motion Pass (20 min): Add keyframe zoom + headline slide.
- Audio Pass (30 min): Add background track, balance with voiceover, sync captions.
- Export as MP4. Watch on mobile.

Congratulations—you just directed your first professional short.

Chapter 2

Mastering Vertical Video: 9:16 Format, Hooks, Rhythm, and B-Roll

There was a time when vertical video was mocked as "the amateur's format." Early YouTube purists dismissed it, filmmakers called it "wrong," and even marketers thought of it as a compromise. But the world changed—not because vertical became trendy, but because mobile became the default screen. Today, more than 80% of video content is consumed on phones. And what do phones favor? 9:16.

Vertical video doesn't just fit the device; it owns it. A vertical short fills the screen with no black bars, no distractions, no wasted space. It feels intimate—like the person speaking is standing right in front of you. That intimacy, combined with the addictive scroll of TikTok, Instagram Reels, and YouTube Shorts, has made vertical the new universal language of video.

But format alone is not enough. Vertical has its own grammar, and breaking it costs attention. You have about three seconds—sometimes less—to earn the right to be seen. Your opening frame, your headline, your energy: all must collide to form a hook. Then comes rhythm: the pacing of cuts, captions, and sound that keeps the brain engaged. And finally, B-roll: the secondary footage that prevents monotony, adds texture, and makes your work look instantly more professional.

This chapter will show you how to master these fundamentals in Canva. You'll learn how to build directly for 9:16, craft hooks that stop the swipe, cut with rhythm like a song, and layer B-roll that transforms a static clip into a dynamic story.

By the end, you'll stop "posting videos" and start directing vertical stories—the kind algorithms push and audiences share.

What You'll Do in 10 Minutes (Quick Win)

Before we dive deeper, let's prove how simple yet powerful vertical video can be in Canva:

- Open Canva and select the Video (9:16) template.
- Import any 10-second clip (your phone or stock).
- Trim to the most dynamic 5 seconds.
- Add a headline text: "Stop Making This Mistake."
- Insert a stock B-roll shot (typing hands, cityscape, or anything that matches).
- Drop a music track and reduce volume to 25%.
- Export and preview on your phone.

That's it: in 10 minutes you've built a vertical short with a hook, rhythm, and a touch of B-roll. Imperfect? Sure. But it demonstrates the rules in action.

Section 1 — 9:16 Format: Filling the Frame With Purpose

Why format matters.

Vertical is not a crop—it's a canvas. Designing horizontal and cropping later leads to disasters: heads cut off, captions hidden under UI, logos lost in corners. Viewers instantly feel the sloppiness. In Canva, you must start with 9:16 and compose every element for the phone screen.

How it works in Canva.

Choose a vertical template. Keep text inside safe zones (the top 70%), away from where TikTok or Reels UI overlays buttons. Place your subject center or slightly higher—this creates eye-level intimacy.

Real Scenario — The Restaurant Fix

A café owner posted wide cooking clips with black bars. They looked amateur. Switching to close-up vertical shots—steam rising from mugs, latte art filmed from above—tripled engagement. Nothing else changed but format.

Pro Tip — Think Thumb Zone

Remember: people hold phones. Keep critical visuals in the middle-top so they're never blocked by thumbs.

Mini Exercise

Take one horizontal video you've already made. Resize it to 9:16 in Canva. Move text and logos to safe zones. Export both versions. Watch on your phone. Which one feels like it belongs in today's feed?

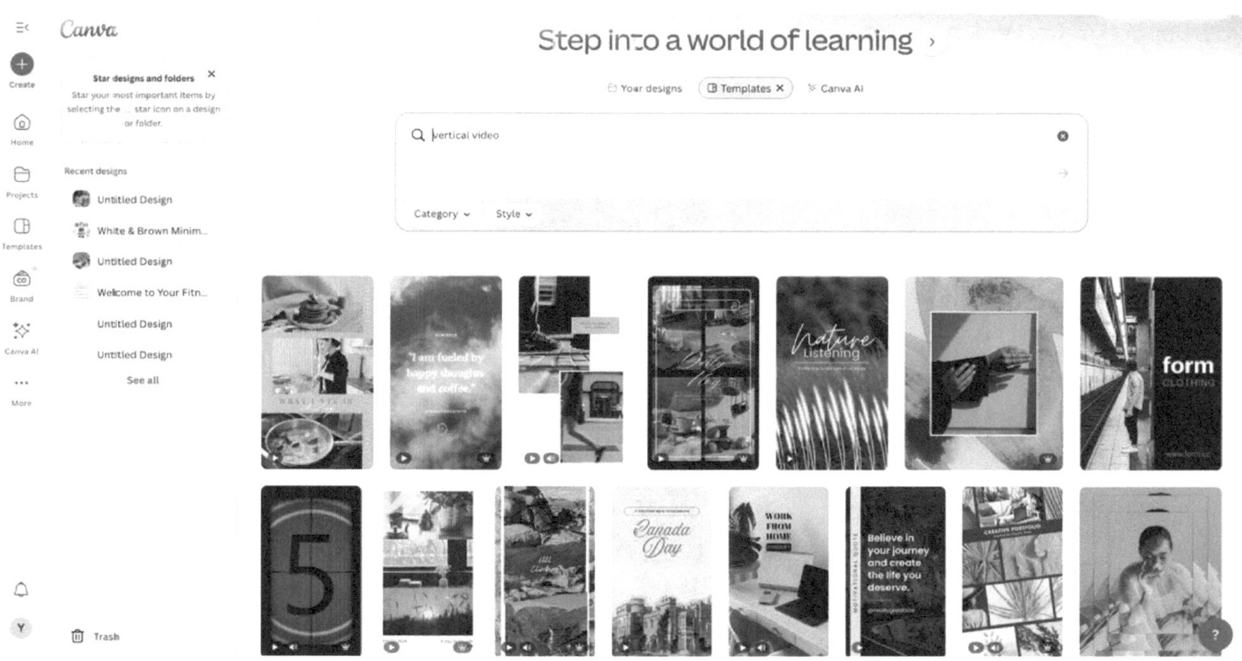

Section 2 — The Hook: Winning the First 3 Seconds

Why hooks matter.

Attention is a ruthless currency. In three seconds, the audience decides: watch or swipe. Too many creators waste those seconds with intros, logos, or "Hi, I'm Marco..." That's a scroll death sentence.

How to do it in Canva.

Use text overlays in the first frame. Add a bold statement: "3 Secrets You're Missing." Or start with an action: drop an object, show a shocking image. Pair it with a sound effect for emphasis.

Real Scenario — Career Coach Breakthrough

A coach used to open with long greetings. Nobody stayed. She switched to starting with "The 3 mistakes killing your job interviews." Watch time doubled overnight. Same message, different hook.

Attention — Don't Waste Branding Up Front

Logos and taglines belong at the end. Use your prime seconds for impact, not introductions.

Pro Tip — Ask a Question

Curiosity buys you more seconds. "Do you know why your videos flop?" is more powerful than "Here's a tip about editing."

Mini Exercise

Write three possible hook headlines for your next video. Place each as a text overlay in Canva's first frame. Export short drafts. Which one makes you want to keep watching?

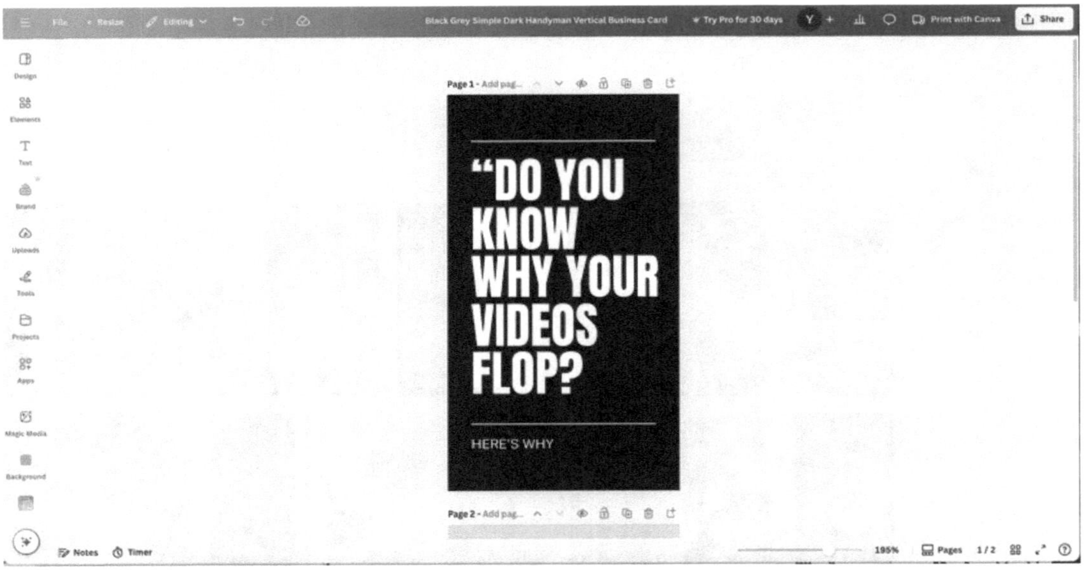

Section 3 — Rhythm: Editing Like Music

Why rhythm matters.

Even with a killer hook, you'll lose attention if the video feels flat. Humans process rhythm instinctively; monotony kills interest. Rhythm means cuts, shifts, and pauses that arrive on beats, like a song.

How to apply it in Canva.

Split clips into 2–4 second chunks. Insert transitions. Add a slide with one phrase. Sync visuals to background music beats. Alternate: talking head → B-roll → bold text → talking head.

Real Scenario — Financial Advisor Revamp

A financial advisor spoke into the camera for 60 seconds. Dead boring. After editing into 3-second clips, adding graphs and testimonial slides, and syncing to upbeat tracks, her retention quadrupled.

Pro Tip — Use "Breather Slides"

A clean frame with just one phrase ("Here's the secret...") gives the brain rest before the next burst. Silence is rhythm too.

Mini Exercise

- Take a 20-second clip.
- Cut it into four beats of 5 seconds each.
- Add one B-roll and one text slide.
- Sync to a track.
- Play it back.
- Does it feel alive?

Section 4 — B-Roll: The Secret Ingredient of Professionalism

Why B-roll matters.

A single talking head feels static. B-roll is your cutaway footage—secondary visuals that support your story. It can be stock or personal, but it must match your words.

How to use it in Canva.

Search Canva's stock for relevant clips: cityscapes, typing hands, office shots. Layer them above narration. Cut on key phrases: if you say "growth," show a graph climbing.

Real Scenario — The Chef's Reel

A chef explained recipes on camera. Retention was low. When he cut in sizzling close-ups, chopping, and plating shots, viewers stayed until the end. Same words, better visuals.

Attention — Don't Overload Stock

Overuse feels fake. Mix authentic clips with stock to keep it human.

Pro Tip — Build a B-roll Library

Create a Canva folder: "Typing," "Smiles," "Nature." Reuse cutaways for speed.

Mini Exercise

Record a 15-second monologue. Add two cutaway clips (one stock, one personal). Export both versions—talking head only vs B-roll layered. Which one would you watch?

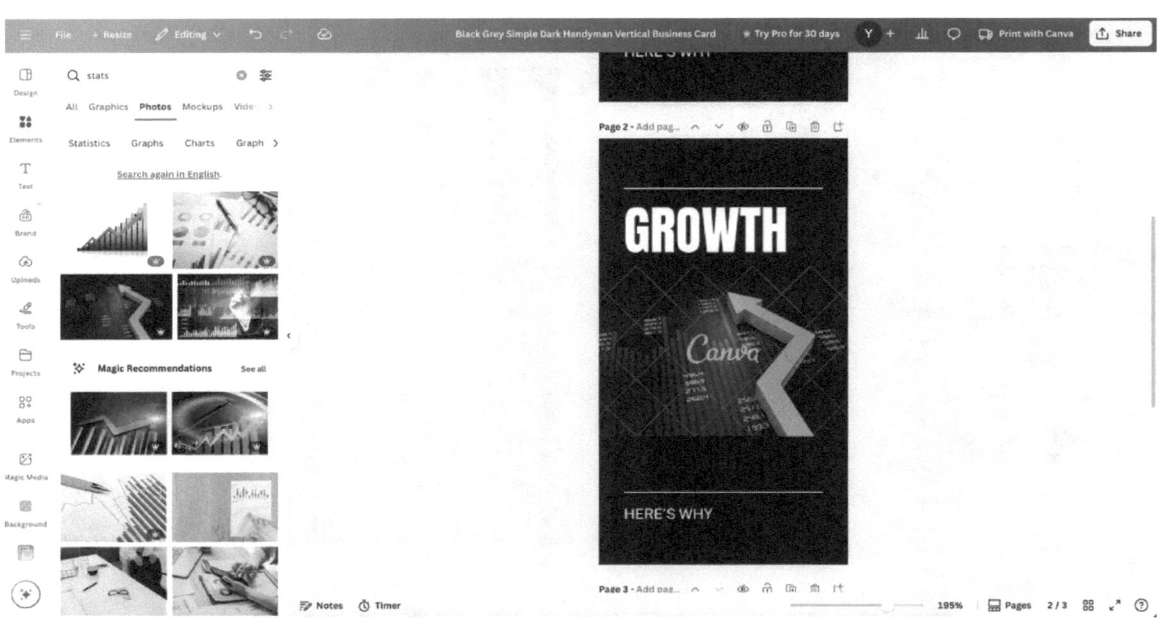

Checklist — Vertical Mastery Locked

You know you've nailed vertical video when:

1. You design directly in 9:16.

Vertical isn't an afterthought, it's the starting point. If you design in horizontal and crop later, you end up with cut-off heads, missing captions, and logos buried under interface buttons. By setting your canvas to 9:16 from the very beginning, every pixel works for the mobile screen. Your video fills the frame, avoids black bars, and respects "safe zones" so that nothing critical is hidden by app overlays. This choice alone makes your video feel like it belongs to the platform, not recycled from somewhere else.

2. You hook in the first 3 seconds.

In the vertical feed, time is merciless. The swipe is always one thumb away. If your first three seconds are vague or slow, you lose. When you open with a bold headline, a surprising action, or a provocative question, you buy the next few seconds of attention. That window is where you can deliver value. A strong hook doesn't just stop the scroll—it signals professionalism. It tells the viewer: "This is worth watching."

3. Your rhythm keeps shifting.

Even a good idea dies if the pacing is flat. Humans are wired for rhythm: peaks and valleys, tension and release. In video, rhythm means you never let one visual or moment overstay its welcome. Every two or three seconds, something changes—whether it's a cut, a caption, a beat drop, or a piece of B-roll. This isn't decoration; it's survival. A shifting rhythm keeps viewers engaged and prevents the dreaded "swipe away."

4. Your B-roll supports the story.

B-roll isn't filler footage—it's the secret sauce of storytelling. A talking head can inform, but cutaways illustrate. When you mention "growth," a rising graph appears. When you talk about "behind the scenes," quick clips of your workspace play. Effective B-roll reinforces your message, breaks monotony, and creates texture. Done well, it makes your video feel cinematic; done poorly or overused, it feels generic. The key is intention: every cutaway should earn its place by deepening the narrative.

When these four align, something powerful happens: your video no longer feels like a piece of content awkwardly adapted to vertical—it feels native. It lives in the feed naturally, flows with the rhythm of the platform, and resonates with how people already consume. That "native feel" is what makes the difference between a clip that gets ignored and one that gets shared.

Common Mistakes — And How to Fix Them

Starting Slow

Many creators open their videos with greetings, taglines, or branding clips — "Hey guys, welcome back!" — thinking it builds familiarity. In reality, it's the fastest way to lose viewers. On social platforms, the first two seconds decide everything. If the audience doesn't feel immediate value or intrigue, they swipe.
Fix: Lead with tension, value, or curiosity. Start with a question, a strong visual, or a statement that hooks attention instantly — "Most creators ruin their first three seconds, here's why..." Introductions and branding can come later, once you've earned the viewer's attention. The goal is not to greet — it's to grab.

Posting Horizontal

A 16:9 horizontal video dropped into a vertical feed feels like a relic from YouTube circa 2015. The moment black bars appear on top and bottom, it signals one thing: repurposed content. Viewers associate that with low effort, and scroll past without giving the message a chance.
Fix: Always plan for 9:16 vertical format from the beginning. Frame your shots, text, and transitions with mobile in mind — full screen, edge to edge. Canva, Premiere, and CapCut all offer vertical templates that make this easy. Designing native for the platform doesn't just improve aesthetics — it shows you respect the medium.

Flat Rhythm

Even strong ideas die in monotone delivery. Long, uncut monologues drain attention because the human brain needs rhythm — pauses, cuts, shifts, and variety. Without these, even passion sounds like background noise.
Fix: Break your story into beats. Alternate between A-roll and B-roll, close-ups and wides, pauses and motion. Add captions to reinforce key lines and make the pacing feel alive. Editing rhythm isn't just about style; it's about guiding the viewer's heartbeat through the story.

Stock Overload

Stock footage can be a lifesaver, but when overused, it becomes a trap. A brand that looks like every other brand loses its soul. Overly polished, generic clips communicate distance — they say "corporate", not "credible."
Fix: Use stock only where it supports your message, not where it replaces authenticity. Mix in your own clips, photos, or behind-the-scenes shots to reintroduce humanity. A slightly imperfect, real moment will always connect better than a flawless fake one. Authenticity scales trust — not filters.

Final Note

Each of these mistakes might seem small in isolation — a slow start, a wrong ratio, a flat edit, a stock clip too many. But together, they compound into a feeling of amateurism. The difference between a forgettable video and a professional one isn't budget — it's intention. When you correct these patterns, your content stops looking improvised and starts feeling designed. You're no longer "posting a video." You're building an experience.

"Do It Now" Homework — 90 Minutes

- Hook Draft (20 min): Create three different 3-second hooks in Canva. Export test clips.
- Rhythm Pass (20 min): Edit a 20s clip into 2–3s beats with music.
- B-roll Build (30 min): Collect 10 stock clips and 5 personal cutaways in a Canva folder.
- Final Draft (20 min): Produce one 20s vertical short with hook, rhythm, and B-roll.

At the end, you'll have a vertical video that doesn't just exist—it belongs in the feed. So, when you master 9:16, hooks, rhythm, and B-roll, you stop making videos that get ignored and start making videos that live where attention already flows.

Chapter 3

Titles, Captions & Transitions: Readability, Timing, and Brand

You could film the most engaging footage in the world, but if your titles blur, your captions lag, or your transitions scream "PowerPoint 2002," the viewer scrolls. In vertical video, words are not optional extras—they are part of the stage. Titles grab attention before the voice can. Captions make content accessible to those watching on mute (which, on social, is most people). Transitions carry the eye forward, smoothing cuts so the story feels deliberate instead of stitched together.

Professional creators know this: text and motion are inseparable. A comedy skit lands because captions punch in sync with the joke. A fitness reel feels premium because every transition matches the beat. A personal brand looks established because titles and fonts are consistent across dozens of posts. Canva gives you tools to build this consistency without a film school degree. The difference is not whether you can add text—it's whether you can make text and motion work together without distracting the story.

In this chapter, we'll go beyond "adding subtitles." You'll learn:

- **Titles**: how to design short, bold, branded statements that hook and orient.
- **Captions**: how to generate, style, and sync them so they're easy to read on the move.
- **Transitions**: how to use Canva's built-in animations with purpose, not gimmicks, so your clips flow like a story.

By the end, your videos won't just be watchable—they'll be readable, memorable, and unmistakably yours.

What You'll Do in 10 Minutes (Quick Win)

Open Canva, start a 9:16 video:

1. Import a 10s talking-head clip.
2. Add a bold headline: "STOP SCROLLING" in your brand font.
3. Generate auto-captions and adjust timing for accuracy.
4. Insert one smooth transition (cross-dissolve or slide) between clips.
5. Export. Watch on mute. If it's clear, you've nailed the basics.

Section 1 — Titles: The Hook That Frames Everything

Why titles matter.

Titles are your first impression. In vertical feeds, the first words on screen act like a billboard on a busy highway: you have less than three seconds to grab attention. A good title doesn't explain everything—it sets the stage.

How to design effective titles in Canva.

- Keep them short: 3–5 words maximum.
- Use brand fonts from your Brand Kit for instant recognition.
- Position strategically: top or bottom thirds, never dead center.
- Contrast with the background—use bold colors, outlines, or semi-transparent boxes.

Real Scenario — Fitness Coach Reel.

A coach titled his reel "10-Minute Core Blast." Before, he relied on voice alone; people muted, scrolled, ignored. After adding the headline upfront, completion rate doubled—because even muted, viewers knew the value instantly.

Pro Tip — Motion Titles.

- Use Canva's "Typewriter" or "Pop" animations sparingly. A moving headline can punctuate a hook but don't overdo it. Professional = subtle.
- Select the text box you want to animate. In the top toolbar, click Animate (right next to "Position" and "Transparency").
- Under the Text Animations section, scroll until you find Typewriter or Pop.
- Click once to preview; click again to apply.
- Adjust speed (slider icon) if needed — slower for emphasis, faster for rhythm. Preview the full video with Play (top-right) before exporting.

Mini Exercise.

- Design 3 title variations for one clip.
- Watch each muted.
- Which one communicates fastest?

That's your winner.

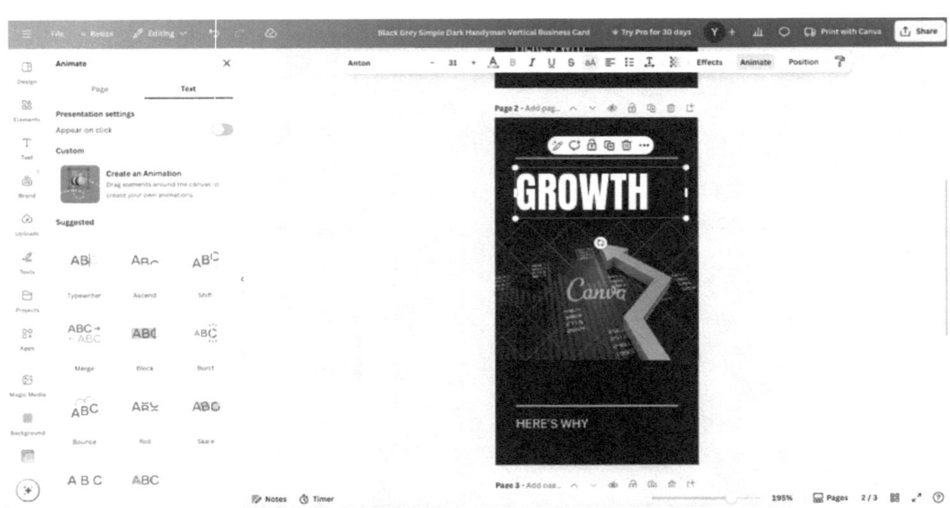

Section 2 — Captions: Accessibility and Engagement on Autopilot

Why captions matter.

85% of social video is watched without sound. If you rely only on voice, you're invisible. Captions don't just make content accessible—they multiply engagement.

How to create effective captions in Canva.

- Auto-generate with Canva's caption tool, then manually proof for accuracy. Select the video on the canvas, then click Subtitles or Captions in the left-side panel (if not visible, go to Apps → Captions).
- Use brand colors for emphasis (highlight one keyword per line).
- Break long sentences into 2–3 words per line. Reading speed must match speaking pace.
- Add a semi-transparent background for legibility on busy clips.

Real Scenario — Career Coach on LinkedIn.

This creator early clips had full captions, but in one block of text. Viewers gave up. She switched to bite-sized captions, synced perfectly. Result: comments and shares grew by 40%, because people could read without sound and still stay hooked.

Attention — Don't Overstyle.

Rainbow-colored captions may look fun but kill credibility. Keep it professional—1–2 colors max.

Mini Exercise.

Upload a 20-second clip. Auto-caption, then edit: shorten lines, highlight one keyword per sentence. Export and preview on phone. Ask: can a stranger grasp the idea in 10s, muted?

Section 3 — Transitions: Flow Without Flash

Why transitions matter.

Raw cuts can feel jarring. But too many wild transitions feel amateur. The art is balance. Transitions should guide the eye naturally, not steal attention from the story.

Canva's key transition tools.

In the timeline at the bottom, hover between two clips or pages — a small "+" icon will appear. Click the "+" and select Add transition. The Transitions panel opens on the left, showing options like:

- **Cross Dissolve** → smooth storytelling.
- **Slide Left/Right** → good for carousels or lists.
- **Fade to Black/White** → ideal for dramatic emphasis.

Real Scenario — Small Business Promo.

A café posted product reels with abrupt cuts. People swiped away. After adding smooth slide transitions synced to music beats, watch time doubled—same content, smoother experience.

Pro Tip — Match Rhythm.

Time transitions to beat drops or pauses in speech. This creates "invisible editing" where the viewer doesn't notice the cut, only the flow.

Mini Exercise.

Create a 3-clip sequence. Add different transitions to each version: dissolve, slide, wipe. Preview side-by-side. Which one feels natural? That's your signature style.

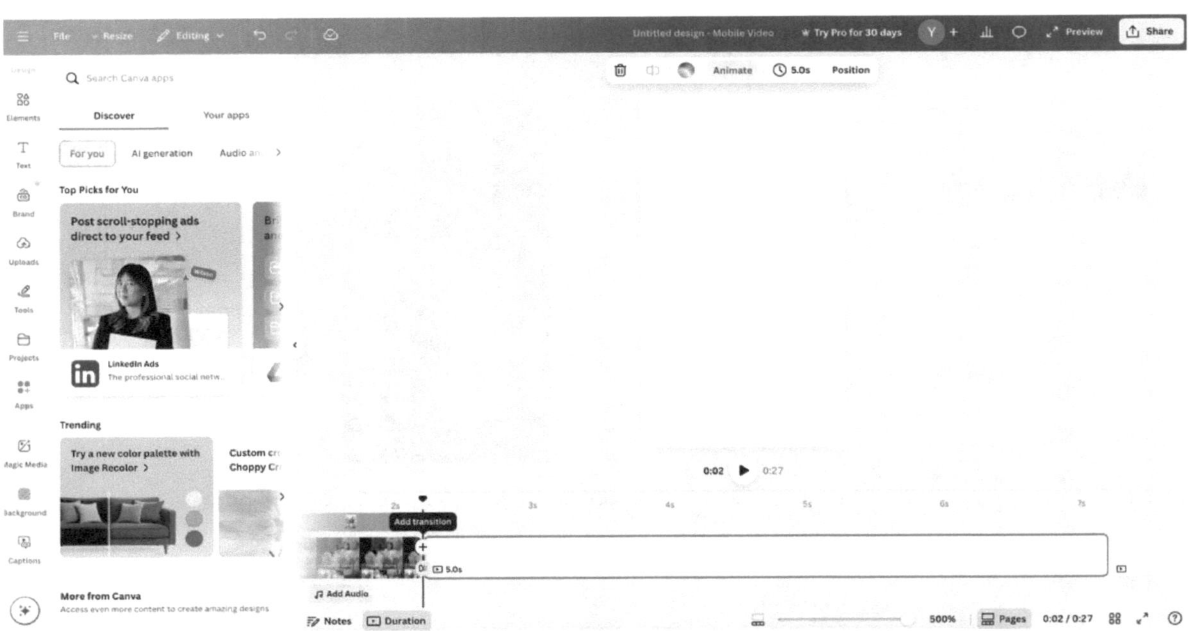

Checklist — Titles, Captions & Transitions Mastered

You know you've locked this chapter when:

1. Titles Orient Instantly.

Your headlines aren't filler—they hook. Viewers know what's coming within three seconds, even with sound off.

2. Captions Are Clear, Not Clutter.

Every line is timed, bite-sized, and branded. They don't overwhelm; they guide. Watching muted feels natural, not like reading a block of text.

3. Transitions Serve the Story.

Your cuts are smooth, timed, and invisible. They support rhythm, not distract. No gimmick spins, no random wipes—just purposeful flow.

4. Everything Feels Branded.

Fonts, colors, and motion styles are consistent across clips. Viewers start to recognize your content by look and rhythm alone.

When these align, your videos carry authority. They feel professional not because they're complex, but because they respect the viewer's time and attention.

Common Mistakes — And How to Fix Them

Overloaded Titles.

Beginners try to cram full sentences. Result: unreadable headlines. Fix: keep it short and let captions carry detail.

Caption Chaos.

Auto-captions left unedited create typos, bad timing, and cringe. Fix: always proofread and time captions manually.

Transition Overkill.

Using every effect Canva offers makes your reel look like a school project. Fix: pick 1–2 transitions and stick with them for consistency.

Brand Inconsistency.

Random fonts/colors break trust. Fix: lock titles and captions to Brand Kit.

These aren't just "oops" moments—they're deal breakers. They make your content look amateur. Fixing them moves you into the professional tier instantly.

"Do It Now" Homework — 90 Minutes

- Titles (20 min): Create 5 bold headlines in your brand style. Test them on old clips.
- Captions (30 min): Auto-caption a 60s video. Proof, style, highlight keywords. Export muted preview.
- Transitions (20 min): Edit a 3-clip reel with smooth transitions synced to music. Export 2 versions, compare.
- Brand Consistency (20 min): Save a Canva template with your title style, caption style, and chosen transitions. Reuse for every future video.

Closing Thought

Words in video aren't "extras." They are the bridge between silence and understanding, between a scroll-past and a watch-through. When your titles grab, your captions guide, and your transitions flow, you've earned not just views—you've earned trust. And trust, in the noisy world of vertical video, is the currency that grows audiences and builds brands.

Chapter 4

Export & Delivery: Bitrate, FPS, File Size, and Cross-Platform Delivery

You can spend hours designing titles, syncing captions, trimming clips, and perfecting transitions. But if your export is wrong—blurry video, pixelated text, or files too heavy to upload—all that work dies the moment you hit "publish." **Exporting isn't a technical afterthought; it's the bridge between your creative vision and your audience's screen.**

Think about it: a great reel ruined by choppy frame rate looks amateur. A beautiful YouTube short uploaded in low resolution screams "unprofessional." A heavy file that takes forever to send to a client wastes their patience. The truth is, the world never sees your Canva timeline. They see the final exported file. That file carries your reputation.

Canva makes exporting simple—one button, a dropdown menu, done. But professionals know the details matter: bitrate, resolution, FPS, file size, and delivery method. Those details decide whether your content looks crisp on Instagram, streams smoothly on TikTok, or impresses a client on a projector screen.

In this chapter, we'll demystify the export stage so you stop guessing and start delivering with confidence.

What You'll Do in 10 Minutes (Quick Win)

- Open your last Canva video project.
- Go to Share → Download → MP4 (Video).
- Select resolution: 1080p (default for social).
- Set frame rate: 30 FPS (safe for most platforms).
- Export, then preview on your phone and laptop.

You've just made a clean export across devices. Next, we'll refine the why behind each choice.

Section 1 — Resolution & Format: The Visual Foundation

Why resolution matters.

Resolution determines clarity. Export too low, and your crisp designs turn into mush. Export unnecessarily high, and your file becomes too heavy without visible benefit.

Best practices in Canva.

- 1080p (Full HD): The sweet spot for Instagram, TikTok, LinkedIn. Sharp, light, fast.
- 4K (Ultra HD): Only if your footage is high-res to begin with and your platform supports it (YouTube, presentations on large screens). Otherwise, wasted space.
- MP4 Format: Universally accepted, small size, and smooth playback. Always export as MP4 for video. GIF is only for very short, looping animations.

Real Scenario — Blurry Client Delivery.

A freelancer sent a client a promo video exported at 720p. On their iPhone, it looked fine. On the client's office projector, it looked unprofessional—blurry, washed out. A re-export in 1080p fixed everything and saved the relationship.

Pro Tip — Design at the Export Size.

If you plan to export 1080×1920, design at that resolution from the start. Upscaling after design leads to fuzzy results.

Mini Exercise.

- Create a 15-second Canva video. Export once at 720p, once at 1080p, and once at 4K.
- Play all three on your phone.
- Notice the difference—and the file sizes. Write down which one is the sweet spot for your platform.

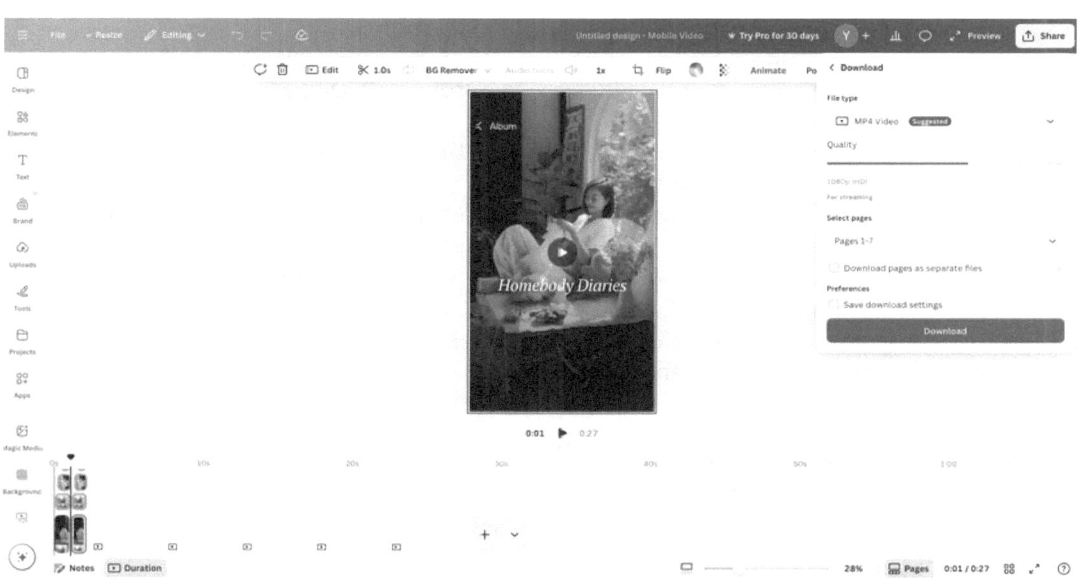

Section 2 — FPS & Bitrate: The Rhythm Behind the Motion

Why FPS matters.

FPS (frames per second) is how smooth motion appears. 24 FPS feels cinematic. 30 FPS feels natural and is the default for social media. 60 FPS feels hyper-smooth—great for gaming or sports, but heavy for uploads.

Best defaults.

- 30 FPS: Universal, lightweight, perfect for social.
- 24 FPS: For cinematic promos or storytelling pieces.
- 60 FPS: Only if you need ultra-smooth motion and have raw footage shot at 60 FPS.

How Canva Handles FPS Internally

- Canva automatically exports videos at 30 FPS by default — the most universal frame rate for web and social media.
- If you upload footage recorded at 24 FPS or 60 FPS, Canva keeps the native motion data when possible, but you can't override it manually.
- Only the Canva Video Editor Beta (for enterprise or advanced users) sometimes shows a hidden "Advanced export" with frame rate options — not available in standard Pro or Free accounts.

Best Practice for Now

- Record and edit your footage at the same FPS you want to export (30 FPS recommended).
- Keep all clips consistent; mixing 24 FPS and 60 FPS in Canva can cause subtle stutter.
- When precision is critical (ads, film, broadcast), do your final export from a dedicated video editor (Premiere, DaVinci, CapCut) where FPS can be set explicitly.

Instagram, TikTok, and LinkedIn compress every video. Don't obsess over perfect bitrate—focus on the right resolution and FPS, then let platforms do their job.

Section 3 — File Size & Delivery: From Canva to Audience

Why delivery matters.

You're not just exporting for yourself. Sometimes you're delivering to platforms, other times to clients. Each requires different optimization.

Social upload.

- Keep files under 200 MB for Instagram/TikTok.
- Stick to 15–60s duration for best performance.
- Export as MP4, 1080p, 30 FPS.

Client delivery.

- Send via cloud (Google Drive, Dropbox, WeTransfer).
- Name files clearly: "ClientName_Project_V1_Date.mp4."
- Provide both high-res (1080p/4K) and lightweight social version.

Cross-platform prep.

One video often feeds multiple platforms. Export once in Canva, then resize duplicates for:

- IG Reels: 1080×1920.
- YouTube Shorts: 1080×1920.
- LinkedIn: 1080×1350.
- Stories: 1080×1920, <15s.

Pro Tip — Always Export Twice.

Export once at full quality for archives/clients. Export again optimized for the specific platform (lighter, resized). This saves headaches later.

Mini Exercise.

Take one 30s Canva video. Export two versions: high-res 1080p for archive, lightweight version (lower resolution, compressed) for Instagram. Upload both. See how long each takes—and how they appear different in quality.

Checklist — Export & Delivery Locked

You know you've mastered export when:

- **Your resolution matches the platform.** No black bars, no fuzzy upscales—everything crisp and intentional.
- **Your FPS fits the context.** 30 FPS for social, 24 FPS for cinematic, 60 FPS only when necessary.
- **Your file size is optimized.** Clients get quality, platforms get speed, you stay efficient.
- **Your delivery is clean.** File names, folders, and versions make you look organized and professional.

When you tick these off, you're no longer "just creating videos"—you're delivering professional assets that work anywhere.

Common Mistakes — And How to Fix Them

- **Exporting Too Low**. 720p looks fine on your phone but pixelates on larger screens. Always default to 1080p.
- **Wrong FPS.** Exporting in 60 FPS for social often backfires with compression. Stick to 30 FPS unless intentional.
- **Bloated Files.** Sending a 1 GB video to a client by email is unprofessional. Compress or deliver via Drive/Dropbox.
- **Messy Naming.** "video-final-v2.mp4" tells no one what it is. Use clear naming: Project + Version + Date.

Each of these errors screams beginner. Correct them, and you're already in the professional league.

Caption Chaos.

Auto-captions left unedited create typos, bad timing, and cringe. Fix: always proofread and time captions manually.

Transition Overkill.

Using every effect Canva offers makes your reel look like a school project. Fix: pick 1–2 transitions and stick with them for consistency.

Brand Inconsistency.

Random fonts/colors break trust. Fix: lock titles and captions to Brand Kit.

These aren't just "oops" moments—they're deal breakers. They make your content look amateur. Fixing them moves you into the professional tier instantly.

"Do It Now" Homework — 60 Minutes

- Resolution Test (15 min): Export one video in 720p, 1080p, 4K. Compare side by side.
- FPS Test (15 min): Export at 24, 30, 60 FPS. Upload privately, check playback.
- Delivery Workflow (15 min): Set up folders: Archive (high res), Social (light res), Client (named by project).
- Naming System (15 min): Rename past exports with clear structure. Example: "Brand_Promo_V1_2025-10-02.mp4."

Closing Thought

Export is the invisible handshake between your creativity and the world. Nobody compliments you on bitrate or file size—but they immediately sense clarity, smoothness, and professionalism. With Canva, export isn't a mystery; it's a skill. Master it, and your videos stop looking like experiments and start looking like assets ready for campaigns, clients, and cross-platform success.

Chapter 5

Templates & Reuse: Series, End Screens, and Covers

Every creator knows the fatigue of reinventing the wheel. You sit down to make a new video and suddenly you're deciding again: which font? Which colors? How should the layout look this time? The process feels fresh, but the result is chaos—your audience can't recognize your brand, and you waste hours polishing things that should already be solved.

This is where professionals separate themselves from hobbyists. They don't start from scratch every week. They use templates as systems. A good template isn't laziness—it's leverage. It creates rhythm, brand consistency, and speed. A recurring video series signals reliability. An end screen signals authority. A consistent cover signals professionalism before anyone clicks.

The truth is, most viewers won't analyze your editing techniques or fonts. But they will feel whether your content looks unified. Inconsistency erodes trust; consistency builds it. Templates are your shortcut to trust, recognition, and efficiency.

In this chapter, you'll learn how to turn Canva templates into a repeatable system that works like a studio behind the scenes.

You'll design:

- Series formats that audiences come to expect and look forward to.
- End screens that close videos with clarity and a call to action.
- Covers and thumbnails that make people actually click.

By the end, you won't just be creating "videos." You'll be running a production system—one where every new video takes half the effort but delivers double the impact.

What You'll Do in 10 Minutes (Quick Win)

Take any short video you've already made.

1. Duplicate the project.
2. Create a branded end screen (logo + CTA).
3. Save it as a reusable Canva template.
4. Design a cover thumbnail with bold text and clean contrast.
5. Duplicate the design and change only the title for 3 variations.

In ten minutes, you've built the foundation of a system. Every future video will feel faster, easier, and more professional.

Section 1 — Series & Themes: Building Recognition

Why it matters.

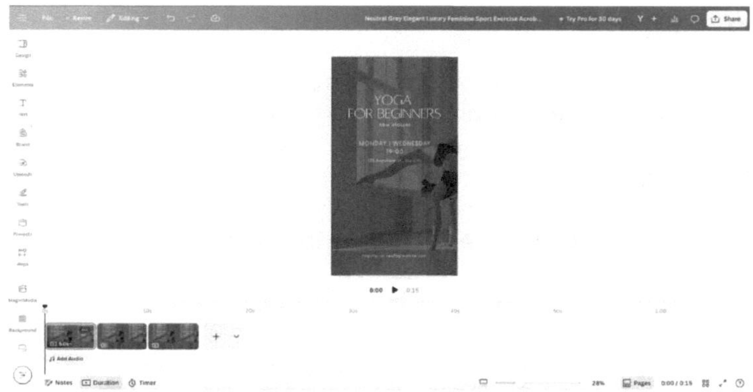

Audiences love familiarity. It's why we binge Netflix shows, why we expect podcasts to follow a format, and why social media series outperform random content. A recurring structure tells your audience: "I'll be here again, with value you can count on."
In Canva, this is simple. Create one base project—set fonts, colors, intro style—and then duplicate it weekly. Swap in new text, images, or clips, but keep the structure intact.

Real Scenario — "3 Tips Monday"

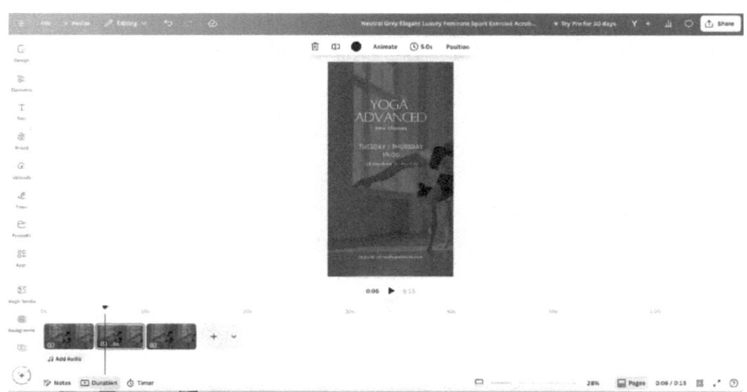

A business coach created a weekly "3 Tips Monday" reel. Every episode opened with the same branded title slide, used the same typography for tips, and closed with the same CTA. Within weeks, her audience began to anticipate Mondays. Engagement grew not because every video was radically new, but because the format was recognizable and trusted.

Pro Tip — Build 3 Core Templates

Don't overcomplicate. Create three base video types:

- Educational (tips, tutorials).
- Inspirational (quotes, motivation).
- Promotional (product/service highlights).
- Rotate them, and your feed stays consistent while your content stays varied.

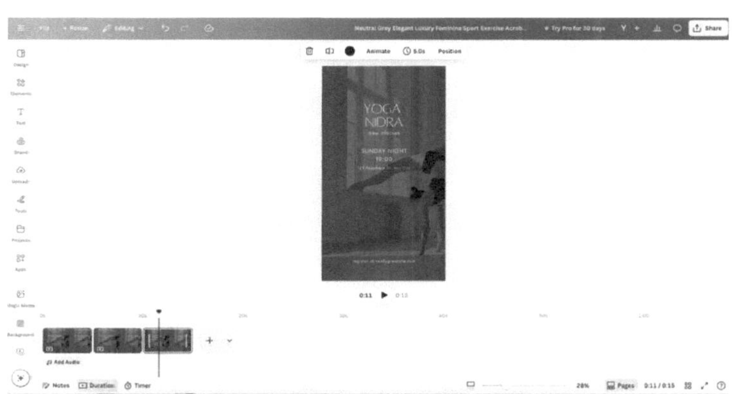

Mini Exercise

- Duplicate one video you've already made.
- Change only the headline and background clip.
- Export.
- That's your first "series" template.

Section 2 — End Screens: Closing with Authority

Why it matters.

Too many videos simply... stop. A fade-out, an awkward cut, and the viewer scrolls away. You've lost the chance to turn attention into action. A branded end screen fixes that. It's your professional signature: "Here's who I am, and here's what to do next."
In Canva, you can design one polished end screen and drop it into every project. Include your logo, a short CTA ("Follow for more," "Download the guide," "Visit our site"), and maybe a tagline. Suddenly, each video ends not with silence, but with clarity.

Real Scenario — From Abrupt to Professional

A freelancer used to let her reels fade out mid-sentence. Engagement was flat. Once she added a branded end screen with "Follow for more design tips," profile visits rose steadily. The content didn't change—only the close.

Attention — Less is More

An end screen should last 2–3 seconds. Don't overload it with text. One logo, one CTA, clean spacing. That's all you need.

Mini Exercise

Open Canva, create a 1920×1080 slide with your logo in the bottom corner and one bold CTA. Save it as a template. Drop it into your next 3 videos.

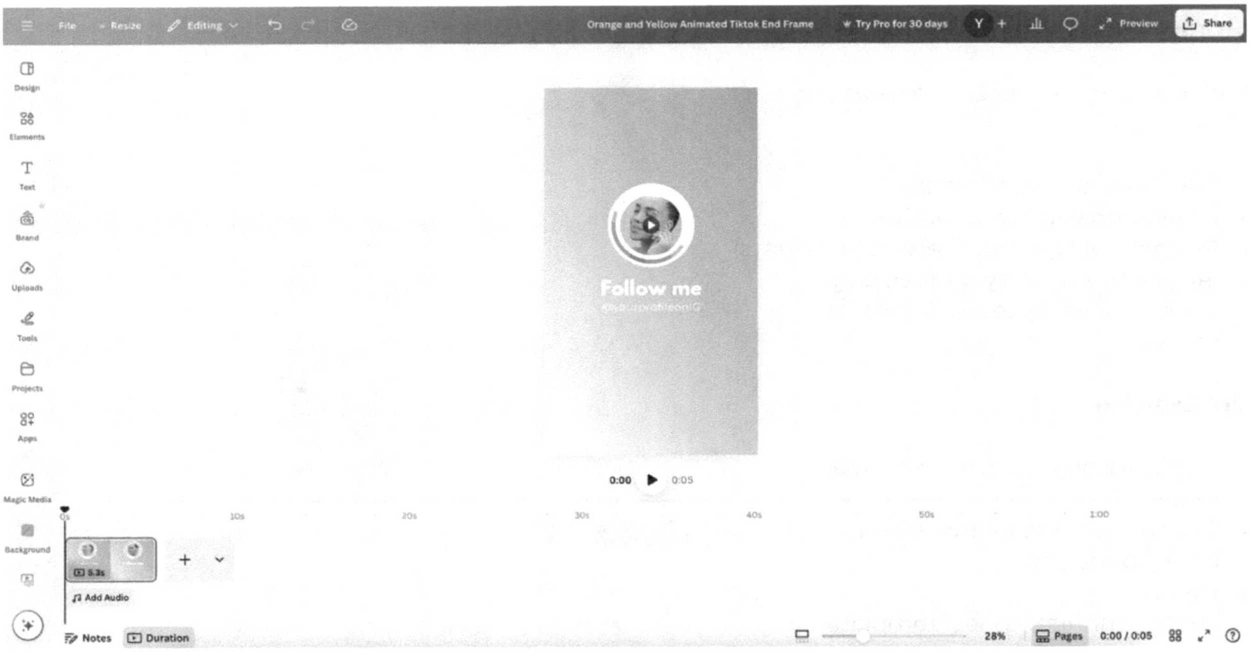

Section 3 — Covers & Thumbnails: Winning the Click

Why it matters.

Your best video means nothing if no one taps "play." Covers and thumbnails are your billboards. On TikTok or Instagram, they decide whether a reel gets opened. On YouTube, they decide whether a short gets buried.
In Canva, build a thumbnail template: bold headline (3–5 words max), large face or image, strong contrast between text and background. Apply the same style across all your videos, so your feed feels unified.

Real Scenario — Chaotic vs Consistent Grid

A lifestyle creator used random screenshots as covers. Her grid looked messy. After standardizing covers with the same font and palette, her profile transformed—suddenly it looked like a brand. Click-through rates rose, because viewers trusted the polish.

Pro Tip — Safe Zones Matter

Always test your cover in-app. On Instagram, the grid crops covers to square. Keep text and faces centered so nothing gets cut off.

Mini Exercise

Create 3 cover variations for the same video. Upload them privately and compare click rates after a day. Adopt the winner as your standard.

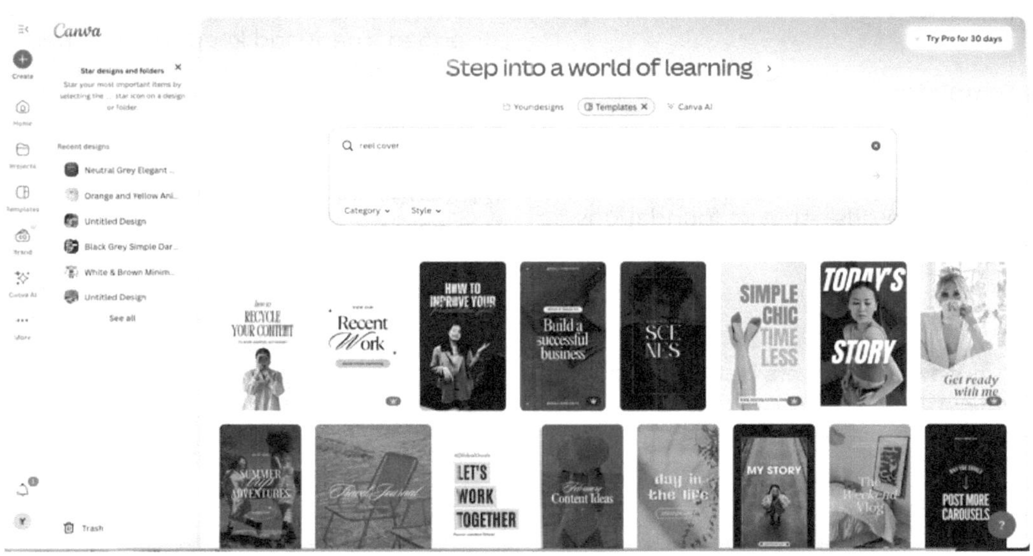

Checklist — Template Mastery Locked

You know your system is working when:

1. You run at least one recognizable series.
Viewers know what to expect, and your content feels like an ongoing story, not random drops.

2. Your videos end with clarity.
Every clip closes with a polished end screen and a call to action, guiding the viewer forward.

3**. Your covers are unified.**
Fonts, colors, and layouts repeat consistently, making your videos instantly identifiable in the feed.

4. Your production feels faster.
Instead of designing from scratch, you duplicate, tweak, and publish—cutting creation time in half.

When these four align, you're no longer just producing content. You're running a content system.

Common Mistakes — And How to Fix Them

1. Ignoring Templates

Some creators design one template, use it once, and never touch it again. That defeats the point. Templates are not one-offs—they're foundations. Build them once, reuse them endlessly.

2. Skipping End Screens

Videos that trail off leave viewers lost. Fix: design one closer and commit to using it. It's your handshake at the end of every piece.

3. Overloaded Covers
Long sentences or cluttered graphics kill click rates, especially on mobile. Fix: short, bold headlines with strong contrast.

4. Chaotic Variety
Constantly switching fonts, colors, and layouts confuses audiences. Fix: commit to one consistent style for at least a month before iterating.

Each of these mistakes alone slows growth. Together, they destroy trust. Correct them, and your channel instantly feels more professional.

"Do It Now" Homework — 45 Minutes

- **Series Sprint (15 min):** Duplicate one of your existing videos. Replace only the headline and main content while keeping structure and style identical. Congratulations — you've just built your first repeatable series format.

- **End Screen Build (10 min)**: Design a branded outro in Canva — include logo, call to action, and social handles. Save it as a reusable template so every video ends with consistency and authority.

- **Cover Pack (20 min):** Create three alternate cover designs for the same video. Test each for engagement and keep the best-performing one as your new brand standard.

Closing Thought

Templates don't restrict creativity—they unlock it. They remove repetitive design labor so you can focus on message, story, and strategy. A recurring series builds anticipation. A polished end screen builds authority. A branded cover builds clicks. Together, they turn you from a hobbyist who "posts sometimes" into a professional studio that produces consistently. In video, consistency is credibility—and templates are how you scale both.

Conclusion:

From Tools to Transformation: You Can...Va!

When you opened this book, Canva might have felt like "just another design tool." A place to drag and drop, maybe create a social post, perhaps an occasional flyer. But as you've walked through each module, you've seen that it's not about the tool—it's about the system you build with it. **Canva, combined with clear workflows, storytelling principles, and AI-powered speed, becomes something more: a platform to create, to publish, and to monetize.**

We started at the very beginning—setting up an account, learning the dashboard, choosing templates. Step by step, you've built confidence, layering skills: layouts, text, images, exports. That foundation became the launchpad for more advanced systems—batch content for social media, business kits for clients, AI hacks for speed, video editing for campaigns. Each module added another brick to the wall of your creative independence.

But here's the real shift: you've moved from consuming design to owning it. No longer dependent on expensive agencies or daunting software, you can now create professional-grade assets yourself—quickly, consistently, and with intention. That's a transformation far beyond "learning Canva." It's about taking control of how your ideas appear in the world.

And the projects? They were never "optional homework." Each final sprint was designed to simulate reality: a business starter kit you can send to clients, a rebrand delivered in hours, a mini-campaign of short videos ready to publish. By completing these, you've proven not just that you understand Canva—you've proven you can operate like a professional creator, delivering results under real-world conditions.

Now, look at the QR codes scattered through these pages. They are your secret weapons.

Each one connects you to bonus templates, checklists, storyboards, and workflows. Use them. Duplicate them. Adapt them. They're not extras—they're multipliers. They take what you've read and turn it into living, working assets you can apply immediately.

Because at the end of the day, learning is only valuable when it turns into action. The more you practice with the templates, the more natural your process becomes. The more you use the checklists, the fewer mistakes slip through. The more you build with the workflows, the faster you scale. These QR codes extend the book beyond its pages, amplifying your experience and anchoring it in reality.

So don't stop here. Open Canva. Revisit the projects. Scan the codes. Build again, but faster this time. And when someone asks, **"Can you design this?" you won't hesitate. You'll know you Can...va.**

That's the real journey this book promised: from zero to published—from tentative first steps to confident creation, from scattered assets to professional systems, from ideas in your head to designs that live, move, and persuade.

Now the stage is yours.

Turn Knowledge into Action

Your Canva Bonus Toolkit

You made it this far — and that already says a lot. This book was written for people who actually want to build something concrete — not just read about it. That's why, as a way to reward those who take action, you'll find a full set of practical bonuses inside.

Each one was created to help you move from learning to doing: templates you can duplicate, checklists to keep you on track, prompt libraries ready to copy, and guides that turn theory into workflow. They're the natural continuation of every module — designed so you can experiment, build, and see results right away. You'll recognize them by the QR codes scattered through the book.

Scan them, duplicate the files, adapt them to your own style, and watch your project come to life step by step. Everything is absolutely doable — as long as you follow the instructions in each chapter and stay consistent.

The real value isn't just in downloading a template, but in using it, testing it, and personalizing it until it becomes yours. So take your time.

Explore each bonus when you finish a section, and use it as a chance to apply what you've learned.
If you do, by the end of the book you won't just understand Canva — you'll have built a full creative system that works for you.

SCAN HERE

Made in United States
Troutdale, OR
06/03/2026

49702785R00097